Preserving Jewishness in Your Family

Preserving Jewishness in Your Family

After Intermarriage Has Occurred

ALAN SILVERSTEIN

A Project of
The Leadership Council of Conservative Judaism

JASON ARONSON INC.
Northvale, New Jersey

This book was set in 11 point Palacio by AeroType, Inc. in Amherst, New Hampshire.

Library of Congress Cataloging-in-Publication Data

Silverstein, Alan.
    Preserving Jewishness in your family : after intermarriage has
occured / by Alan Silverstein.
        p.   cm.
    Includes bibliographical references and index.
    ISBN 1-56821-543-6
    1. Jewish families—Religious life—United States. 2. Interfaith
marriage—United States. 3. Interfaith families—United States.
4. Proselytes and proselyting, Jewish. 5. Conservative Judaism—
United States.   I. Title.
BM723.S59   1995
296.4'44—dc20   95-8310
                                                                                      CIP

Manufactured in the United States of America. Jason Aronson Inc. offers books and cassettes. For information and catalog write to Jason Aronson Inc., 230 Livingston Street, Northvale, New Jersey 07647.

To

Rita, David, and Rebecca

Contents

Foreword

Ismar Schorsch

I ntermarriage is what stands behind the anxiety over the Jewish future. Wherever I travel, the question is raised: "How do we relate to our children who are intermarried?" There is no house in American Jewry that is unaffected. It is not *their* children, it is *our* children. This is a problem that is affecting all of us. And the survival of American Jewry will depend on how we can effectively respond to the challenge of intermarriage.

So what do I tell these questioners as I travel? Their question reflects the communal fear, the erosion and attrition sweeping the American Jewish community. My response is, "After our children intermarry, our response must be to love more, not less." They did not marry out because they hate us. They did not marry out because they are in rebellion against Judaism. Assimilation is not an ideology anymore—it is simply a brute social force. And we shall never succeed in getting them to return if we break our relationships. We need to remain in touch. We need to reach out. We need to reinforce whichever residues of Jewish identity are left, because we love them and because we know that people grow and change.

Beyond that, we need to create moments when our children can experience Judaism with us, as a family and as a community. Judaism is not a creed and it is not a catechism. Judaism is a way of experiencing God. It is a way of experiencing the holy, and we need to create for the intermarried, for our children, as many opportunities as we can conjure to allow them the joy of savoring God Jewishly. We need to dwell on the positive and not the negative. Judaism will sell itself, if given half a chance. And to do this, we must muster and project love and not anger.

This is not a modern take. The Talmud, for example, teaches that God is a compassionate Being and His blessing exceeds His cursing. However, for human beings, creatures of passion, our cursing exceeds our blessing. So we are obligated, as creatures of the Divine, to continue to love and draw our children in, irrespective of what they have done.

At the same time, in our confusion and our pain, we ought not to ask of Judaism things it cannot do. We cannot demand of Judaism that it adopt strategies that violate its integrity. We ought not to expect rabbis to officiate at mixed marriages, no matter how great the pressure at the local level. We ought not to shift to the patrilineal principle. We ought not to compromise the standards of traditional conversion. The Jewish position on these issues is legitimate, defensible, and holy. And no amount of desire should push us to violate our conscience.

On the other hand, sincere adult conversion and raising one's children as Jews are praiseworthy goals. Conversion will create Jews by Choice who are an asset, an enrichment, and a strengthening of Judaism. Conversion has always been a Jewish way of opening. It is a way for creating valuable new Jews who will contribute much.

We should not be intimidated by accusations of discrimination. Religion gets its sense of holiness precisely by drawing boundaries. At the same time that we seek to be loving and caring, we need to have a fence of self-respect and self-confidence that expresses itself in defending the integrity of the tradition.

This volume is intended to offer precisely that balance between love, caring, and openness with authentic Jewish standards of practice.

Acknowledgments

I am indebted to the Leadership Council of Conservative Judaism and its constituent organizations: the Jewish Theological Seminary, the Rabbinical Assembly, the United Synagogue for Conservative Judaism, the Women's League for Conservative Judaism, and the Federation of Jewish Men's Clubs, as well as to Jason Aronson Inc., publishers, for their assistance and support in making this volume a reality.

In particular I wish to acknowledge the crucial involvement of the following individuals: to Rabbi Brad Artson of the Rabbinical Assembly; to Dr. Anne Lapidus Lerner of the Jewish Theological Seminary; to Ginger Ignatoff and Rabbi Charles Simon of the Federation of Jewish Men's Clubs for thorough and insightful editorial work; to Rabbis Gerald Zelizer, Avis Miller, and Neil Weinberg of the Rabbinical Assembly and Dr. Lawrence J. Epstein of the United Synagogue for careful reading and suggestions; to Eileen McGrath and to Muriel Jorgensen for superb copyediting; to Alan Ades, Mark Sternfeld, and other lay leaders of the United Synagogue for their encouragement; to the many members of Congregation Agudath Israel in Caldwell, New Jersey, for reading and critiquing the manuscript from the point of view of our laity; and to Arthur Kurzweil of Jason Aronson Inc. for bringing this material to the public-at-large.

Finally, I want to thank my wonderfully supportive family for their love and understanding during my countless hours of involvement in composing and reediting this material: to my parents, Sol and Doris Silverstein; to my mother-in-law, Cili Neufeld, and father-in-law, Sol Neufeld, of blessed memory; to my children, David and Rebecca; and most of all to my wife, Rita.

Introduction

I f intermarriage has occurred, does this necessarily mean no future efforts should be made to preserve Judaism in one's family? The answer of this volume—*most emphatically*—is *No*!!

As will be discussed in the following chapters, there are gradations of involvement in Jewish life on the part of the intermarried:

- If the non-Jewish family member converts into Judaism, then the household is no longer intermarried but rather a *fully Jewish home* in every sense.
- If a non-Jewish parent does not convert into Judaism but does support the effort to rear the children meaningfully as Jews, transmission of Jewish religion can still be achieved.
- If a mixed couple is uncomfortable in engaging their offspring in Jewish experiences but will permit the Jewish in-laws to share their own Jewishness, then Jewish grandparenting can be the crucial link.
- If an intermarried family is religiously undecided, it is never too late to discuss conversion and to make the case for selecting Judaism for the sons and daughters.

In each case, Conservative rabbis and congregations will be ready and able to assist you in your quest. As is stated by Rabbi Avis Miller, the national chairperson of *Keruv* (Outreach) among Conservative rabbis, in this regard:

After intermarriage has occurred, we try to bring interfaith couples into the community and retain them with open and cordial communication. We can amplify the beauty of Jewish observance involving pageantry and community (such as Shabbat, Sukkot, or a Passover seder). The role of rituals and community can be emphasized and we should not underestimate the power of community (reflected during *shiva*—house of mourning—for example). (Avis Miller, "Support and Guidance for the Parents, Family, and Friends of Intermarried and Interdating Couples," pp. 24–25)

There are effective ways to draw the intermarried into some aspects of Jewish life. Some innovative programs create new "gateways" into synagogues of the Conservative movement. A welcome extended to the non-Jew can help that person begin to appreciate the holiness and beauty and meaning of the religious heritage of his or her Jewish spouse.

There are a growing number of congregations and rabbis who are seeking the best way to bring the non-Jewish spouse into literacy programs in a noncoercive way. Others have established sensitive counseling programs and social settings to enable intermarried couples as well as Jewish in-laws to cooperate in the creation of a viable Jewish home for the Jewish spouse and children. Dr. Steven Bayme of the American Jewish Committee has written:

We must maintain lines of communication [to the intermarried]. We must enable them to raise their children within the Jewish faith. Let us, therefore, discuss openly our concerns with them. Let us share with them our cherished values and beliefs. Let us expose them to the beauties of Jewish peoplehood. Let us dialogue with them on the role of Israel in Jewish life, our concerns for endangered Jewish communities, and our joy and celebration in contemporary Jewish renewal. Let us develop support groups within our synagogue to enable us to maintain such an honest dialogue with intermarrieds rather than signal to them their rejection from the Jewish community. (Steven Bayme, "Communal Policy and Program Direction," pp. 64–65)

Each of the following chapters is intended for distinct audiences and stages in the process of assisting mixed-married families to grapple with preserving Jewishness in their family.

1

Remaining Jewish: Jewish Identity and the Intermarried Jew

The intermarried Jew remains a very important person for the Jewish community at large. We are concerned that your Jewish identity continue to be nurtured and that your personal involvement in Judaism continue to grow. This chapter is divided into two aspects of our concern: first, Judaism's views of efforts to lead intermarried Jews into paths that claim to offer harmony for mixed-married homes while at that same time remaining "consistent" with Jewish religion; second, a discussion of the joys, the pride, the reasons why remaining Jewish is a blessing for you.

QUESTIONABLE PROSELYTIZING

1. What about Messianic Judaism as a compromise choice?

Messianic Judaism (Jews for Jesus) takes advantage of widely held misconceptions about alleged compromise positions between Christianity and Judaism. To assume that entry into Jews for Jesus does not involve an exodus from Judaism is to fall into an ideological trap.

Messianic Judaism *is* Evangelical Christianity proselytizing to the Jews. The founder of Jews for Jesus, a deceptive proselytizing technique, was Martin Rosen, a former Jew who converted to Evangelical Christianity in the mid-1950s. Rosen was ordained as a Baptist minister in 1957 and was assigned to serve the American Board of Missions (missionaries) to the Jews. In this capacity Rev. Rosen became sensitized to the theological vulnerability of many American Jews. When approaching those who knew little about Jewish belief, Rosen represented himself as an "authentic Jew," Moishe Rosen. Yet even the most assimilated Jews resisted formal conversion out of Judaism.

By 1970 Rosen had developed a solution to his dilemma. Dov Aharoni Fisch writes:

> [Rosen was able to] synthesize a new missionary ideology, based on his earlier successes in confusing young Jews [largely] from non-observant homes by asserting that it was he who was the authentic Jew, not their rabbis. Summoning all of [his ample] . . . marketing skills, he decided to send forth [from his base in San Francisco] individuals portraying themselves as "Jews made kosher by Jesus." Preying on the lack of Jewish knowledge . . . Rosen would claim that his movement was not less Jewish than the typical Reform or Conservative Jewish temple [e.g., it was just one more Jewish denomination]. To help reinforce this deception, Rosen's evangelists occasionally would wear yarmulkas (skullcaps) or other Jewish symbols [tallis, Hebrew names of the "congregation," Torah scrolls, *menorahs, matzah,* etc.]. (Dov Aharoni Fisch, *Jews for Nothing,* p. 26)

Over the last 20 years, Rosen's fledgling efforts have grown into a full-blown missionary effort called Messianic Judaism. Misleading advertisements are targeted at Russian, Iranian, Israeli, and other immigrant Jews arriving in America, as well as toward the alienated and *intermarried* among native-born Jews. Free admission is offered for "High Holiday Services,"

"Passover *seders*," "Jewish Day Camp and/or Child Care," "Hebrew Song Concerts," and other recruitment events. Guidelines for missionaries include the following:

> Words that elicit strong negative reactions among Jews [are] . . . avoided at all costs — at least in initial stages of contact. Jesus [is renamed] . . . "Yeshua," Christ [becomes] . . . "Messiah," or better yet, the Hebrew "Mashiach," a Hebrew Christian [becomes] . . . "a Messianic Jew," baptism [becomes] . . . "immersion in the mikveh." The wearing of crosses and crucifixes [is] . . . strongly discouraged [instead] a Jewish star. . . . Most crucial [are] . . . the out-of-context memorization of purported messianic prophecies from the Hebrew Bible. (Larry Levey, "Why I Embraced, Then Rejected Messianic Judaism," pp. 18–21)

Once ensnared by this bait, vulnerable Jews are met with classic, cult-like "love-bombing" via intense interpersonal contact by missionary operatives. These Jews are gradually persuaded that one need not leave Judaism to become "completed as a Jew" through faith in Jesus and Christian doctrine. Dennis Prager has commented:

> There is no such thing as a "Jew for Jesus." . . . The deceit lies in the fact that these Jews who come to believe in Jesus as their God, Savior and Messiah do not acknowledge that they have become Christians. . . .
>
> The fact that the first Christians were Jews is pointless, since the first Mormons were Christians, the first Buddhists were Hindus, and the first Protestants were Catholics. Yet . . . Protestants [have not] called themselves "Catholics for No Pope" . . . Jews do not demean Christianity or Judaism by calling [the tens of thousands of] Christians who convert to Judaism "Completed Christians" or "Christians without Christ."
>
> Why, then, among all religious groups in the world do some [Evangelical and missionizing] Christians believe that there can be

"Jews for Jesus?" . . . [Because] the only way to attract any [significant] number of Jews to Christianity is to deceive Jews who are ignorant of Judaism into believing that they can keep their Jewish identity while adopting Christian beliefs. (Dennis Prager, "Is There Such a Thing as 'Jews for Jesus'?" pp. 6–7)

It is incorrect to assume that if you opt for so-called Messianic Judaism, you or your future children or spouse are doing anything other than converting out of Judaism and into Christianity.

2. What about Unitarianism as a neutral ground?

Some Jews, wrongly assuming that Unitarianism is not a Christian faith, seek this perceived middle path as a solution to their intermarriage religious dilemmas. Yet Unitarianism is Christianity! Judy Petsonk and Jim Remsen have surmised:

Unitarianism [is part of] Protestantism. . . . [Most] Unitarian congregations . . . have a definite Christian flavor to them. They [are] . . . called churches. Their officiants are known as ministers. They . . . sing hymns, have responsive [Christian] readings, refer frequently to Jesus, have a [Christian-style] invocation and benediction, perhaps offer a form of communion . . . a naming ceremony [for infants that is called] a christening. . . . Adolescents . . . are welcomed into membership through . . . confirmation. (Judy Petsonk and Jim Remsen, *The Intermarriage Handbook*, pp. 272–273)

In addition, the heavily cerebral approach of Unitarianism, while appealing to some adults, is quite frustrating to future offspring. For most children, Unitarianism lacks the drama of either Jewish or Christian ritual, with the sounding of the *shofar*, the multiple stimuli of the Passover seder, the warmth of the Hanukkah lights or Christianity's Christmas mass, communion ceremony, and so on. Affiliating as a family with a Unitarian church may be too bland to satisfy the religious needs of future sons and daughters. Furthermore

[Unitarian churches] seem to have limitations as identities for children. There are few Unitarians . . . overall, so a child can easily feel isolated. Their intellectual thrust can be difficult for small children to grasp. It can be hard for a child to explain to peers what a Unitarian . . . is or believes. [And it does not have] . . . deep roots in history, or the coherent belief system which makes either Judaism or Catholicism [or mainstream Protestantism] such a powerful identity base. (Judy Petsonk and Jim Remsen, *The Intermarriage Handbook*, p. 206)

3. Are there Perils in a Jew's selecting Transcendental Meditation as an alternative?

Transcendental meditation (T.M.) *is* an Eastern religion. Some intermarried Jews play out their spiritual needs in T.M., which they are told is nonreligious in nature. "Meditation is a general technique of concentrating one's consciousness on one point or idea, increasing the intensity and duration of this concentration until separation between self and non-self is overcome" (Elimelech Lamdan, "Judaism and Transcendental Meditation," p. 209).

Jews are informed that there is nothing inconsistent in engaging in T.M. while remaining Jewish. Rabbi Elimelech Lamdan posits that some Jews are drawn to T.M. because of its secrecy, its novelty, its apparent ease of access, and its claim of simply offering techniques for enhancing one's awareness of oneself in lieu of a religious system.

At first glance, T.M. appears perfectly compatible with Judaism. At its introductory stages, T.M. seems to be simply a technique and appears to make no mention of one's soul or faith. However, as one is brought into more serious encounter with this Hindu system, tutors probe into the Eastern religious philosophies. Rabbi Lamdan writes:

> Our problem worsens when the [vulnerable] Jewish student of T.M. [unfamiliar with Jewish spirituality] becomes more curious and begins probing deeply into its philosophy. . . . He now accepts answers which, previous to his spiritual experiences with the Self [via T.M.], he would have scorned as "religious answers." . . . Not having a previous standard of [Jewish] spiritual experience with which to compare and evaluate [T.M.'s] answers, he tends to accept them uncritically. (Elimelech Lamdan, "Judaism and Transcendental Meditation," p. 214)

Transcendental Meditation was originated by a Hindu religious luminary called Gurudev, the teacher of the current T.M. leader, Maharishi Mahesh Yogi. Recruits are invited to lectures presenting T.M. in seemingly scientific terms. Interested students are then paired with a teacher, who will gradually tutor the novice in his own personal mantra (a sound or syllable) around which the T.M. discipline focuses. Initiation includes an offering to Gurudev, and a picture of Maharishi Mahesh Yogi is presented to the newcomer, to be hung on a wall over a small table that is to receive future student offerings. A flower, burning incense, as well as prayers of thanks to Gurudev and Maharishi are further components of the ritual. In its final stage of evolution, the T.M. practitioner is urged to practice the mantra repetition for 40 minutes a day. By this point, an elaborate religious ideology has been introduced.

> Focusing this mental energy [of meditation] into the depths of the soul, eliminating thereby the limitations of the ego and merging into the infinite being of God . . . [the first basic premise is] the belief that man is a soul which is temporarily bound to a physical body in its earthly lifetime. A second basic premise is that this soul

is inherently pure, peaceful, and complete, for it is part of the infinitude of God. The resulting conclusion is the third basic point: that man's purpose in life is to purify himself, and that can be accomplished by living a natural life in accordance with the nature of his soul and not with the outside physical world. Man must use his mind to direct his thoughts to the spiritual side of life and away from the physical. (Elimelech Lamdan, "Judaism and Transcendental Meditation," p. 209)

Once a person fully accepts the religious edicts of T.M., one has left Jewish religious life, with its emphasis upon finding holiness within this physical world, and has fully entered into Eastern religion, rejecting the body and material existence.

4. What about turning instead to discipline of the mind such as Scientology?

Scientology was started in 1950 by L. Ron Hubbard via a book entitled *Dianetics: The Modern Science of Mental Health*. Within five years, it had become a religion with more than 4 million members, 22 churches, and 100 missions in 33 countries. Its ministers deliver sermons and preside over life-cycle ceremonies including christenings, weddings, and funerals. Scientology's theology includes a concept of "Thetan," a spirit that lives on after death in another body. This Thetan, a "prime mover unmoved," is likened by Scientologists to God. Hubbard claims that Scientology is an extension of Buddhism. Hubbard is the Church's sole prophet. His wife, Mary Sue, holds the title of Worldwide Guardian of Scientology. Ministers are organized in different levels. Branches and missions are arranged in a hierarchy called "Orgs."

Recruiters into Scientology do not initially indicate that this ideology represents a distinct religious ideology. They simply tell prospective initiates that Scientology is a means to sharpen

one's mental awareness, enhance one's ability to communicate, and improve one's physical health and spiritual serenity.
They claim that newcomers need not abandon their previous
religion to be a Scientologist. In particular, The American
Jewish Scientology Committee targets activities at Jews both in
North America and in Israel. Recruitment involves a four-step
strategy:

> The first step is "contact," the initial friendly approach to the
> potential member. The second step is to "handle" the recruit, i.e.,
> to overcome his reservations about Scientology. The third is to
> find the "ruin," or vulnerable area, of the potential member's life
> such as drugs, sex, a past crime, or incest. In the fourth step,
> "salvage," the recruiter assures the potential member that he
> knows other people who have overcome similar problems
> through Scientology. (James and Marcia Rudin, *Prison or Paradise:
> The New Religious Cults*, p. 87)

Recruits are enrolled in Scientology courses, leading gradually
into excessive expenditures of money. Initiates are persuaded
to work increasingly long hours for the Scientologists with no
payment. According to James and Marcia Rudin:

> [For example,] "Sue Anne" [a former member] reports she was
> under constant pressure to get new members and to encourage
> them to spend money on auditing [courses]. . . . Most who are
> heavily involved in the movement live in Scientology centers or in
> houses or apartments with other Scientologists. . . .
> Ex-members maintain one cannot question church teachings
> and that authoritarian Scientology leaders keep tight discipline by
> paramilitary methods . . . [administered by] "Ethics Officers" . . .
> [and] "Ethics conditions." . . . Many former Scientologists believe
> they were hypnotized and their thoughts controlled during audit-
> ing. (James and Marcia Rudin, *Prison or Paradise: The New Religious
> Cults*, pp. 86–87)

The Rudins conclude that Scientology exhibits the basic characteristics common in religious cults, such as the Unification Church, the International Society for Krishna Consciousness, The Way International, Tony and Susan Alamo Christian Foundation, the Divine Light Mission, the Children of God, the Church of Armageddon/Love Family, and the Body of Christ. These qualities are:

1. Members swear total allegiance to an all-powerful leader whom they believe to be a messiah.
2. Rational thought or questioning is discouraged or forbidden.
3. The cult's recruitment techniques are often deceptive.
4. The cult weakens the follower psychologically and makes him believe that his problems can only be solved by the group.
5. The new cults expertly manipulate guilt, and members may be forced to "confess" their inadequacies and past "sins" before the group or certain individuals.
6. Cult members are increasingly isolated from the outside world and cut off from their pasts.
7. The cult or its leader makes every career or life decision for members.
8. Some cults promise to improve society, raise money, work for the poor, and so on. However, their energies are channeled into promoting the well-being of the group rather than improving society.
9. Cult followers often work very long hours, for little or no pay, and they are made to feel guilty or unworthy if they protest. (James and Marcia Rudin, *Prison or Paradise: The New Religious Cults,* pp. 20–23)

Be cautious when accosted by recruiters for allegedly secular "mental health" groups or unspecified meetings. Cults may have targeted you as a vulnerable, prospective initiate.

5. What about stepping aside from organized religion and joining a humanistic cause such as Ethical Culture?

In a free society like the United States, you certainly can opt for secular humanism. Perhaps this will be a satisfactory synthesis for you in the present. However, unlike Judaism, modern secularism has not withstood the test of time. What will be your feelings toward your discarding of Jewish religion 10 or 20 or 30 years from now? An example of how a secular person's perceptions can change during the course of adulthood is Anne Roiphe's memoir *Generation Without Memory*. During her young adult years, Ms. Roiphe comfortably cast aside her Judaism. "I thought of myself as tribeless, stateless, countryless, classless, religionless" (p. 80).

Later, when she was a married woman and a mother, this secular synthesis became less and less satisfactory. For example, when comparing her daughter Becky with Becky's Jewishly identifying friend Hannah, Anne Roiphe observed, "My child has no Jewish identity. She has no non-Jewish identity. She hasn't yet heard the word [Jewish]. . . . My child has many questions [about religion] I can't answer. She is already more burdened than [her Jewish friends]" (Anne Roiphe, *Generation Without Memory*, pp. 52, 14).

More and more, Ms. Roiphe came to acknowledge her mistake in so casually casting off Judaism and Jewish identity for her family and her future offspring.

> I can see that we made an error [casting Jewish traditions aside]. . . . The sense of connection to past and future that are lacking in our lives are serious losses. . . . We atone for nothing and are thankful for little. . . . We have no group cultural past and no group cultural future—this is not adequate. (Anne Roiphe, *Generation Without Memory*, p. 214)

Similarly, Letty Cottin Pogrebin's *Deborah, Golda, and Me* is an autobiographical statement by a prominent secular woman who later in life realized the value of the Jewishness that she had disdained in her young adult years. The poignant moment of awareness for Ms. Pogrebin came during the *bat mitzvah* of a friend's daughter. She was called upon to say a few words to the young honoree. Being struck by the power of this rite of passage into Jewish womanhood, Ms. Pogrebin reflected with sadness upon the lost Jewish ritual opportunities of her own daughters' childhood years.

> My daughters could not fly out to Colorado for the bat mitzvah, but I gave them my text to read. The truth is, I had written it for them as well as for Amy [the honoree]. I owed it to them. . . . My daughters have the sad distinction of having been denied by their mother what she had herself. . . .
>
> I wish I had written a sermon like this while my daughters were young enough to learn from it. I wish I had sent them to Hebrew school. I wish I had discovered my current synthesis of ritual and revisionism early enough to fuel their growing identities as Jewish women. But none of us can relive our children's childhoods. I can only hope that when they are parents, they will revert to the [Jewish] tradition. . . . Maybe then, there will be some bar mitzvahs and bat mitzvahs in my future. (Letty Cottin Pogrebin, *Deborah, Golda, and Me*, p. 142)

What Letty Cottin Pogrebin was reflecting at the time of Amy's *bat mitzvah* was the value of time-tested rituals for coping with life's moments of significant passage. As Rabbi Harold Kushner has written:

> There are events in the lives of each of us which we don't want to have to face alone. . . . Religion [and its rituals] teaches us to face them in the company of others, our neighbors around us and our ancestors before us, who faced similar situations and left records of their experiences to enlighten and guide us. (Harold Kushner, *Who Needs God?* p. 34)

Organized religion is a critical weapon in combating existential loneliness, a normal human tendency. Here again, Rabbi Kushner commands our attention.

What does religion offer that we lonely human souls need? In a word, it offers community. . . .
   Can you remember a time in your life when something very good or something sad happened? Wasn't your first impulse to call someone up, to tell about it? . . . [We] needed to share it. Marriage ceremonies, funerals, and mourning customs are all ways religion gives us of taking a private event and giving it a public expression, so that we are not left alone on those emotional mountain peaks. (Harold Kushner, *Who Needs God?* pp. 103, 104–105)

How disheartening it is to encounter a person who is unaffiliated, unconnected, and uncomfortable with organized religion and who experiences a tragedy or wants to rejoice in a happy occasion. Who can they tell? With whom can they exult? Upon whom can they depend? In what fashion can they deal with the void, the emptiness of not having a ritualized routine for marking this critical passage?

SO WHY BE JEWISH?
WHAT'S THE GAIN, THE PRIDE, THE JOY?

With so many Jews contemplating whether to remain within Judaism, we must take seriously and respond to the inquiry: "Why be Jewish? What's the gain?" Here I shall share with you some of the personal excitement, joy, pride, and commitment in being Jewish. I shall do so in terms of two genres of finding meaning in one's life: meaning sought in self-fulfillment and meaning found in commitments to larger ideals such as God, family, a distinctive peoplehood, and the world at large. Seven Jewish approaches to finding meaning will be discussed. Each has resonated with significance for many Jews. Each answers the question, "Why be Jewish?"

Self-Fulfillment via Judaism

North American society is best characterized by personal freedom, by "not having other people's values, ideas, or styles of life forced upon [us]" (Robert Bellah et al., *Habits of the Heart*, p. 23). Personal freedom expresses itself in the quest for fame, sexual conquests, quality relationships, inner peace, popularity, career and financial achievements, material possessions, levels of learning, and so on. One's "human potential" is generally viewed independently of requirements of family, religion, community, or tradition. "The search for self-fulfillment expresses itself in . . . the need to 'keep growing,' the urge to express one's 'potentials,' to 'keep in touch with one's own true feelings,' to be recognized for 'one's self' as a 'real person' " (Daniel Yankelovich, *New Rules: Searching for Self-Fulfillment in a World Turned Upside Down*, p. xviii).

These desires are widespread among American Jews and Gentiles alike. Americans from every walk of life are eager "to find fuller self-expression and add a touch of adventure and grace to their lives" (Daniel Yankelovich, *New Rules: Searching for Self-Fulfillment in a World Turned Upside Down*, p. 5). The influential psychologist A. A. Maslow has defined five levels of human needs. The fifth in his hierarchy is self-actualization (self-fulfillment). This need must be addressed in our discussion of "Why be Jewish?" Being Jewish offers many opportunities for self-actualization, providing a variety of modes for different types of people.

The historian Gershom Scholem has defined three categories of Jews in terms of Jewish identity and personal enrichment: Heart Jews, Hand Jews, and Head Jews. Heart Jews seek serenity via holiness, spirituality, ritual, and prayer as routes to intimacy with God. Hand Jews are best inspired by communal, political, or philanthropic acts—by deeds that transform the lives of individuals, society, or the doer. Head Jews are cerebral, finding meaning and fulfillment in the realm of books, ideas, and discussions.

The Jewish tradition speaks simultaneously to Heart, Hand, and Head aspects. Nevertheless, each Jew does have a dominant mode—whether intellectual, spiritual, or communal. Individuals might manifest different facets of themselves at different stages of life, in varying contexts, and as their level of Jewish interest fluctuates. In seeking self-fulfillment within Judaism, we should aim to sample and savor those qualities that best meet our personal needs.

As is reflected in Conservative Judaism's ideological statement *Emet Ve-Emunah*, each of us should endeavor to be a willing Jew, a serious Jew, a learning Jew, and a striving Jew. We should locate ourselves on an infinite symbolic pyramid, with the three sides serving as ladders of commitment. We ought to be striving to ascend the rungs of these ladders, moving toward increasing levels of personal involvement, knowledge, practice, and meaning. By seeking to ascend the three symbolic ladders of commitment—Head, Hand, and Heart—each of us will grow in our behaving, believing, and belonging within Judaism.

Heart Jews—Spirituality and Ritual Expression

Judaism's path to spirituality is particularly significant at this time of widespread spiritual longings. The quest for meaning, for finding a spiritual core, is expressed by Vice President Al Gore in his best-seller *Earth in the Balance*:

> I have for several years now been engaged in an intensive search for truths about myself and my life; many other people I know are doing the same. More people than ever before are asking: Who are we? What is our purpose? There is indeed a spiritual crisis in

modern civilization that seems to be based on an emptiness at its center and the absence of a larger spiritual purpose. (Albert Gore, Jr., _Earth in the Balance: Ecology and the Human Spirit_, p. 367)

For many of us—Head Jews and Hand Jews—this quest goes unnoticed. We are like the deaf man in a hasidic parable who is puzzled by the strange movements of people in a courtyard because he does not hear the music to which they are dancing. Yet for many others, for Heart Jews, Al Gore is correct. When we observe the incredible success of parapsychology, holistic healing, meditations, together with New Age literature and tapes; when a feature film appears, entitled "Stranger Among Us," lauding the spiritual dimension of Brooklyn's _hasidim_, is a box-office success; something must be afoot. Rabbi Harold Kushner, coming in contact with people during his lecture tours throughout North America, has noted this spiritual thirst: "[People are beginning to realize that] there is a kind of nourishment our souls crave, even as our bodies need the right foods, sunshine, and exercise. Without that spiritual nourishment, our souls remain stunted and underdeveloped" (Harold Kushner, _Who Needs God?_ audiotape). What is this spiritual concern? And how does Judaism relate to the needs of Heart Jews?

Prayer can be an effective mode for fulfilling spiritual needs. But we must have patience. Peak moments in formal prayer come unexpectedly and require a momentary suppression of our ego. Jews habitually involved in prayer aspire for those rare sensations of immersion in a "prayerful mood." The Tanzer Rebbe was asked by his disciples how he prepares for his daily prayer. He answered, "I pray that I might be able to pray." The Rebbe pleads that he might attain peak moments in which "heaven and earth symbolically kiss" and then return to their distant realms.

Rabbi Lawrence Kushner's _God was in this PLACE and I, i did not know_ describes the biblical patriarch Jacob, upon awakening from a divinely inspired dream, uttering: "God was in this place and I, I didn't know it." The repetition of the pronoun "I" implies that as long as the "I," Jacob's ego, gets in the way of spiritual illumination, true fulfillment is impeded. But once our obsession with ourselves recedes, as we deepen our immersion into prayer, we find that the realm of God opens wide.

On the holiday of Sukkot, for example, we are commanded to eat and to reside in the *sukkah* for seven days. The only valid exception is inclement weather. When we see that it is raining, we may say the *Motzi* blessing and resume our meal inside our house. For the rabbinic tradition, this leniency can be understood to imply that while seeking spirituality in the *sukkah*, if we still notice rain making us wet, if we are still attuned to *the self*, then we should return to our mundane dwellings. Awareness of our physical lives is a clear indication that we have not entered the spiritual realm.

In a similar fashion, Jewish legend tells of two Jews, Reuven and Shimon, privileged to be among the generation crossing the Reed Sea. They had experienced the miraculous Ten Plagues in Egypt and now the awesome parting of the waters. Nevertheless, all the way across the river bed they persisted in *kvetching*. They complained that the ground was slippery. They were annoyed that other Israelites were pushing and shoving. They were perturbed by shortness of breath. Soon enough they reached the other side of the Sea. However, by the time their complaining ceased, they had missed the miracle, the incredible spiritual moment at hand. Reuven's and Shimon's chances to open their souls to God in prayer had been squandered by an obsession with the self. Their opportunity to be fulfilled for the moment as Heart Jews had been missed.

For prayer to be a route toward Jewish spirituality, we must move beyond our rational, analytical first level of awareness into the realm of our soul. When we repeat and repeat the same refrain on the High Holy Days, especially on Yom Kippur, we try to move beyond the rational side of our mental processing and into our spiritual, emotive, feeling side. It is that mode we are in when we meditate, when we light *Shabbat* candles, when we repetitively chant a hasidic melody. This spiritual mode is available to Heart Jews via prayer.

I am always struck by the sense of awe, of mystery, on the faces of young children when they lead the *Havdalah* (ending of *Shabbat*) prayers on Saturday night. The youngsters who chant the prayers do not intellectualize about their meaning. They probably are not able to translate many of the Hebrew words. Yet their spirits are totally immersed in the prayerful mood, the dimmed lights overhead, the smell of the spice box, the flicker of the candle, and the cup of wine. Picasso remarked that "it has taken me 50 years to draw like a child." Abraham Joshua Heschel, too, pointed to the innate, unblemished spiritual gift of youngsters. Small boys and girls have not yet "learned" to feel embarrassed by genuine responses to the wonder of sacred words, of a beautiful sunset and the first three evening stars. Children still are dominated by spirituality. Judaism, in its prayers and in its rituals, offers a way back into that God-given mode.

Jewish spirituality also means learning how to view life differently. It teaches us to understand spiritual messages, to view the world through the lens of religion. As Rabbi Abraham Joshua Heschel taught: "We do not step out of the world when we [have spiritual experiences] . . . we merely see the world in a different setting." For spiritual access, we need a point of view, a religious perspective, "religious spectacles." An eye surgeon in my congregation once said to me: "Rabbi, a religious person does not need just excellent eyesight, but also superb vision."

The ultimate test for Moses in the Bible was not his defense of a Jew against a violent slave taskmaster, or his rescue of Jethro's daughters from abusive shepherds, but rather his viewing a "burning bush that was not being consumed." In the arid desert, hundreds of bushes burn on a weekly basis. How could Moses have become aware that this bush was a miracle? To realize that the bush was not being consumed by its fire, Moses had to suspend his tasks as a shepherd. He had to be willing to become immersed in watching this part of nature. Moses had to demonstrate the ability to see the universe through the lens of religion and to see divinity at work. He had to respond to the mystery, the awe that most of us take for granted. He had to answer the call that Heschel speaks of as "God in search of Man."

In order for us to be fulfilled as a Heart Jew, religion asks us to take note of the miraculous in our lives. In a valuable parental primer called *Something More: Nurturing Your Child's Spiritual Growth*, Jean Grasso Fitzpatrick recommends:

> Set aside some quiet time to think of a miracle in your life today. Did a 3-year-old offer a playmate a lick of his ice cream cone? Have roses bloomed on the garden fence? Has a toddler's scraped knee healed? Did you and your child read a poem together, or hear some music, that touched your hearts? Think of a few such gifted moments you may have noticed in the past week. (p. 55)

Sensitizing us to the miracles in our lives is precisely the purpose of Judaism's system of saying blessings ("*barukh attah* . . . "). *Brakhot* are intended to awaken us to holiness, to the spiritual in our everyday encounters.

At a workshop for clergy, Rabbi Elie Spitz distributed one raisin to each person. He urged us to take a moment to feel the raisin's texture, to note its unique colors, to smell its distinctive fragrance, to chew it, slowly sensing its crunchy nature, and then to recite the blessing of gratitude: "*Barukh attah Adonai* . . . " ("Blessed are You, O God, Ruler of the Universe, Who brings forth produce from the earth"). The exercise was intended to emphasize the attitude of gratitude in Hebrew blessings, the appreciation of the miraculous qualities of God's creations. If only we always could view nature through the lens of religion, our souls, not just our bodies, would be nourished. "[Judaism] is an inventory of moments in our lives in which we do and have things happen to us, in ways in which our eyes are opened to see God. God, in a world which can be so beautiful and so holy, so full of meaning and satisfaction, if we only opened our eyes to look" (Harold Kushner, *Who Needs God?* audiotape). Involvement in Jewish prayer and its system of blessings can give us a sense of holiness, of contact with cosmic meaning. One Jew by Choice in my congregation observed:

> This is precisely why [one] . . . converts, because of some sort of experience of something spiritual that has never been accessible prior to undertaking this perilous journey. A window was somehow miraculously opened. At the time of illumination the convert may be in awe as his whole disposition reflects the extraordinary process of transformation going on within . . . the power of God at work.

If you are a Heart Jew, in search of spiritual satisfaction, carefully investigate Judaism, its meditative prayers, its parables and sacred wisdom literature. Heart Jews can also be inspired spiritually by Jewish rituals. These holy acts have their own intrinsic value. There is a spiritual power in a Jewish life that puts us in touch with the Ultimate, with God. Judaism sanctifies life. Unlike some other spiritual modes, Judaism does not seek to remove us from other aspects of life. We need not adopt a life of celibacy or separate ourselves from our families.

Jewish ritual structures our life in a way that makes it more fulfilling. For example, Jewish ritual offers a meaningful process for dealing with emotion-laden points in our lives. Many of us have witnessed the healing power of a house of *shivah*, mourning the loss of a loved one. One local outreach worker of Jewish Family Services had continually articulated the psychological value of Judaism to clients. However, only after experiencing Jewish mourning practices firsthand did she truly comprehend the power of this message. After the death of her father, this woman said: "Only now did the total therapeutic impact of the Jewish response to death become a reality for me."

Other Jews have been equally moved by the awesome transitional moments of bestowing a Jewish name upon an infant male at the *bris* or upon an infant female during the baby-naming at synagogue. These celebratory formulas for rejoicing at a birth mirror the world around us. They reflect participation both in the miracle of creation and in the formation of the newest link in the Jewish tradition, spanning centuries. Equally moving for many Jews is the religious pageantry shared under a Jewish wedding canopy (*huppah*), sanctifying marriage. Moreover, Judaism provides a rich medley of holidays, with emotions ranging from the serious introspection of Yom Kippur to the hilarity of Purim and the home hospitality of Passover. "Marriage ceremonies, funerals and mourning customs [as well as bar/bat mitzvah, *bris,* and baby-namings] are all ways religion gives us of taking a private event and giving it public expression, so that we are not left alone on those emotional mountain peaks" (Harold Kushner, *Who Needs God?* pp. 104–105). "Ritual is food to the spiritually hungry. Ritual has the potential to heal and warm; to glorify God and reify human devotion; to make objects and places sacred; to create community" (Letty Cottin Pogrebin, *Deborah, Golda, and Me*, p. 56).

We should not allow our rituals and Jewish laws to be a source of awkwardness to us, but rather they should be a source of pride. Many Jewish parents cringe at explaining to their young children why we do not celebrate Christmas. What they neglect to point out to their children is the various celebrations and holidays we do have. Jews are not impoverished in ritual life. Our calendar is filled with an elaborate array of holidays with rituals that provide a context of interpersonal emotional and spiritual health.

I vividly recollect my initial years as an undergraduate when I was not observant. As a type-A personality I studied around the clock each semester for fourteen consecutive weeks. I would take final exams and then, totally exhausted, return home for recuperation. There was no rhythm to my life, no pacing of energies. Each day and each night were interchangeable. All of this tedium ended once *Shabbat* entered into my life. Every seventh day I was mandated to break the frantic pace of my activities and allow my physical and spiritual self to be regenerated. In the words of Abraham Joshua Heschel, the Sabbath offered me "holiness in time" (Abraham Joshua Heschel, *The Sabbath*, p. 82). It provided a weekly 25-hour sacred window of escape. On *Shabbat* I could not do errands or finish tasks; I could not keep myself glued to the telephone, the typewriter, and other addictive technologies; and I could not roam far from home or from the *Shabbat* dinner table. As one of my congregants reflected: "On Monday morning, when I get hassled at work, I simply begin the countdown to *Shabbat*." *Shabbat* offers a special pace for our lives. Conversely, the absence of ritual creates a terrible void.

> If one abandoned the synagogue, the High Holy Days, the Sabbath Queen, the Torah, the Talmud, the Midrash, what replacements are made in the building of the soul? How are the crises of life marked: birth, marriage, death? How are festivals managed? . . . What do we do—we who once thought only of abandoning the ways of our parents and parents' parents and gave no heed to necessary replacements, substitutes, we would need to make—what do we in our empty apartments do to make furniture and fabric for ourselves? (Anne Roiphe, *Generation Without Memory*, p. 18)

Judaism's prayers and rituals offer religiously satisfying opportunities for Heart Jews. For those who delve seriously into our rich legacy of teaching and observances, Judaism opens a sanctified view of the world. In *The Search for God at Harvard*, *New York Times* writer Ari Goldman observed: "[For me Jewish spirituality] makes everything holy, ties me back to history and connects me with the spirit of God" (p. 45).

Another powerful dimension of Jewish spirituality relates to
Jews in recovery from addictions (to alcohol, to drugs, to food)
through the 12-Steps programs. It was my privilege for several
years at my synagogue to host a group for Jews in Recovery. In
this setting, I heard the following apocryphal tale of a rabbi
who turned to his congregation on Yom Kippur, just before *Al
Het* (the confessions of our sins), and told them he wanted to
give a sermon about the addiction to lying. The rabbi pro-
ceeded to ask those assembled, "How many of you have read
the chapter in the Book of Proverbs about lying and liars?"
Numerous hands went up. "Good," he said, "you are just the
group I wanted to address. You see, there is no such chapter."

Recovery from harmful habits and addictions begins with
an end to denial, to lying to oneself. It teaches the 12-Step
process, with a recognition of our spiritual need. Recovery
commences with an acknowledgment that we might have
become powerless over habitual lying, over alcoholism, over
drug addictions, over unhealthy sexual relationships, over
excessive food intake, over squandering money, or over pro-
crastination. The program offers a way out of addiction. It does
so by teaching people to "work on their spirituality." Rabbi
Abraham Twerski, a pioneer in this field of recovery, has
commented: "Human beings differ from animals in that, beyond satisfying biological drives, we need spirituality, different people in different degrees. When spiritual needs [for
some] are not gratified, some people feel disoriented. . . .
[We work on our spirituality] . . . to become the persons [we]
are capable of becoming" (Abraham Twerski, "Animals and
Angels: Spirituality in Recovery," videotape).

Heart Jews, seeking sobriety and spiritual succor in Alco-
holics Anonymous, Overeaters Anonymous, or the plethora
of other recovery groups, often have questioned whether this
approach is consistent with Judaism. They ask, "Rabbi, what
does Judaism have to offer to those of us in recovery, seeking to
work on our spirituality?" Rabbi Neil Gillman, the foremost

theologian of Conservative Judaism, has indicated that the 12-Step program is very much in harmony with aspects of Judaism. It bears many similarities to Maimonides' classic description of the steps necessary for *teshuvah* (sincere repentance), for "turning one's life around" to a new path.

In the first of the 12 steps, as in *teshuvah*, we must acknowledge our powerlessness over the addiction and our need for change. This is what Maimonides called *hakarat ha-het* (the acknowledgment of the sin). We must sense our impotence, the fact that we have reached the depths. It is time for the death of our old self and of birth anew. As our next step, we must accept the existence of a "higher power," God, who is both our Father (merciful) and our King (just). We need to place our total dependence upon God, the all-powerful Creator of Heaven and Earth. As a third step for recovery and for *teshuvah*, we need to feel remorse, *haratah*, for any harm caused to ourselves, our loved ones, and our acquaintances. The next step is expressed in *vidui*, our confession. As in the repetitions of the Yom Kippur prayers, there is something therapeutic and spiritually cleansing evoked by verbalizing our shortcomings. It is equivalent to when a parent insists that a child say, "I'm sorry." Mother and Father are not just being stubborn; rather, they realize that doing this is a transformative act. People need this spiritual release.

In addition, as in 12 Steps, *teshuvah* requires that we apologize to those whom we have harmed, whether intentionally or unintentionally. We are enjoined to recite the following formula: "If I in any way have either intentionally or unintentionally offended you, I apologize and seek your forgiveness." I would also add the following corollary, suggested by one of my congregants: "I also express appreciation for all that you have done for me during the past year." Furthermore, *teshuvah*, like 12 Steps, insists upon a "New Year's resolution," *kabbalah le'atid*, to do better in the year ahead. Finally, 12 Steps and *teshuvah* require *azivah*, that is, transforming our behavior when the same situation arises again. For Judaism and for 12

Steps, "working on our spirituality" is a remedy to bringing us back into contact with our true selves.

Hand Jews—Assisting Fellow Jews and Social Activism

Some Jews do not relate to their Judaism primarily through the spiritual dimension of their lives. For Hand Jews, self-fulfillment might best be achieved via religion in action—helping one's fellow human beings.

Judaism offers a hands-on sense of community, an opportunity to assist and to interact with one's fellow Jews. Jews can be involved in the diverse institutional world of synagogues and Jewish organizations—B'nai B'rith, National Council of Jewish Women, ORT, American Jewish Committee, and Jewish Federation agencies such as Jewish family service, Jewish vocational service, and Jewish homes for the aged.

We are committed to helping all people in need, both Jews and Gentiles overseas and those in our local communities. We offer our skills in Jewish cooking, in Judaica crafts, our expertise via committee work, and *tzedakah* in the form of monetary contributions. In 1992 more dollars were contributed nationally to the United Jewish Appeal (UJA) than to any other philanthropic cause including the Salvation Army, the United Way, and Catholic Charities, although Jews comprise less than 2.5 percent of the American population.

Something special can be said about persons who opt to spend their limited spare time at committee meetings of synagogues, Sisterhoods, Men's Clubs, and Federations in lieu of a card game, bowling, or tennis. Let no one ever feel that he or she is not a "good Jew," if his or her commitment to God and the Jewish people is primarily in the form of direct service to the institutions of Jewish life. Synagogue officers, chairpeople, and other lay leaders are to be accorded an honorable place on the ladder of Jewish commitments. Similarly, there is something sacred about individuals willing to contribute meaningfully of their wealth to maintain congregations, Israel, and Federation agency projects. For Jewry, *tzedakah*, giving of time and/or money, does not mean "charity" – an outpouring of the heart – but rather "righteousness," expressing with our hands what God wants us to do among our fellow human beings. Jews who are *ba'alei tzedakah*, who make this type of contribution, are exemplary hands-on Jews.

Hand Jews can also be religious enablers. These people feel closer to God by enabling others to observe Jewish holidays in a traditional fashion. My mother-in-law, for example, is an outstanding cook and baker. She provides delicious Eastern European delicacies for Passover, the High Holy Days, and for other sacred occasions. Many other exceptional Jewish men and women preserve the flavors and memories of Ashkenazic and Sephardic Jewry via recipes, fragrances, and aromas.

Other Hand Jews express themselves via Jewish crafts and artistry. Some congregational sanctuaries, for instance, are adorned by magnificent ark covers embroidered by members. At our synagogue one gentleman in particular displayed extraordinary "hands-on" dedication. Among his many contributions, he designed and constructed a High Holy Day Ark, a smaller replica of our permanent ark. He also joined with another temple member to create a magnificent stained-glass window arrangement for our chapel.

Hand Jews also express their commitments via a connectedness to other Jews in need. I recollect the remarkable efforts of members of our congregation and of so many other congregations in "adopting" Russian Jewish families. Adoption meant meeting the newcomers at the airport; transporting them to apartments that had been stocked with food, linens, and other basic necessities; and connecting these immigrants with Jewish agencies for assistance in learning English and locating employment and health care.

Devoted Hand Jews are available to help others in need. They aid families in setting up and maintaining a house of *shivah* after a death. They coordinate the provision of meals for the mourners, cover mirrors, and prepare a basin of water for washing hands after the funeral. They also provide support groups for divorced persons, single parents, new mothers, Jews in Recovery, and other clusters formed as the need arises. These wonderful Hand Jews are religiously motivated to visit and assist shut-ins, the elderly, and persons recuperating from surgery.

Jewish youth, too, have been motivated to respond as Hand Jews. One young woman, celebrating becoming a *bat mitzvah*, was outraged by the death of a child in her town caused by the negligence of a driver under the influence of alcohol. The youngster used part of her monetary gifts to purchase video equipment for local police to facilitate the arrest and conviction of drunken drivers. Another young woman, whose mother has been suffering for years with complex illnesses, used the occasion of becoming *bat mitzvah* to launch an international pen-pal support network of boys and girls whose parents are struggling with disease. Thirty-three of our religious school children raised funds to assist a family of Righteous Gentiles, Yonas and Stase Ruzgias—non-Jews who risked their lives during the Holocaust to save endangered Jews and who were now impoverished in Vilnius, Russia.

I vividly remember many hands-on experiences in my own Jewish life. For one notable example, during my first year in Caldwell, New Jersey, I was contacted by our Jewish Federation's Chaplaincy Office to bring Passover greetings to the six Jewish elderly, long-term residents of a state psychiatric institution. In fulfilling this imperative of *ahavat Yisrael*—love for one's fellow Jew—I brought *matzah* and other holiday items to this isolated hospital setting. Five of the residents were unable to speak and showed no awareness of my presence. I felt discouraged. The sixth person, however, provided me with an unforgettable moment of holiness, of fulfilling the commandment of *bikkur holim*, visiting the sick. I was told that this woman was 85, received no family visits, and had not uttered a word for 30 years. When I entered the room and presented her with the Passover gifts, she suddenly opened her eyes wide, threw her arms around me, kissed me on the cheek, and said, *"Matzah, matzah."* Her holiday and mine had come alive. In the spirit of talmudic wisdom: A hands-on *mitzvah* had served as its own reward.

A by-product of the commitment of Hand Jews is a strong sense of community. The interconnectedness among Jews offers a powerful sense of personal identity. Judaism tells a person who he or she is and from where they all came. It links Jewish people to other Jews throughout the world. We sense this bonding every time we travel, seeking fellow Jews in American cities or when touring abroad. Los Angeles radio personality Dennis Prager has written: "Judaism . . . provides the sense of community and belonging for which Judaism is uniquely known . . . the instant intimacy that I have experienced with fellow Jews in Morocco, the Soviet Union, and elsewhere throughout the world" (Dennis Prager, "Why I am a Jew: The Case for a Religious Life," p. 27).

Prominent Jews have testified to their indebtedness to Jewish collective memory for their Jewish identity and values. The founder of modern psychology, Sigmund Freud, in a speech to the B'nai B'rith in 1926, observed: "Plenty of . . . things . . . make the attraction of Jews and Jewry irresistible—many obscure emotional forces, which were the more powerful the less they could be expressed in words, as well as a clear consciousness of inner identity" (cited in Anne Roiphe, *Generation Without Memory,* pp. 179–180). In his bestseller *Chutzpah,* Boston attorney Alan Dershowitz commented: "My Jewishness is a very important part of my life. Indeed, though I live and participate quite actively in the secular world, my Jewishness is always with me, both consciously and unconsciously" (pp. 10–11).

A hands-on approach to Jewish identity can lead not only to involvement with Jewish communal affairs but to benevolent interactions with society at large. Judaism is committed to the mending of the world, to *tikkun olam*. Jewish teaching insists that humankind must not be content with the imperfections in societies. As in other traditions based on divine ethics, we are mandated to be God's partners in improving the human condition. Reform, Conservative, Reconstructionist, and Orthodox Jewish groups all are in agreement about this moral imperative, evident in Conservative Judaism's ideological platform, *Emet Ve-Emunah:*

> The [biblical] Prophets fought vigorously against any attempt to limit Jewish faith to the sacral or cultic domain. While not denying the beauty and significance of Jewish ritual, they also pointed to the world outside and to God's demand that we carry our faith beyond the Temple and to incorporate it in our relationships with our fellow human beings. Our imperative was clear: "Justice, justice shall you pursue" (Deuteronomy 16:20). The Prophets never tired of calling on us to loose the bonds of the oppressed, to feed the hungry, clothe the naked, and shelter the homeless. . . . Their vision was that of the just and humane society intended by God as the goal of creation. . . . There is an unfinished agenda before us: *le-takken olam be-malchut Shaddai*, "to mend and improve the world under God's Kingship." (Robert Gordis et al., *Emet Ve-Emunah: Statement of Principles of Conservative Judaism*, pp. 44–46)

Author, philosopher, and Holocaust survivor Elie Wiesel has commented: "A Jew cannot remain indifferent to human suffering, whether in former Yugoslavia, in Somalia, or in our own cities and towns. The mission of the Jewish people has never been to make the world more Jewish, but to make it more human" (American Jewish Committee advertisement in the *New York Times*, September 27, 1992). In addition to advocacy efforts on behalf of Jewish causes, American Jews have established many organizations to serve universal human needs at home and abroad, among them:

Joint Distribution Committee (assistance to earthquake vic-
tims, etc.)
Jewish Federations (personal assistance, hospital support,
etc.)
Jewish Community Relations Council (advocacy of socially
responsible public policies)
Jewish Vocational Service (vocational training and placement)

Similarly, Israel has set up medical emergency camps in
Ruwandi, rescued numerous Vietnamese boatpeople, welcomed hundreds of endangered Bosnian Moslems into the
Jewish State, trained physicians for Third World countries,
and performed numerous other acts of benevolence.

Jews also have been disproportionately prominent in non-
sectarian struggles for equality, compassion, and human dig-
nity. In the evaluation of Rabbi Daniel Gordis:

> It would not be fair, of course, to suggest that socialism, feminism
> or other similar political movements are Jewish movements. Many
> crucial contributions to these movements have been made by non-
> Jewish men and women. But at the forefront of each of these
> movements were Jews who, whatever their level of commitment
> to Jewish life and community, seem to have been profoundly
> influenced by their Jewish roots. Could this be the fulfillment of
> Isaiah's dream that Jews would serve as . . . a covenantal commu-
> nity which acts as a model for the other nations? (Daniel Gordis,
> *Am Kadosh: Celebrating Our Uniqueness*, p. 48)

Most parts of the Hebrew Bible echo the sentiment of the
Psalmist, "Those who love God, hate evil." Biblical ideals of
social justice constantly remind us of having been slaves in
Egypt. The memory of bondage has a sobering effect. It sensi-
tizes Jews to the vulnerability of orphans, widows, and other
impoverished or dependent persons:
Jews are enjoined to be a "light unto the nations," bringing
God's standards of justice and morality to the interpersonal

and international realms. Whatever political philosophy the
Jew chooses, liberalism or conservatism, the individual Jew
is commanded to be committed to the mending of society. We
can best achieve this goal of social justice by acting not only
as individuals but also as part of a sacred people sharing
this quest. "If we act as individuals, our lives would be
too short and the extent of our influence too small to effect
much toward . . . righteousness on earth. But acting cooper-
atively, through [our] historic groups that have a longer life
and a wider range of activity than any individual, we can
each of us render service [to this transformative goal]" (Sidney Greenberg, ed., *A Modern Treasury of Jewish Thoughts*,
pp. 49–50).

Head Jews—Religious Beliefs and Intellectual Strivings

Perhaps you are a Head Jew. Perhaps you relate to life primarily not through prayer or ritual acts but rather through ideas,
thoughts, and concepts. Judaism has been known throughout
the ages for advocating study, education, reading, discussion,
inquiry, and grappling with ideas. We are a learned tradition,
the "People of the Book." Judaism is insistent that study of
Torah, which can be understood as intellectual engagement
with the full range of Jewish experience, can bring a person
closer to God. For nearly 3,000 years we have read our Torah,
the sacred scroll, in a public setting rather than among a
cloistered few, the clergy.

All Jews have been expected to spend some time in study.
Our texts praise the *matmid*, the person who studies virtually
all the time. Aspects of rabbinic literature regard all distrac-
tions from study as *bittul Torah*, diversions from encounter
with the Divine. The greatest Jewish thinker, Maimonides,
regarded inquiry into traditional Judaic writings and secular
subjects as ultimate expressions of what God demands from
us. For Maimonides, study was holier than prayer, more pious

than ritual observance. Rabbinic midrash teaches: "If you wish to come to know Him [God] who by His word created the world, study [rabbinic texts]. . . . For by doing this you will come to know Him . . . and will cling to His ways" (*Sifre* Deuteronomy, *Ekev* 49). In Judaism, study is not merely an exercise of the brain; it is a spiritual act.

For a Head Jew, the Jewish religion offers beliefs with which to contemplate sanctity and holiness in our world. Judaism's tradition has much to nurture and challenge the modern thinker—ideas regarding heaven and hell, the fate of the soul after death, the messiah, sin and repentance, God's role in our lives, and revelation of the divine will. Judaism posits that human beings are born free, free of any "original sin." For Jews, there are no intermediaries between the believer and God. In Judaism, the divine preference is more for deed (acts of goodness) than for creed (beliefs). We regard human indiscretions not as the result of sinfulness but rather as *het*, "missing the mark." Persons are not inherently flawed when they err. Instead, we are like unskilled archers with poor technique in using the bows and arrows of living. We are in quest of *teshuvah*, "returning our aim" to the correct path.

Jews do not claim to have exclusive possession of salvation in God's hereafter. We echo the Bible's assertion that all races and creeds are descendants of Adam and Eve. Judaism posits that each ethical person (Jew or Gentile) has a portion in the world to come. Furthermore, we reject any bias against women or against men. Both sexes stem from the original Adam, initially a combination of male and female. In addition, age-old Jewish sources declare a concern for life. We affirm humankind's "stewardship" over nature and an eternal concern for animal life. Our concept of the messiah does not focus on our personal salvation. Rather, Judaism emphasizes the potential of this chaotic world ultimately to reach a state of perfect peace and justice. Moreover, Jews insist upon a God-given impetus to engage in medical science. Being "made in God's image" means that men and women have the capacity for being "like the Almighty," correcting flaws within nature.

The Torah provides us with revolutionary moral innovations of eternal significance. Among them are:

Unlike ancient societies based upon slave labor, the Bible abolished slavery among Jews. A Jew who fell into debt did not become a slave. Instead he or she became an indentured servant. The Jewish servant possessed human rights, guarantees of equitable treatment, and a limitation upon the duration of servitude (Exodus 21:2, Leviticus 25:39–52).

Jews were reminded of their experiences as "strangers" in Egypt, a foreign land. This humbling memory sensitized them to proper treatment of strangers in their midst (Exodus 23:9).

A code of sexual morality was mandated for the Jews. They were commanded to be "holy" in sex acts. They were to remain distinctive from the pagan cultic practices of the Egyptians and Canaanites around them (Leviticus 18:3ff).

A Jewish person was to behave with honesty in business, with correct weights, scales, and other suitable tools for the ethical conduct of affairs (Leviticus 19:35–36).

Jews were enjoined to be helpful to the poor. Interest was not to be charged for loans needed to feed, house, or clothe less fortunate members of the community (Leviticus: 25:35–38).

Special consideration was offered to the widow, to the orphan, and other dependent persons (Deuteronomy 16:11–12).

A Jewish farmer was to leave part of the crop for the poor to glean, and provide for the support of community institutions (Deuteronomy 24:20–21).

"Murder" was to be forbidden under all circumstances. "Killing" could be sanctioned in self-defense or in wartime. In contrast, murder of the innocent or of the defenseless was never to be tolerated.

We also are blessed with a comprehensive system of Jewish values whose wisdom is available through Jewish laws, parables, tales, and philosophical discussions. Some of the prominent value concepts of the Jewish religion are the following: We place a high priority upon comforting the mourners (*nihum avelim*) after a death in a family. We are committed to the *mitzvah* of visiting the sick (*bikkur holim*). We are enjoined to bring joy to bride and groom (*lesame'ah hatan vekallah*) at the sacred milestone of Jewish marriage. We are warned to be careful with our speech, lest we engage in slander (*lashon hara*), thereby harming the speaker, the listener, and certainly the person maligned. We are commanded to show respect for the aged members of the community (*hiddur p'nei z'kenim*) as a source of memory, of wisdom, of tradition. We are encouraged to be active in the organizational life of our synagogues and Jewish and civic groups, to avoid separating ourselves from the community (*tzorkei tzibbur*). We must return lost objects to their rightful owners (*hashavat avedah*) and stay away from falsely acquired possessions.

We are expected to be respectful to our parents (*kibbud av ve'veim*), whether or not we comply with their wishes. We ought to rebuke persons who commit moral infractions (*hochiah tochiah*), lest misdeeds become habitual. We should always seek to be the peacemaker (*rodef shalom*) among friends, family members, neighbors, congregants. We work on the Jewish assumption that momentum can be created for either reconciliation or alienation. We ought to make whatever sacrifices are necessary to redeem captives or hostages (*pidyon shevuyim*) and to save human lives (*hatzalat n'fashot*). We are enjoined to feel a special bond with our fellow Jews (*ahavat Yisrael*) and to love humankind (*ahavat habriot*). We are commanded to give everyone the benefit of the doubt (*dan lekaf zekhut*) in forming evaluations of them.

Judaism realizes that it is human nature to mistreat other human beings and to enter into the manipulative mode Martin Buber called "I-It." "I-It" implies interacting with others only to exploit their qualities—physical attractiveness, wealth, intelligence, or social status. Judaism offers a value system of *mitzvot* to transform selfish inclinations into acts of "I-Thou"— treating human beings in a moral, caring fashion. "I-Thou" is a selfless meeting of two entire personalities, not just isolated personal qualities. Some persons, perhaps, can attain "I-Thou" relationships independent of organized religion. However, Judaism's life-enhancing value system both transforms us and passes values on to future generations.

Several years ago a Conservative rabbi was approached by a Jewish young man who boasted of achieving a level of "I-Thou" human interactions independent of *mitzvot*. The young person, son of a rabbi, claimed to have attained Judaism's ethical ideals of feeding the hungry, sheltering the poor, comforting the bereaved, and visiting the sick. "Of what value," he insisted, "is organized religion?" The rabbi responded in a twofold fashion. First, these moral deeds are the fulfillment of *mitzvot*. Second, without being part of an ongoing religious tradition, this righteous man would become a "cut flower." He would look morally beautiful but would be cut off from his ethical roots. He would risk not being able to lead his children and grandchildren down a similar path.

Judaism remains ever open to personal exploration, questioning, challenge, and investigation. It teaches that the pursuit of truth is equivalent to searching for the signature of God. No scientific theory, no archaeological discoveries or theories, no aspect of secular learning is off limits. Judaism has never been harmed by challenges, only by indifference.

It is our obligation not to stick our heads in the sand. Instead, we wish to integrate Judaic ideas and the best concepts held by society. Out of the ensuing ideological dialogue, we derive new syntheses and vitality. Novelist Chaim Potok, for example, has shaped his fiction around "core-to-core culture conflict." In his nonfiction, Potok's history of the Jewish experience, entitled *Wanderings*, portrays Judaism's ability throughout the millennia to encounter the best of ideas available within the world.

For Head Jews, Judaism is a treasure chest of books, of issues, of opinions, of values, of striving for answers. Ongoing inquiries into Jewish religion are available in community newspapers as well as in a wide range of Jewish magazines and journals (e.g., *Commentary, Tikkun, Moment, Sh'ma, Midstream, Conservative Judaism, Judaism*).

Jewish religious ideas are facing the challenges posed by technology and by ever-changing societal mores. From the values of Judaism and the work of learned scholars, Jews have guidance with regard to abortion, life-support systems, surrogate motherhood, genetic engineering, fertility medication, test-tube babies, organ transplants, autopsies, and the permissible limits of human sexual behavior.

Ours is a religious history filled with inspiring ideologies—Zionism as a powerful force in modern Jewish history, the collective vigilance against anti-Semitism, feminism in Judaism. Reform, Conservative, Orthodox, and Reconstructionist Jewries all offer views to be investigated by Head Jews in books and published reports, historical analyses and theological pronouncements.

When I was an undergraduate at Cornell University, it was my encounter with Jewish studies that triggered my involvement in Jewish religion and social action. As a Head Jew, I found books, ideas, and issues to be the first line of appeal in my growth as a Jewish young adult. I was intrigued by reading Jewish history, assessing our people's interaction through the millennia with every major culture. It was incredible to learn historian Salo Baron's thesis that Jews under medieval Islam and Christendom lived better than 99.9 percent of non-Jews. Most Gentiles were penniless serfs of feudal overlords; they were denied education, the opportunity to travel, and the prospect of a better fate for their children. In contrast, many Jews lived unattached to the soil and thus were eligible for commerce, for cultural contact, for learning. Jewish status became so lofty that laws were passed making conversion to Judaism illegal.

I was mesmerized by the range of issues addressed in Jewish philosophy classes: How can we believe in God if bad things happen to good people? Are we able to reconcile God's knowledge of future deeds with our free will to choose? I also was drawn to the dilemmas emerging from the Holocaust: Did Jews resist or were we passive, like "sheep led to the slaughter"? Why did world leaders refuse to intervene? To what extent did Gentiles risk their lives to save our brethren? What are the motivations of those groups who question the historicity of the Holocaust? How shall we pursue and prosecute Nazi war criminals? Ultimately, I began to find personal fulfillment in interacting with Jewish sacred texts.

Other Head Jews have been stimulated by Jewish studies courses on many campuses, the presence of Jewish titles at most bookstores, and the frequent media attention to Jewish issues. Paraphrasing the words of the former chancellor of the Jewish Theological Seminary, Louis Finkelstein, to rabbinical students: "Physicians are equating longevity in life with physical exercise. They are only partially correct. The real secret [of octogenarian JTS scholars still producing seminal books and articles] is mental exercise, *talmud torah* [the study of Torah]."

The Talmud records that the question was asked: "What is more meritorious, *talmud* (study) or *ma'aseh* (deeds)? Rabbi Tarfon said *ma'aseh*. Rabbi Akiba said *talmud*. They finally agreed that study takes precedence, for it motivates and induces good deeds" (Simon Greenberg, *A Jewish Philosophy and Pattern of Life*, p. 302).

Jewish devotion to learning, *keneged kulam*, "above all else," has brought countless persons closer to Judaism. The 1977 Nobel Laureate Dr. Rosalyn Yalow reflected: "Throughout the ages, we have taken pride in being known as the 'People of the Book.' . . . The Jewish people, never satisfied with conventional answers, have always valued intellectual inquiry and continued to honor wisdom and learning" (American Jewish Committee advertisement in the *New York Times*, March 7, 1993).

The Jewish route to self-fulfillment via Torah study is described in Vanessa Ochs's personal memoir, *Words on Fire: One Woman's Journey into the Sacred*. Ms. Ochs chronicles her spiritual odyssey from disinterest to curiosity and then to passionate study of the Torah, its commentaries and existential issues. As a product of secular universities, she initially expressed reluctance: "I thought it would be boring. Hebrew school had been horribly tedious. Along with history and language, Torah was just another subject that only minimally engaged me" (p. 12). Beginning with a small study group of women, Ms. Ochs's interest was aroused. "Studying together, you develop a profound sense of personal intimacy. You open up spiritually to each other. If you're learning Torah seriously, you bring your whole being into it, share your deepest inner experiences . . . and become close personal friends" (pp. 93–94). As she read and discussed Jewish texts, Vanessa Ochs came to appreciate their transformative power. "The rushes I [now] get reading Torah . . . it's like falling in love. . . . I feel so many associations reading the text . . . I have an overwhelming sense of returning home . . . to my place and people. . . . I reclaim a vital, missing part of myself" (p. 195).

Self-fulfillment via Judaism's intellectual tradition is more accessible than ever. There are thousands of English-language volumes, magazines, and newspapers on topics ranging from Jewish beliefs and values to Jewish history and lore, Bible and Talmud, Jewish literature and the arts, Jewish law and practice, as well as views of contemporary political, moral, and scientific concerns. Judaica courses for adults are offered by institutions of Jewish studies as well as at community centers. Judaica also is

provided at many universities. Jewish museums, within most
major metropolitan areas, offer Jewish art and public lectures.
For the Head Jew, as for the Heart Jew or the Hand Jew,
Judaism offers an array of opportunities for self-fulfillment.
Many Jews find their interaction with Judaism to be not primarily through prayer or ritual practice but rather through
books, journals, ideas, and inquiry. Rabbi Finkelstein used to
assert: "When I pray, I speak to God. When I study Judaism,
God speaks to me."

Judaism as a Source of Commitment

To be a Jew is to be potentially enriched in many different
ways. It is an inspiring religious system, yet it is more than
involvement in Jewish rites and sacred symbols. Judaism also
can involve the intellectual and the hands-on dimensions of
one's personality. In none of these three domains—Heart,
Hand, or Head—is Judaism all or nothing. Furthermore, Judaism offers commitments that transcend the self and connect us
with larger ideals—to Jews throughout the ages, to Jews
around the globe, to the world at large, and to God.

In 1979 social scientist Daniel Yankelovich identified a societal trend of seeking "an ethic of commitment" beyond simple
self-gratification, beyond a "Yuppie lifestyle":

> The word "commitment" shifts the axis away from the self (either
> self-denial or self-fulfillment) toward connectedness with the
> world. The commitment may be to people, institutions, objects,
> beliefs, ideas, places, nature, projects, experiences, adventures
> and callings. It discards the Maslowian checklist of inner needs
> and potentials of the self, and seeks instead the elusive freedom
> Arendt describes as the treasure people sometimes discover when
> they are free to join with others in shaping the tasks and shared
> meanings of their lives. (Daniel Yankelovich, *New Rules: Searching
> for Self-Fulfillment in a World Turned Upside Down*, p. 250)

Rabbi Harold Kushner's volume entitled *When All You've Ever Wanted Isn't Enough* offers the following analogy:

A rabbi once asked a prominent member of his congregation, "Whenever I see you, you're always in a hurry. Tell me, where are you running all the time?" The man answered, "I'm running . . . after fulfillment." The rabbi responded, "That's a good answer if you assume that all . . . blessings [are achieved in that fashion] . . . but isn't it possible that God [and family, and our ancestors, and the world] has all sorts of wonderful [meaning] . . . for us . . . but we in our pursuit of [fulfillment] . . . are so constantly [oriented toward seeking self-fulfillment] . . . that God [and family, and ancestors, and the world] can't find us [ready to be encountered]?" (p. 146)

To whom do we owe commitment? First, we owe it to God. Jews have had more than 3,000 years of an unbroken chain of tradition, a covenantal bond to represent ethical monotheism in this world. Three thousand years represent at least 150 generations of bringing to humankind the message that God and God alone is to be worshiped; God's message is that all human beings must be moral in their behavior toward one another and toward the universe as well. We owe it to God to remain Jewish and to keep Judaism alive.

Second, we owe it to our ancestors. They kept alive this unbroken chain of tradition, sometimes at great peril to their lives, in order to pass this precious legacy on to the next generation and ultimately on to us. Some of our ancestors may have been pious and others secular, but each link in the chain recognized that unless they passed the baton on to the next in line, they would deny their sons and daughters and grandchildren the opportunity to choose whether or not to be intimately involved in the riches of Jewish ritual, values, learning, wisdom, and spirituality. We owe it to our ancestors and to our descendants not to be the end of that millennia-long chain of transmission.

Third, we owe it to our fellow Jews of today. As was demonstrated by the tragedies of the Holocaust and by the euphoria accompanying the creation of the modern State of Israel, in a modern age of technologies of genocide and mass destruction, more than ever individual Jews in distress rely upon one another for support and help. Uniquely among the peoples of the world, Jewry sustained the morale of Jews behind the Iron Curtain of the U.S.S.R. and is bringing unprecedented hundreds of thousands into freedom. In unmatched acts of bravery, while other civilizations witnessed the deaths of thousands of Ethiopians of all religions due to famine, civil war, and lawlessness, Jewry alone rescued tens of thousands of Ethiopian Jews, by plane, by ship, by bribe, by whatever was necessary to save the lives of our people. And in unparalleled outpourings of philanthropy, world Jewry has consistently aided the unequaled struggle for survival and for the absorption of diverse immigrants within Israeli society over the past four decades. We owe it to our fellow Jews to remain Jewish.

Fourth, we owe it to the world. Judaism and the Jewish people have made profound contributions to world culture, science, and ethics, far in excess of our tiny numbers and dispersion. Prominent persons of Jewish heritage have been as diverse as Karl Marx, Sigmund Freud, Albert Einstein, Louis Brandeis, Jonas Salk, Maimonides, Saul of Tarsus (Jesus' primary disciple), and even some of the sailors who arrived with Columbus on his maiden voyage to North America. Our religious imperative for learning, for scientific inquiry, for improving upon God's world, for creating a moral society has set the groundwork for ongoing profound Jewish contributions to virtually every sector of societal evolution. We owe it to the world to remain Jewish.

The Jewish tradition asserts that to find meaning in life Jews must connect with transcendent values, institutions, the Jewish people, and God. Jewish lore suggests that the Ten Commandments and other laws given on Mount Sinai to Moses as *harut* (engraved in stone) were actually our source of *herut* (true freedom). True freedom comes about when a person makes a commitment to a discipline. Consider the analogy of a violin string that hangs loose in its natural state but gains the freedom to express a full range of notes and fulfills its destiny once it is tuned and disciplined by a musical system. Similarly, my children become bored if we play tennis without rules, volleying aimlessly, not keeping score, ignoring infractions; however, once rules are added to the game, excitement and meaning enter as well. Music and sports need laws and commitment to standards that convey meaning. So too with the human spirit. We are blessed with opportunities for significant living through our commitment to tradition, to Jews throughout the globe, to the world, and to God. All of these potential commitments can have a claim upon us and can add significance to our lives.

Our Destiny as Jews

Being Jewish is our destiny. The permanent departure from Judaism by an individual Jew is not so easy to achieve. Although a Jew may decide to cast aside Judaism, he or she cannot predict how much *Yiddishkeit*, Jewish sensibilities, lifestyle will mean in later life. A superficial rejection of one's Jewishness belies deeper, subconscious strivings to remain true to one's real self. Author Anne Roiphe offers a personal testimony to the persistence of Jewish identity: "[As a young adult] I had thought that since I had removed God from my life, the thin, watered-down Jewishness I had learned as a child would wither and disappear. . . . The tree [of Judaism] without its roots has surprised me with its staying power" (Anne Roiphe, *Generation Without Memory*, p.180).

Dramatic turnabouts with regard to Jewish identity are predicted by Jewish lore. Kabbalistic tradition teaches that even alienated Jewish individuals still possess a *pintele yid*, a mystical spark of Jewishness. At times, the spark burns at low ebb. At other times, unpredictably, its flame begins to glow with greater intensity.

In a High Holy Day sermon in 1992, Rabbi Jeffrey Wohlberg of Washington, DC, related an apocryphal episode in the life of Louis D. Brandeis:

> In his senior year of law school, his pre-eminence could not be denied. Jewish or not, he was invited to join the exclusive Honor Society. On the evening of the official induction, the atmosphere was thick. All eyes were on him as he walked to the lectern. Slowly, he looked around the room. "I'm sorry I was born a Jew," he said. The room erupted in applause, an explosion of shouting and cheers. They had prevailed upon him at last [to convert to Christianity]. Brandeis waited. When silence was regained he began again. "I am sorry I was born a Jew, but only because I wish I had the privilege of choosing Judaism on my own." This time there was no shouting, no explosion, no cheers; this time there was respectful silence. The members of the society were awed by his conviction and strength of character. When he finished they gave him a standing ovation. (Rabbinical Assembly Homiletics, 1992)

Given the enormous blessings Judaism can provide, do not forego such a heritage. Judaism has a rich and compelling legacy that speaks powerfully to us today, as it has to Jews throughout the ages.

Being Jewish is a multifaceted blessing. It is a source of pride and of joy. It enriches our lives in a variety of ways. In this age of unprecedented choices, be appreciative of your Jewishness. Do not take for granted this precious legacy and its ability to speak to you even today. Before you ignore or discard this incredible heritage, study it, savor it. It will enrich your life and the lives of those around you.

2

Making Conversion a Priority

Jewish partners in an intermarriage as well as Jewish in-laws are sometimes uncertain regarding the significance of potential conversion by a Gentile relative. They also may be unclear about how to raise this issue or how to proceed if the non-Jewish person expresses further interest. The following questions and answers are intended to assist in making conversion a priority.

1. Does it make a significant difference for Jewish continuity when a non-Jewish spouse converts to Judaism?

Conversion into Judaism has become ever more common over the past several decades. "Probably fewer than a thousand gentiles per year became Jews-by-Choice before 1965. . . . The rate more than doubled between the mid-1960s and the early 1970s, to about 1,800 per year . . . and [increased again] to 3,200 between 1975 and 1984. By the end of the 1980s and in the early 1990s, the number has risen to around 3,600 per year" (Egon Mayer, "Why Not Judaism?" p. 29).

As early as 1979, studies published by the American Jewish Committee (AJC) and confirmed in all subsequent work have underlined the dramatic, positive impact of transforming an interfaith household into a Jewish home. Conversionary families join synagogues, seriously involve themselves in Jewish traditions, and transmit Judaism to their children in a fashion similar to that of most families in which both parents are born Jews.

Children of conversionary marriages are three times as likely to identify as Jews as those of non-conversionary [inter]marriages. When conversion occurs, the chance of a generally successful marriage too is much higher than with no conversion. In a recent study of 6,500 Jewish families married within the last five years, divorce occurs among intermarriages without conversion at a rate three times higher than in marriages between two Jewish partners, whether born or converted to Judaism. (Gerald Zelizer, High Holiday Sermon, September 1991)

In contrast, dual-faith households are generally not effective environments for passing on Jewish heritage. In the AJC's 1983 investigation of dozens of adults raised in interfaith settings, more than 80 percent of the questionnaire respondents had lost even the most limited sense of identification as a Jew:

- If born anew, they would not care whether or not they were Jewish.
- They do not feel any special closeness to other Jews in need.
- They do not express any unique ties to the State of Israel.
- They would not be troubled if their own children were not Jews.

Paraphrasing Shimon Peres's comments to the Conference of Presidents of Major American Jewish Organizations during their February 1994 Mission: "Do not worry about the survival of the Jews of Israel. Your interfaith households are the dwindling population of world Jewry. Less than 10 percent of the sons and daughters of such homes eventually will regard themselves as Jews!"

In contrast, sincere conversion offers positive prospects for the Jewish future of our family members. In the assessment of Rabbi Ismar Schorsch, chancellor of the Jewish Theological Seminary: "Sincere conversion will create Jews of Choice who are an asset, an enrichment, and a strengthening of Judaism. Conversion throughout the ages has always been a Jewish way of providing an opening. It is a way for creating valuable and contributing new Jews" (Ismar Schorsch, keynote speech to Conservative Movement Conference on Intermarriage and Conversion, March 2–3, 1987).

In light of the dramatic difference between conversionary and interfaith homes, the results of the Council of Jewish Federations 1990 National Jewish Population Survey (NJPS) are particularly discouraging. Whereas prior to 1980 many Gentile spouses of Jews opted for conversion, the numbers have rapidly dwindled. Some attribute this decline to patrilinealism, which has created the false impression that conversion is inconsequential to the family. Thus, the NJPS indicates that among interfaith marriages that occurred between 1985 and 1990, 95 percent of non-Jewish spouses did not become Jews. Moreover, only slightly more than half of the remaining 5 percent formally converted to Judaism.

Nevertheless, many nonconverts remain receptive to Judaism. They often consider themselves identifying with the Jewish religion, but have never officially converted under rabbinic auspices. Yet, unless we assist them in formal, knowledgeable, and observant conversion and affiliation, they will have precious little to transmit Jewishly to their offspring.

The NJPS data indicated that we have nearly 200,000 converts in American Jewish life, plus a rapidly growing group of 739,000 Gentile spouses of Jews. We face an uphill battle to unify intermarried families as Jewish homes. The stakes are high. We cannot afford to be indifferent or neutral to the choice of becoming Jewish when a non-Jewish family member is involved. After all, as Rabbi Harold Schulweis has noted: "There is a *mitzvah* in the Torah called *keyruv geyrim*, which means bringing close those that seek to identify with us" (Harold Schulweis, High Holiday Sermon, September 1990). And doing a *mitzvah* is what being Jewish is all about.

2. Why and when do people consider conversion to Judaism?

We must first identify those spouses most likely to be candidates for conversion into Judaism. The research conducted by the AJC in the early 1980s revealed the following general profiles. Persons were most likely to contemplate conversion into Judaism:

- if at least one of their Jewish in-laws was an immigrant [e.g., authentic representation of the European Jewish experience] or was intensely religiously observant
- if they viewed their own Christian parents as less religious than their Jewish in-laws
- if they saw their spouse as religiously observant or strongly desiring to remain Jewish
- if their own Christian family had a history of intermarriage [e.g, Protestant father married to a Catholic mother, siblings married to persons of a different faith]
- if their family was from a lower socioeconomic background than their Jewish in-laws
- if they had an "unchurched" background
- if they had been alienated from their parents since teenage years
- if they came from a foreign cultural background perceived to be of lower status than American culture

Furthermore, the AJC studies indicated certain points in the life cycle when they were most prone to consider conversion:

- during the engagement period
- soon after marriage
- prior to or soon after the birth of the first child
- prior to or soon after enrolling the first child in a Jewish school (nursery, Sunday school, Aleph class, etc.)
- prior to the *bar/bat mitzvah* of the first child
- after the death of a Christian parent who might have disapproved of conversion into Judaism

Many converts have made explicit statements about the motivations for their entry into Judaism. One such articulate description was offered by columnist Mary Hofmann in an essay entitled, "Why Did I Convert to Judaism?"

1. [Judaism] offers rich spiritual experiences without insulting our intelligence.
2. . . . allows for—even encourages—questioning and debate.
3. . . . is the fount from which Western religions sprang (and I like to make decisions based on original sources rather than editorializations).
4. . . . consists of a binding social contract I can respect rather than a nebulous "faith thing" based on declarations and testimonials rather than substance.
5. . . . emphasizes this world and the things that need to be done to repair it, rather than looking at life as merely a prelude to an afterlife.
6. . . . assumes a partnership with God and stewardship of the world—monotheism strikes me as particularly ecological in philosophy, since it assumes an interrelationship of all living things.
7. . . . truly celebrates life and fills my life with spiritual nourishment and cultural traditions without demanding that I abrogate common sense.

8. . . . doesn't purport to have corner on salvation.

Lots more could be said but, in effect, Judaism is the only religion I've ever studied that makes sense. (Mary Hofmann, "Why Did I Convert to Judaism?" p. 11)

After years of firsthand experience with converts, Rabbi Harold Schulweis has come to the following conclusions:

What do they [prospective converts] see in Judaism? . . .
They see . . . a religious civilization that has overcome millennia of intimidation, and tyranny, and derision, and persecution and survived. They see in us a passion for learning, and an ability to think, and a right to doubt that they have not always seen in the religions that they come from.
They see in us a this-worldly religion that has no puritanical hangups about sex or wine or food, something that they have not always seen in the religions that they come from.
They see in us the warmth of the family, and they see in us the hospitality of the people. . . .
[And] I see in these people remarkable souls. . . . Midrash Tanhuma says: "The converts who come on their own accord are more precious to God than are all the tribes of Israel who stood at Mt. Sinai, for these *geyrim* did not hear the thunder and did not see the lightning, and yet they came, by choice, and took upon themselves the yoke of heaven. Is there anyone dearer to God than these? . . ."
(Harold Schulweis, High Holiday Sermon, September 1990)

3. What are the barriers that impede conversion to Jewish life?

During the past fifteen years, practitioners have helped us to identify barriers that have inhibited non-Jewish spouses from considering conversion into Judaism.

Some individuals claim that selecting a specific religion is unnecessary. They incorrectly assume that one can have content in one's religious life without identifying with a distinct tradition. Yet author Rabbi Harold Kushner has counseled: "I don't believe you can practice religion in general any more than you can speak language in general. You have to speak a specific language and to follow a specific, consistent, coherent religion" (Harold Kushner, *Who Needs God?* pp. 18–19).

Other persons assume that although they identify with Judaism, formal conversion is unnecessary. Astonishingly, the NJPS indicated that for every 100 converts into Judaism, there are 43 other individuals who regard themselves as Jews without having formally entered into Judaism. These "fellow travelers" are well intentioned but misguided. We must provide them with accurate and helpful information, exemplified in the following letter:

> In the same way that others have spent time in France and learned the language and culture so well that they consider themselves to be French, you have come to know us and consider yourself to be one of us. The fact is that until a temporary resident applies for and is granted citizenship, he or she has neither the rights nor obligations of that nationality. So, too, it is with Judaism. Until you fulfill the laws of citizenship of the Jewish people, you remain a beloved fellow traveler, a close friend of the family, but not a relative. (Sharon Strassfeld and Kathy Green, eds., *The Jewish Family Book*, p. 34)

There also are individuals who represent the totally opposite problem. They assume that Judaism is a closed clan that does not permit conversion. This misconception is fostered by the reluctance of Jewish spouses and other relatives to openly discuss conversion (for fear of offending the non-Jewish person). I vividly remember a conversation with the Gentile father of a child in my synagogue school who had decided to enter into our conversion program. I asked him why he had not considered this religious affirmation earlier in his twelve years of marriage. He responded: "Rabbi, since neither my wife nor my in-laws ever brought up the topic, I assumed that it was not an option. Either you were born Jewish or not; conversion was out of the question. Only when I heard your recent sermon about the blessing of sincere conversion into Judaism did I realize that I could actually pursue my desire to religiously unify our family."

Thus we must empower Jewish families with the vocabulary to express themselves on this crucial dimension of Jewish family life. Jewish husbands/wives as well as mothers- and fathers-in-law might feel comfortable in articulating the reality that they would welcome and encourage the entry of their non-Jewish relative into Jewish learning, observance, and commitment, and that they too will sincerely partake in that process of study, ritual practice, holiday celebration, and prayer. The collective goals must be to grow together as Jews involved in Judaism. Keep in mind that very few people will be content to relinquish the Christianity of their youth without filling their innate religious need with substantive involvement in Jewish religion.

Another barrier to conversion is that Jews and non-Jews alike generally lack the information about how and where to begin the process. The Jewish community has characteristically left this information solely in the hands of the local rabbi, but most non-Jews are intimidated about approaching the rabbi as the first step in investigating conversion. Therefore it is vital to have access to literature that is both informative and brief. (For this purpose, the Rabbinical Assembly has published and is distributing my booklet, *Are You Considering Conversion Into Judaism?* [reprinted in this volume as chapter 3].) Chapter 3 offers the opportunity for a Gentile spouse to get answers, generally in the form of direct quotes from Jews by Choice, to a wide range of concerns:

- Does traditional as well as liberal Judaism accept converts?
- Will I have to forsake my Gentile family?
- Should I be troubled that Orthodox Jews question non-Orthodox conversions?
- Will I find spiritual fulfillment?
- Will I find meaning in Hebrew prayers, Jewish history, the land of Israel?
- Is it reasonable that my interest has been triggered by a wish to unify my family?
- Is my quest valid if it was sparked by contact with my Jewish spouse's extended family?
- Is it understandable that my love for my husband/wife brought me to this point of interest?
- Is it okay that my attraction sprang from my admiration for Jews throughout the world?
- If I am an Asian/Hispanic/African American, are there racial barriers to conversion?
- Am I the only prospective convert who seeks to reconnect with a Jewish ancestry?
- Is it acceptable that my desire was created by positive association with Jewish friends?
- Is it plausible that reading books and seeing films about Jewish subjects started my quest?
- How do rituals such as *mikvah* and circumcision relate to conversion?
- What is involved in studying for and preparing to become a Jew by Choice?

After reading chapter 3, prospective converts need to make an appointment to meet with a local rabbi in order to have a "sponsor," a religious mentor. Here, too, some non-Jewish spouses unfortunately encounter difficulties. Many phone calls regarding conversion are ineffectively handled by synagogue secretarial staff. Unless adequate briefing is provided, the office personnel, swamped with clerical details and unfamiliar with issues of conversion, often indicate either lack of interest or bewilderment when called by a potential Jew by Choice. How many times have I met with a candidate for sincere conversion who begins his or her personal story with: "Rabbi, thank God I got through to you. You have no idea how many temple offices I called until I finally succeeded in talking directly with a rabbi." Keep in mind that rabbis are interested and willing to discuss these issues and welcome genuine interest in conversion! Do not allow the person who answers the congregation telephone—secretary or volunteer—to mislead you into thinking otherwise!

Yet one more barrier to conversion often occurs once the candidate has established telephone contact with a rabbi. The non-Jew may hear some discouraging facts about Introduction-to-Judaism courses.

Fact: Tuition often is charged for the instruction and textbooks, ranging perhaps from $250 to $500 for 18 to 26 weeks of learning. The fees are necessary to cover the costs of teachers, social workers, publicity, books, and materials. Interested, supportive Jewish spouses and/or in-laws should help prepare the would-be convert for these charges. They should also be committed to making certain that money is not a barrier to conversion. They should be prepared either to assist with the payment or to speak privately with the rabbi regarding tuition abatements based on need. Whether or not you are in agreement with the charging of tuition, do not allow dollars to prevent the religious unification of your family!

Fact: In many communities, Introduction-to-Judaism courses are offered only on certain evenings and in certain locations, which might prove inaccessible to the potential convert. For example, if our regional school in the New Jersey Rabbinical Assembly is in session on Thursday nights, and Thursday is impossible for your Gentile relative's schedule, help him or her find an alternative course on a different night. Similarly, if the regional program's location is too far from your home, inquire at the regional office of the United Synagogue for Conservative Judaism to find more convenient locations. Furthermore, if our regional instruction is based on a semester system and your family member's inquiry is too late for entering the current class, do not be dissuaded. Instead, either arrange for private instruction with your sponsoring rabbi or help find an Introduction-to-Judaism course that starts on a different date.

Fact: Different programs of instruction are conducted in different ways. Some are lecture format with dozens of students. Some are one-on-one with student and rabbi. Some require the Jewish partner to be in attendance. Some are part of general Introduction-to-Judaism sessions with born Jews and prospective converts, studying for a wide range of different reasons. Some courses last 18 weeks, while others are as long as a full year. Although at times confusing, this medly of options is intended to be advantageous to converts. Help your inquiring family member to assess which type of learning setting is best suited to the needs of your family. Under no circumstances should you allow any frustration regarding this range of choices to thwart the quest to convert.

Fact: Participation in an Introduction-to-Judaism course usually is supplemented by individual sessions with the sponsoring rabbi, as well as affiliation with the rabbi's synagogue. This matching process is important. Help your non-Jewish relative select a rabbi with whom you will be able to bond both religiously and personally. And choose a "user-friendly" synagogue, one where people your own age attend *Shabbat* and holiday services and where programs are available for networking with other member families. Keep in mind that sincere conversion is most likely to occur once a new Jew links effectively with other religiously involved Jews of similar age and family stage-of-life. How many times have I seen the sense of frustration of a person who converts under the sponsorship of his Jewish in-laws' rabbi and thereby enters a congregation whose core of active members is primarily from a much older generation. In contrast, how many wonderful success stories have emerged from positive encounters of conversionary young couples with warm, welcoming, nurturing *Shabbat* clientele of similar age and family circumstances.

Barrier: A major barrier to conversion is the indifference of many Jewish partners to the virtues of unifying the household as a Jewish home. "The saddest observation of all is . . . that when we [rabbis] meet with a couple who is considering conversion, how very often it is the Jewish partner who is recalcitrant, who is obdurate, who is difficult, who is unwilling, who is unJewish!" (Harold Schulweis, High Holiday Sermon, 1988). Yet Jewish spouses/fiances must become aware of the importance of this process for their future marital contentment and for the solace in providing a Jewish identity for future offspring. A conversionary home is much less likely to encounter divorce than is an interfaith home. Children raised with one religion are most likely to develop a sense of comfort with the spiritual dimension of life. Furthermore, Judaism is best experienced in the context of a total Jewish family unit. Most important, the attitude of Jewish spouses often determines whether the non-Jewish partner will convert. After completing a study of dozens of intermarried couples for the AJC, Egon Mayer concluded: "Most non-converts reported that religion was not sufficiently important, either to themselves or to their spouses, to prompt conversion. By contrast, the converts . . . saw the religious issue as important to their spouses and their Jewish in-laws" (Egon Mayer and Amy Avgar, *Conversion Among the Intermarried*, p. 32).

4. How can I open a discussion with my non-Jewish spouse/ fiance with regard to my positive feelings about conversion to Judaism?

A pamphlet entitled "Inviting Someone You Love to Become a Jew," by Lydia Kukoff, offers a useful initial perspective:

It's not always easy to begin to talk about conversion with someone you care about deeply. We often hear: "I don't want to pressure her." "I wouldn't convert, so I could never ask him." "I'm afraid she'll be upset and our relationship will suffer." "It's not my place to intrude."

Jews often express concern about "pressure" and "intruding" when they think about asking someone to consider conversion. . . . When a relationship is precious, no one wants to raise issues that may be uncomfortable. Yet lovingly asking someone you care about to consider Judaism is simply an invitation. It is not coercion or pressure. It is an expression of concern about your future and a desire to share a precious tradition.

How can you begin to talk about conversion? Simply, honestly, and respectfully, with whatever words work best for you: "I've had something on my mind that I'd like to talk about." "I've been thinking about our family." "I'd like to talk with you about my feelings about Judaism." "I've wondered what it was like for you to have been with our family for seder." It doesn't matter where you begin.

Commentator Dennis Prager has offered an example of an open invitation to consider Judaism:

> You do not have to be Jewish to be saved—Judaism holds that God rewards all good people.
>
> Therefore, if you are presently involved in a religion, this notice does not apply to you.
>
> But if you are searching for religious meaning in this life, you may want to be Jewish. Contrary to what many people—including many Jews—believe, Judaism has always sought new adherents. This is why the Jewish tradition emphasizes that Abraham, the first Jew, was a convert.
>
> If you are on a quest for truth, or for meaning, or for a moral way of life, or for sanctity in a secular world, or for religious meaning, or for all of these, we [I] invite you to consider Judaism.

Contact any of the organizations listed here for further information on classes which culminate in a Sabbath experience with a Jewish family. And pick up any of the books listed below to better understand how Judaism can enrich your life. (Dennis Prager, "Judaism Seeks Converts," p. 6)

At a more personal level, two prominent experts have authored sensitive recommendations for Jewish partners facing this important juncture in their relationship. One is Professor Lawrence J. Epstein of Long Island, New York, who has gathered extensive survey data about conversion and has published a valuable primer entitled *Conversion to Judaism: A Guidebook*. The other is therapist Lena Romanoff of the Philadelphia area, a Jew by Choice and director of the Jewish Converts Network. The following recommendations are offered by Dr. Epstein.

First, consider why you value your Jewishness [read the first chapter of this volume]. What is it about Judaism that makes it important to you? . . .

Consider why you would like your partner to consider becoming Jewish . . . [such as] family unity . . . the opportunity to bring up children who will not be confused about their religious identity, and others.

There are good times and bad times to discuss the subject. . . . Good opportunities include a time of engagement, marriage, or the birth of a child. Bad times include religious holidays such as Christmas and Easter. . . .

One possibility is to discuss why you feel Judaism is important and to say: "Would you consider sharing the Jewish way of life?" followed by a discussion of what you see as the mutual benefits of your partner becoming Jewish.

Other people I spoke to invited their partner to a Seder, or Bar or Bat Mitzvah, or raised the issue in the context of discussing what kind of family they were going to have.

Others gave introductory books about Judaism or a book about conversion as a present. . . .

A talk with a rabbi, an Introduction to Judaism class, visiting Jewish sites, and other means of learning are vital for deliberation. (Lawrence J. Epstein, "Setting the Stage to Discuss Conversion," p. 8)

An alternative set of guidelines is provided by Lena Romanoff in *Your People, My People: Finding Acceptance and Fulfillment as a Jew by Choice*.

5. What is an Introduction-to-Judaism course for prospective converts?

There are many purposes for these programs:

- To transmit a conception of Judaism as a way of perceiving and acting that can provide direction to life.
- To transmit, through study and experience, the central practices and concepts of Judaism as well as an understanding of how these give meaning to the lives of committed Jews.
- To help participants decide to what extent they want to shape their own lives within the framework of Jewish tradition and to help them extend and develop Jewish tradition to make doing that possible.
- To foster a sense of community in class, creating an environment in which participants can experience the meaning of communal study and observance and can help one another to define their perspectives and commitments.
- To help participants clarify and deal constructively with their underlying feelings about Judaism and Jewish peoplehood.
- To encourage participants to take part in synagogue communities and to help them find congregations in which they feel comfortable.

- To provide participants who wish to convert to Judaism with the educational foundation they need to make their decision and to help them find outside rabbis to sponsor their conversion.

As for curriculum, I recommend a variety of necessary components. Keep in mind that only some of these essential elements will be present in any Introduction-to-Judaism course. It is the responsibility of Jewish family members to assist the Gentile relative in supplementing any gaps in this process.

- How to observe Jewish holidays and practices (*Shabbat*, High Holy Days, Hanukkah, Passover, etc.)
- Jewish life-cycle ceremonies (birth to death)
- Jewish beliefs (God, messiah, afterlife, chosen people, revelation, the soul)
- An awareness of Jewish peoplehood, the grandeur and pride of 3,200 years of Jewish history
- What Judaism says about modern issues (abortion, transplants, environmentalism, nuclear weapons, etc.)
- Jewish values such as visiting the sick, welcoming guests, *tzedakah*, respect for parents, and so on
- Jewish identity concerns such as the Holocaust, the State of Israel, Anti-Semitism
- Learning Hebrew prayers and the concepts behind them [note: fluency in conversational Hebrew is an entirely different skill and is rare among American Jews]
- Sacred texts, such as Bible, Talmud, midrash, codes, responsa
- Jewish heroes of biblical times (Abraham, Moses), rabbinic times (Hillel, Akiba), Middle Ages (Rashi, Maimonides), and modern times (Abraham Joshua Heschel, Mordecai Kaplan, David Ben-Gurion, Golda Meir, Elie Wiesel)

- Hebrew instruction to enable the student to feel comfortable in reading and understanding basic Hebrew prayers
- The American Jewish community today

In addition to these cognitive elements in studying for conversion, a candidate should begin to build Jewish memories. After all, our tradition regards a Jew by Choice as a "newborn" Jew, a person who needs to create a storehouse of positive Jewish memories. To help achieve this goal, a Jewish spouse should affiliate with a local synagogue and local rabbi and also should select some of the following:

- Ask to be paired with a "mentor couple," a family in a similar stage of life yet more experienced in Jewish home practices. These "mentors" should be willing to invite you to their home for an occasional *Shabbat* and/or holiday meal, to attend a synagogue function, to work together on a congregation committee, and so on. And you should feel free to reciprocate with invitations to your home.
- Help to build a network of Jewish peers by requesting involvement in one of your synagogue's *havurah* groups or other forms of couples' clubs.
- Build a pattern of religious practice by systematic attendance at *Shabbat* services (once or twice a month or more).
- Benefit from a total Jewish learning experience by partaking of a synagogue *Shabbat* retreat or a weekend session at Camp Ramah.
- Seek to enhance the would-be convert's comfort level for Jewish peoplehood by planning a trip to Israel.
- Many rabbis also suggest gaining familiarity with Jewish community resources:

  1. Jewish bookstores
  2. Jewish day schools
  3. Jewish homes for the aged

4. Jewish bakeries
5. Jewish meat markets
6. Jewish museums
7. Local bureaus of Jewish education
8. Local branches of Jewish organizations such as Hadassah, National Council of Jewish Women, B'nai B'rith, Synagogue Sisterhoods and Brotherhoods, American Jewish Committee, American Jewish Congress, UJA/Federation, etc.
9. Individuals who have converted to Judaism and are willing to discuss their experiences with you.
(Ronald Isaacs, *Becoming Jewish*, p. 11)

- Rabbi Neal Weinberg, of The University of Judaism (Los Angeles) Louis and Judith Miller Introduction To Judaism Program encourages candidates and Jewish significant others to explore the following areas:

  - Take a Jewish home tour of a typical modern Jewish home. Tour the kitchen in detail, practice candlelighting, and observe a typical *Shabbat* table setting
  - Consider support groups intended for successfully coping with the needs of Jewish and non-Jewish family members:

    - How do I tell my friends and family about my decision to convert to Judaism?
    - How do I include both families at religious functions?
    - How do I deal with the Easter/Passover and Christmas/Hanukkah conflicts?
    - Do I say *kaddish* for a non-Jewish parent who has passed away?

  - Consider Jewish peoplehood

    - How do I make that emotional connection with Israel as an ancestral homeland?

- How do I begin to feel Jewish?
- How can I find my place in the Jewish community?

Through the process of study combined with religious and communal experiences, many potential converts are able both to reaffirm what they already believe and to find added meaning through the lens of Jewish tradition. Frequently, the Jewish partner also is inspired by seeing Judaism anew through the eyes of the Gentile partner. Yet while experiencing mutual growth, Lena Romanoff reminds Jewish spouses/fiances to keep in mind that ultimately the process of deciding whether to convert to Judaism rests with the prospective Jew by Choice.

> The decision has to be "right" for each individual. It should be based on the person's exposure to Jewish experiences and Jewish study. One cannot convert into a religion that one does not understand or know. Yes, Jews should be open, welcoming, and encouraging of conversion under the right circumstances. Anyone who seeks information about conversion should be embraced and shown the way—no one can decide to convert into a religion in a vacuum!
>
> There may well come a time when a person is no longer content to passively observe the Judaism of others by standing on the sidelines. Instead the person will want to be an active participant.
>
> The choice to convert is seldom simple. It often is complex and conflictive, intertwined with the feelings of significant others. It is a choice which can only be made in a private moment of introspective thought, and the moment of that decision is known only to the individual. (Lena Romanoff, "How Does One Decide to Convert to Another Religion?" p. 6)

6. How shall conversionary couples handle the inevitable challenges of the December Dilemma (Christmas and Hanukkah season)?

To assist Jews by Choice and their born-Jewish spouses in this difficult season, the Federation of Jewish Men's Clubs

published an outstanding resource guide entitled *Hanukah* in
Dr. Ron Wolfson's "Art of Jewish Living Series." Dr. Wolfson
skillfully identifies the emerging challenges to be navigated by
conversionary couples each winter.

> All of a sudden, we are not confronting Christmas [only] in the
> shopping mall; we must respond to an invitation of a non-Jewish
> relative to celebrate Christmas with a part of our family. All of a
> sudden, we are not just debating whether to sing Christmas songs
> in the school choir; we are asked to accompany a family member
> to Midnight Mass. It is one thing to say "no" to a child wanting to
> sit on Santa's knee, but quite another to refuse an invitation from
> in-laws to celebrate their holiday. (Ron Wolfson, *The Art of Jewish
> Living: Hanukkah*, p. 155)

As a means of addressing these mounting concerns, Dr. Wolfson case-studies the Bobrow family, Claudia being a convert
and her husband Shlomo a Jew by birth.

> Reflecting on an oft-repeated story, Claudia's conversion to Juda-
> ism also prompted Shlomo's commitment to Jewish religious
> life. . . . Yet, the winter holidays bring the family face-to-face
> with the fact that while Claudia converted to Judaism, her family
> did not. . . . The Bobrows' solution to their family's December
> Dilemmas has been reached after years of debate and experimen-
> tation. (Ron Wolfson, *The Art of Jewish Living: Hanukkah*, p. 31)

Rabbis and Jewish educators recommend that conversionary
families are best served by establishing clarity within their
home during the holiday season. This means that the family
must *not* have a Christmas tree in its own home.

> Claudia: That was a real hard thing to give up, but I knew
> that . . . [it] was right. It seemed rather obvious. So that is how
> we worked it out. I know other couples where the Jewish partner

wavers on that issue, which I think is a mistake. (Ron Wolfson, *The Art of Jewish Living: Hanukkah*, p. 161)

More difficult is the question of whether to accept invitations to spend Christmas evening at the home of Christian relatives. Certainly the simplest solution is to schedule visits to Christian relatives at times other than Christmas and Easter, such as Thanksgiving, July Fourth, or Labor Day Weekend. However, if a conversionary couple does decide to attend Christmas dinner at grandparents' or other relatives' homes, they must make clear that they will not attend church services.

> Claudia: We are only there [at Christmas dinner] to be with the family. . . . We are not going to church with them. I would draw the line at that. (Ron Wolfson, *The Art of Jewish Living: Hanukkah*, p. 162)

Nevertheless, Christmas can pose a serious conflict for the evolving Jewish identity of Jewish children and even for some Jews by Choice unless they are continually nourished by the rich spiritual flavor of Judaism's full calendar year. Lena Romanoff told my class of rabbinical students at the Jewish Theological Seminary:

> It is preferable to instruct converts to visit Christian relatives at secular holidays such as July 4 or Thanksgiving.
>
> If you do visit, bring the Christian family Christmas gifts, and have them give Hanukkah gifts to you and your family.
>
> Kids will not be confused as Jewish kids, if during the rest of the year you have content-filled Jewish homes [weekly *Shabbat*, holidays throughout the year].

This admonition is borne out in the experience of the Bobrow family. Claudia astutely remarked:

> I realized . . . what you have to do. You have to celebrate all of the holidays the rest of the year. Then when you get to Hanukah, you

really don't have a big conflict. If your life is filled with Jewish festivals and a Jewish calendar is part of your life, by the time you get to Christmas, it's no problem. (Ron Wolfson, *The Art of Jewish Living: Hanukkah*, p. 161)

Claudia and Shlomo had learned the wisdom offered by Ron Wolfson and other experts that parents explain to their children that Christmas is someone else's party, not ours. We can appreciate someone else's birthday celebration. We can remark at how lovely a Christmas tree or lights are, but Christmas is not our party. Our party comes every Friday night and Saturday morning. It comes on the High Holy Days, Sukkot, Passover, Shavuot, Hanukkah, Purim, Simchat Torah, and other special occasions.

7. What emotional pitfalls might arise for my non-Jewish relative contemplating conversion?

In chapter 2 of *Your People, My People*, Lena Romanoff takes note of discernible stages in the emotional process of conversion:

* Introspection. Who am I? Where did I come from? Where am I going?
* Intellectualization. Intense learning about Judaism
* Drifting betwixt and between. I'm no longer Episcopalian but I'm not yet Jewish. What do I call myself?
* Fear of the unknown. Who will be my Jewish role models?
* Feeling overwhelmed. There's too much to know, to read.
* Conversion day: apprehension and relief.
* Post-Conversion highs and lows. I'm officially a Jew, but when do I begin to feel Jewish?

Concerned family members should also provide context and emotional support for the potential Jew by Choice who encounters frustrations in dealing with other Jews. Here Rabbi Ronald Isaacs's volume *Becoming Jewish* offers useful pointers:

> Some born Jews will find it easy to accept you and will see your decision to convert as an endorsement of Judaism and the Jewish way of life. Some will try to be accepting but nonetheless feel uncomfortable around converts. Some find it difficult to understand why anyone would want to convert to Judaism in the first place. (This is often the case with less knowledgable Jews.) . . .
>
> Occasionally there may be guilt and ambivalence on the part of born Jews who feel threatened by a convert who knows more than they do and who is more enthusiastic about Judaism than they are. (p. 19)

The following is a list of guidelines for enhancing the Jewish self-esteem of the prospective or recent convert by offering step-by-step growth in Jewish involvement. Encourage or help the future or new Jew by Choice to:

- Celebrate *Shabbat* on a weekly basis
- Begin to use a Jewish calendar, noting Jewish holidays
- Practice and learn basic prayers and rituals
- Purchase books and magazines of Jewish interest
- Visit local Jewish museums
- Obtain ritual objects for your home use
- Acquire pieces of Jewish art, tapes, and CDs of Jewish music
- Utilize a family *tzedakah* (charity) box
- Build and decorate a family *sukkah*
- Prepare your own Passover *seder*
- Make costumes for use at Purim's *megillah* reading

Converts will feel more and more confident as they acquire "ownership" of hands-on aspects of Jewish living.

As you begin your life as a Jew, try to see each new day as an opportunity to practice your Judaism. Continue to study and increase your repertoire of knowledge and fulfillment of mitzvot. Practice the mitzvot with joy! Make prayer a regular part of your life. Practice your Hebrew skills. Discover the happiness of celebrating Jewish holidays throughout the year. Because Shabbat comes every week, try to make it an opportunity for personal recreation. (Ron Isaacs, *Becoming Jewish*, p. 39)

Jews by Choice should continue their formal study beyond the Introduction-to-Judaism curriculum by continuing to learn Hebrew, enrolling in Adult Education courses, entering into an adult *bar/bat mitzvah* one- or two-year program leading toward a group *bar/bat mitzvah* ceremony, participating in a *Shabbat* morning learners' *minyan* (prayer service), attending holiday workshops, utilizing Judaica videotapes, audiotapes, Jewish cookbooks, and other Jewish educational materials. This additional learning will help the new Jew to become comfortable with Hebrew prayers and to develop a rhythm of Jewish living.

Also consider useful books within Conservative Judaism specifically about the conversion experience:

- Alan Silverstein, *Are You Considering Conversion into Judaism?* (New York: Rabbinical Assembly, 1992). Rabbi Silverstein provides a series of answers to questions frequently posed by prospective Jews by Choice, often citing the experiences of converts currently active within congregations such as his Conservative synagogue.
- Lena Romanoff, *Your People, My People: Finding Acceptance and Fulfillment as a Jew by Choice* (Philadelphia: Jewish Publication Society, 1990). This is an easy-to-read and insightful guidebook written by a convert for other converts.
- Lawrence J. Epstein, *Conversion to Judaism: A Guidebook* (Northvale, NJ: Jason Aronson, 1994). A comprehensive guidebook for conversion to Judaism.

- Simcha Kling, *Embracing Judaism* (New York: Rabbinical Assembly, 1987). Rabbi Kling offers a text of basic Jewish knowledge used by many Conservative Jewish converts.
- Ronald H. Isaacs, *Becoming Jewish: A Handbook for Conversion* (New York: Rabbinical Assembly, 1993). Rabbi Isaacs has written a valuable summary of personal issues that confront Jews by Choice, as well as a curriculum for Jewish holidays, life cycle, and living an ongoing Jewish life.
- Harold Kushner, *To Life: A Celebration of Jewish Being and Thinking* (Boston: Little, Brown, 1993). Rabbi Kushner discusses basic concepts in Judaism and how the Jewish religion offers guidance for modern living.

8. Do all conversions result in successful commitment to Judaism?

Rabbis caution family members not to leave the convert "dripping at the *mikvah*." In other words, the Jewish tradition wisely regards a Jew by Choice as a religious newborn. Lawrence Epstein cautions: "The role of the partner does not stop at raising the issue of conversion . . . [but also includes] the ramifications for raising children, celebrating holidays, making life-style choices, joining religious and other institutions, and other issues" (Lawrence J. Epstein, *Conversion to Judaism*, p. 46). Spouses, in-laws, and friends must help this important person in our lives to gain positive Jewish memories, skills, and experiences. If we fail to assist in this process of resocialization, there are risks of varying degrees of failure. In his extensive research about this range of successes, Steven Huberman noted seven types of converts to Judaism:

1. Integral converts—live a "Jewish rhythm"

2. Participants – involved in Jewish life on a regular basis
3. Associated converts – affiliated with Jewish institutions in some concrete way
4. Contributors and consumers – give money and/or use the services of Jewish institutions periodically
5. Peripheral converts – identify as Jews but completely uninvolved in Jewish life
6. Marginal converts – quasi-Jews, neither completely in or out of the Jewish commmunity
7. Non-Jews – have repudiated Judaism and their conversion. (Steven Huberman, "From Christianity to Judaism: Religion Changers in American Society," p. 22)

In order to maximize the integration of new Jews, all experienced observers stress the need for the Jewish family to become more involved than ever in the religious dimensions of Judaism. One convert told researcher Steven Huberman: "I will always know I am different. I can't be like my husband; he was born Jewish. I was born Italian. To be a good Jew I have to be a religious Jew" ("From Christianity to Judaism," p. 25). Lacking the ethnic dimension of born Jews, converts define their Jewishness in terms familiar to them from their Christian upbringing: prayer and ritual observance. Make sure to become involved in the religious, educational, and social life of your local synagogue or, if you relocate, to get a referral to a suitable congregation in your new neighborhood. Sisterhoods or Men's Clubs are often useful vehicles for networking into congregational life. In Women's League for Conservative Judaism's guidebook, *And Teach Them Diligently: Sisterhood Welcomes the Jew by Choice*, for example, editor Penny Leifer writes:

> The intent of this publication is to impart some very basic information about holidays, Shabbat and kashrut to the Jew By Choice, who does not have the benefit of childhood experiences or memories. We have given some tips that have been learned through our

own experiences, and also some information that can only be
learned by doing, preferably in someone's house.

We look to our Sisterhood leaders to reach out and teach, to
walk beside the Jew By Choice and show the way. There is no limit
to what can be done. . . .

Having chosen to accept Judaism, Jews By Choice have taken
the first big step. It is now up to us to reach out . . . "And Teach
Them Diligently." (p. 1)

It is also recommended that you seek postconversion support groups. Linda Fife of the United Synagogue regional
office in Los Angeles has drawn up guidelines for such programs, which can be offered by individual synagogues or on a
regional basis, either as six-week sessions or on a drop-in basis
with topics announced in advance. Ms. Fife has noted:

For those who convert, there are many challenges that must be
faced. Family concerns, the process of joining a people and not
just a religion and their lack of Jewish memories to name but a
few. . . . Support groups are designed on a topical basis in an
effort to provide support for the new Jew as he/she makes his/her
way as a Jew. . . .

- Feelings about becoming Jewish—How do I develop Jew-
  ish authenticity and identity?
- What about my non-Jewish family (and my children)
- My spouse (and/or) in-laws as ambivalent
- What about the part of me that was formed by my non-
  Jewish family and memories
- Holidays How? Where?
- Life cycle events—Can I say Kaddish for my parents?
- Acceptance and Rebuffs by the Jewish community
- How do I tell my non-Jewish family?
- I'm single
- How will I ever learn Hebrew?

- Israel
- Holocaust
- Peoplehood vs. religion (Linda Fife, "Welcoming Converts into Synagogue Life")

Linda Fife also urges Jews by Choice to network with other converts in their community: "If you know of other converts in your congregration and they are willing to be available by phone, provide their names and numbers to new converts. Often speaking to someone who has 'been through it' can be very helpful" (Linda Fife, "Welcoming Converts into Synagogue Life"). She also suggests that supportive friends provide the new Jew with a Jewish "shower," to celebrate the ceremony of conversion. Guests might bring a gift of Jewish content: a book such as a *siddur*, a Bible, or others; or a ritual object such as a *Kiddush* cup, *hallah* board/cover/knife, *havdalah* set, Passover plate, *matzah* cover, or a *tallit* (prayer shawl), which symbolize the *mitzvot* (commandments) of Judaism. The newly converted Jewish adult might also seek a Torah *Aliyah* or Ark Opening or Dress/Lifting the Torah during the synagogue service as a symbol of formal acceptance into the Jewish religious community.

Rabbi Joseph Tabachnik and Dr. Brenda Foster have observed:

The process of becoming a Jew is a process of resocialization, not just learning a few new religious holiday rituals. Converts indicate that even in the religious realm, major changes in life-style and beliefs are required. In addition, the ethnic dimension, feeling, talking, reacting like a Jew, and being accepted as a Jew by Jews, takes even more time and effort. A commitment to life-long study and involvement must be made and followed through. (Joseph Tabachnik and Brenda Foster, *Jews by Choice: A Study of Converts to Reform and Conservative Judaism*, p. 153)

For ongoing support, new Jews also might investigate whether their area has a Jewish Converts Network (JCN). The JCN in Philadelphia, created and directed by Lena Romanoff, is the national coordinating center for these programs. The JCN's "statement of purpose" indicates that "after 'formal conversion' is completed, a long period of 'acculturation' begins, in which the convert must discover how most of the information he or she has previously learned translates into the realities of Jewish life" (Lena Romanoff, "Jewish Converts Network"). Thus, the JCN seeks to help converts:

1. Experience the pride, excitement, exhilaration, and joy of making Judaism a living, integral aspect of one's life
2. Achieve intellectual understanding of some of the factors . . . of Jewish identity, such as pride in one's heritage, the ability to assert one's ethnic and religious rights and the handling of values conflicts
3. Examine the delight, ecstasy, enthusiasm, and spontaneity of Jewish observance, worship, and learning—[via] music, dance, meaningful prayers and relevant study, and group interactive learning experiences
4. Learn about new skills, techniques, and programs for use in the Jewish family and in educational, organizational, and communal life
5. Examine personal values and priorities and to analyze factors which impede stronger Jewish identity and commitment, as well as to explore new methods to intensify personal Jewish values and commitments
6. Establish closeness and warmth and meaningful one-to-one relationships within the JCN group. (Lena Romanoff, "Jewish Converts Network")

To begin the process of inviting and supporting your spouse's conversion into Judaism, you may contact the nearest Rabbinical Assembly Introduction to Judaism program. This information can be obtained by:

- contacting the Rabbinical Assembly International office – (212) 678-8060 – at 3080 Broadway, New York, NY   10027.
- contacting the Rabbinical Assembly's Conversion Chairperson, Rabbi Neil Weinberg, in Los Angeles – (310) 476-9777 – at University of Judaism, 15600 Mulholland Drive, Los Angeles, CA   90077.
- or contacting the Rabbinical Assembly's 800 number for Conversion and Outreach – 800-WELCOME.

Here are some other resource persons who may be of help to you:

Dr. Lawrence J. Epstein – author, regarding conversion issues – (516) 751-5013

Rabbi Marvin Labinger – a resource person for information regarding conversion programs in the Pacific Southwest region of Conservative Judaism – United Synagogue of Conservative Judaism, 15600 Mulholland Drive, Los Angeles, CA   90077

Rabbi William Lebeau – Dean of the Rabbinical School at the Jewish Theological Seminary

Rabbi Stephen Lerner – The Center for Conversion to Judaism, (212) 877-8640 or (201) 837-7552.

Rabbi Avis Miller – chairperson of the Rabbinical Assembly *Keruv* (Outreach) Committee

Meryl Nadell – Jewish Family Service of MetroWest (NJ), specializing in counseling conversionary and interfaith couples and their families

Lena Romanoff – author, lecturer, director of Jewish Converts Network in Philadelphia area, with affiliated programs in other states – 1112 Hagysford Road, Narbeth, PA   19072   (215) 664-8112

3

Considering Conversion
to Judaism

Perhaps you are considering conversion to Judaism. Your interest may stem from reading Jewish books or taking courses at college, from contact with Jewish friends, a love relationship with a Jew, an unfulfilled spiritual quest, an awareness of Jewish parentage or ancestry, or a positive image of Jewish religion conveyed by films and the media. You may be wondering: what are the benefits and challenges of entering the Jewish faith? Have others who have chosen Judaism faced the same concerns and questions I have?

This chapter presents a series of questions and answers borrowing from converts' personal testimonies, to help you answer your own questions. These questions are partially based on categories listed in *Jews by Choice: A Study of Converts to Reform and Conservative Judaism*, by Conservative rabbi Joseph Tabachnik and Dr. Brenda Foster. On the basis of over 400 questionnaires, Tabachnik and Foster provide "reasons proposed to explain Gentile [affiliated as well as unchurched Christian] conversion to Judaism." Following is a partial restatement of their total list of reasons why people convert to Judaism:

Religious-related

- Belief that Judaism is a better religion
- Identification with Jesus as a Jew
- Feeling that God is leading them down this path
- Feeling that Jewish beliefs make sense
- Liking Jewish worship
- Liking the realism in Jewish routine practices
- Sense of spiritual or religious need
- Search for a better religious identity
- Serious personal event that caused questioning of faith

Marriage-related

- Concern for religious identity of children
- Desire for a Jewish wedding
- Desire to provide children with a coherent family tradition and religion
- Wish to avoid dissonance in the home
- Wish to please the Jewish in-laws
- Wish to please the Jewish partner
- Desire to share faith and practice with partner

Community-related

- Admiration of Jewish accomplishments in the face of hostilities
- Desire to belong to a close community
- Desire to be part of an ancient heritage that has withstood the test of time
- Feeling that Jews live desirable lives
- Many Jewish friends
- Identification with the Jewish fate

Although not every one of the following questions may reflect your personal state of mind, perhaps some of them will accurately portray your feelings and help move you toward exploring a profound religious decision.

1. Does traditional Judaism accept converts, or is only the Reform movement liberal enough to be welcoming of Jews by Choice?

Don't assume that the traditional segment of the Jewish community does not accept sincere converts. Representing modern Orthodoxy, for example, Rabbi Maurice Lamm's new volume entitled *Becoming a Jew* includes a final section, "Welcome Home: We Are Keeping the Lights On," in which he articulates the warm affinity of traditionalists for pious newcomers. " 'Those who stood at Sinai' [to receive the Torah via Moses] is a phrase that comprises those who are born to Jewish ancestors, all of whom originally converted at Sinai, those whose ancestors heroically converted since that time, and those who will convert today and tomorrow" (Maurice Lamm, *Becoming a Jew*, p. 417).

Rabbi Lamm and the rest of us in Jewry eagerly await the "return home" of persons whose destiny is to join ranks with the Jewish religious community.

As for Conservative Judaism, we are a huge movement of more than 40 percent of American Jewry, blessed with thousands of sincere Jews by Choice. Among converts into our ranks, we are proud to number some rabbis, cantors, Jewish educators, many local synagogue, Men's Club and Sisterhood presidents, and countless well-respected members of our Boards of Trustees, committees, and *minyanim* (those who attend prayer services). The chancellor of the Jewish Theological Seminary, Rabbi Ismar Schorsch, in addressing a 1987 national conclave for the leadership of Conservative Jewry, observed:

[Conversion is] an instrument that accords with our religious integrity. . . . Conversion opened up the Jewish community to the Greco-Roman world. There were many non-Jews who entered Judaism because Judaism pioneered the institution of conversion back [then]. . . . So I wish to make myself very clear. I think that conversion properly used is still the most effective way [in terms of responding to existing interfaith marriages] for us to be consistent with our past . . . while at the same time addressing the real needs of the present. (Ismar Schorsch, keynote speech to Conservative Movement Conference on Intermarriage and Conversion, March 2–3, 1987)

All suitably prepared and involved Jews by Choice are welcomed by Reform, Reconstructionist, Conservative, and Orthodox groups within the mainstream of American Jewish religious life, in accord with each movement's standards of practice.

2. "Will I have to forsake my Gentile family in order to become a Jewish person?

This is a sensitive problem that must be treated with care. Rabbi Sanford Seltzer has written:

It is true that initially one's parents may be hurt and resentful when informed that a son or a daughter has decided to leave their former faith. These feelings may exist even when one's family has not been particularly religious. . . . The impact of conversion to Judaism upon parents and other loved ones should be thoroughly evaluated before one decides to become a Jew. (Sanford Seltzer, "On Becoming a Jew," p. 2)

One of the paramount commandments of the Jewish tradition is the *mitzvah* of honoring one's father and mother. Judaism opposes cutting off ties with non-Jewish family members. Christian and unchurched relatives ought to be respectful of a convert's new religious needs as well. In her excellent guidebook for new Jews, *Your People, My People: Finding Acceptance and Fulfillment as a Jew by Choice,* Lena Romanoff, a convert and committed Conservative Jew, offers the following advice, based on hundreds of case studies:

> A convert should explain to the family that he or she is the same person as before, with a different religious and cultural orientation. He or she should never criticize or ridicule the family's—and his or her former—faith. . . . Converts should provide details about the conversion process and describe how they intend to incorporate Judaism into their lives. (p. 107)

Rather than sending Christmas cards to you, Christian family members should send Hanukkah greetings, and you should reciprocate with Christmas regards to them. Rather than beginning home meals with prayers to Jesus Christ when you are present, they might more suitably invoke the name of God. You should respect that Christianity is their religion, and they should respect that Judaism is yours. Once such mutuality is achieved in religious matters, your family interpersonal relationships ought to remain warm and respectful.

3. Should I be troubled with the prospect that Orthodox Jews will question the validity of my conversion under Conservative Jewish auspices?

America is a land of freedom in decision-making. There are no government-mandated religious authorities. Instead, our country separates church and state. Neither in Christianity nor in Judaism can anyone dictate uniformity of practice.

Thus, for example, many rituals and practices of Catholics are unacceptable to Protestant groups. Evangelical Protestants question the validity of mainline Protestant commitments. A convert to Methodism may be regarded as inauthentic by born-again Christians. A neophyte Unitarian might be considered unacceptable to right-wing Christian faith communities. Mennonites and Amish are regarded as exotic, sectarian groups. Diversity and disagreement are characteristic of American Christian denominations. The same divergence is true among America's Jews.

Orthodox Judaism represents less than 10 percent of American Jewry. It has its own criteria for valid ritual practice, theology, and conversion. So too does Conservative Judaism, which represents the largest number of affiliated Jews in the United States. Our conversions are consistent with the nature of Jewish religion as practiced within our more than 800 congregations and more than 1.5 million adherents. Jews by Choice who enter Judaism under the auspices of Conservative rabbis find their status as Jews acceptable to our entire religious movement, as well as to Reform, Reconstructionist, and unaffiliated Jews, collectively totaling more than 90 percent of American Jewry.

In the remote event that you subsequently became involved in an Orthodox community, they would not recognize your conversion as valid any more than they would recognize a Conservative rabbi as a rabbi or a Conservative congregation as a synagogue. However, keep in mind that different standards would be only part of a fundamental reorientation for *any* non-Orthodox Jew (born Jew or convert) entering Orthodoxy, a reorientation in ritual practice, in prayer, in belief, in every aspect of religious life. Just as a convert into a mainline Protestant group would not be concerned about the opinions of Evangelicals or of Roman Catholics, as a Conservative Jew by Choice you need not worry about the minority views of Orthodox Judaism.

4. Will entry into Judaism resolve my personal faith concerns? Not having been satisfied with previous religious affiliations, will I find spiritual fulfillment within Judaism?

Jew by Choice Gail Saville offers an eloquent articulation of the attraction of Jewish beliefs in contrast to her previous faith experiences:

> I find great comfort in Judaism. Jewish children are born innocent [of original sin]. . . . Jewish children are not born with the burden of guilt. They do not come into this world tainted with original sin, but rather blessed with original purity. . . .
> There are no intermediaries between Jews and God. Jews believe that all people have close, personal access to God. As a Jew, I don't have to go through an ecclesiastical switchboard . . . in charge of human affairs to reach God. . . .
> There is also security in knowing that as a Jew I am part of a people and a way of life that has survived and will survive. (Gail Saville, "Why I Chose to Become a Jew," p. 20)

The testimony of a former Protestant minister, Richard Kajut, is equally forceful. He writes:

> The decision to break with my former Christian faith was the culmination of a lengthy process of religious search. . . . There was no flash of lightning which prompted my choice to convert. Ironically, it was the desire to know more about the character of Jesus the man, the historical Jesus, which eventually led to the renunciation of my Christian heritage. . . .
> During my college years, I spent many spare hours in the religion stacks of the university library pulling texts on the "historical" Jesus. [Albert] Schweitzer led me to R.H. Charles, Charles to Albright, and Albright to Powell Davies. I graduated soon to Joseph Klausner and Abba Hillel Silver. . . . A whole new understanding of the zeitgeist of the early first century opened before my eyes: apocryphal and

pseudopigraphical theology . . . Greek mystery religions, Sadducees, centrist Pharisees, apocalyptic Pharisees, Essenes, Zealots, Hillel and Shammai. . . . If I was to serve the one God of Moses and the Prophets in the manner I was drawn to Him, I could do so only as a Jew. (cited in Maurice Lamm, *Becoming a Jew*, pp. 29–30)

In addition to finding comfort with our beliefs, many converts to Judaism discover that membership in the Jewish community sparks a new sense of spirituality, of religious vitality. Paul Cowan's personal odyssey, *An Orphan in History*, describes his wife Rachel's spiritual rebirth via conversion under the supervision of Rabbi Wolfe Kelman, the former Executive Vice President of the (Conservative) Rabbinical Assembly. "She [Rachel] said that she had been thinking about the idea [of conversion] for months, ever since she discovered that worshipping as a Jew released something inside her which enabled her to think about God; to feel, at rare moments, a faith whose intensity startled her" (Paul Cowan, *An Orphan in History*, p. 217). In a related assessment, one of my own students for conversion into Judaism, Ben Asher, explains:

That is precisely why [one] . . . converts, because of some sort of experience of something spiritual that has never been accessible prior to undertaking this perilous journey. A window was somehow miraculously opened. At the time of "illumination" the convert may be in awe as his whole disposition reflects the extraordinary process of transformation going on within . . . The Power of God at work. (Conservative Congregation Agudath Israel, Caldwell, New Jersey)

5. Having been raised as a non-Jew, will I ever find religious meaning in the Hebrew prayers or in sacred sites of Jewish history, such as the land of Israel?

Don't be intimated by what might seem to be a chasm between Jews and Gentiles in religious vocabulary and experiences.

Once a person sincerely enters into Judaism via conversion, Hebrew prayers, *Eretz Yisrael*, and other internal Jewish symbols not only open up to you but will become enormously inspiring. Conservative convert Lucy Katzen observes:

> It took time for Jewish tradition to grow and it is logical that it should take time for someone to grow into it. If I had waited for every custom to have meaning before I observed it, I'd still be waiting. I learned instead that customs can grow to have meaning because you observe them. I had to give myself time to make memories and the two years I had when I [prepared for being] converted cannot compare to the ten years of experiences I've had now. (Lucy Katzen, "A Ten-Year Retrospective," p. 5)

In *Lovesong*, Julius Lester, the involved member of a Conservative congregation, emotionally expresses the birth of the love for Hebrew language, ritual, and the liturgical beauty of Judaism through the eyes of a New Jew.

> I am in love!
> What an odd thing to say about a religion, but it is true. I am in love with Judaism, with being a Jew. . . . I am having a love affair with my soul. . . .
> I have begun my second semester of modern Hebrew. . . . Knowing Hebrew will give me the confidence to go anywhere among Jews. And Jews are the only ones with whom I can share my great love. (Julius Lester, *Lovesong: Becoming a Jew*, p. 202)

Joann Boughman, a Jew by Choice, was initially moved during a professional conference in Israel by the spiritual power of a visit to the Western Wall (Judaism's most sacred spot, at the site of the ancient Temple in Jerusalem) and by subsequent encounters with Jewish ritual.

> I was absolutely overcome with emotion [when I saw the Wall]. My knees got weak and I started crying. One of my colleagues had

to help me sit down on the pavement. . . . [It was the feeling that] thousands of years had come crashing down on me all at once.

I fell in love with the incredible richness of Jewish tradition and ritual. For example, one thing I always liked about Christmas was the candlelighting services on Christmas Eve, the warmth and beauty of it. Well, [Christians] light candles once a year. I do it every Friday night. (Alyssa Gabbay, "Jews By Choice," pp. 52–53)

These powerful spiritual experiences are not at all uncommon among converts to Judaism. For example, Judith Lee traced her receptivity to entering into Judaism to a shared search among candidates in a Board of Rabbis' (Conservative and Reform) conversion class. In many cases, they were seeking a stronger religious identity. Recounting personal sharing among classmates, Judith writes:

Those of us who were not Jewish at that time had given a great deal of thought to many things before we decided to come together that [first] night [of class]. We had thought about ourselves and how, despite the fact we were all educated and professionally successful, we were somehow missing a needed sense of individual and communal spiritual connectedness. . . .

We each had felt a strong pull towards Judaism for several years and had sensed that living as a Jew would make it possible for each of us to realize our potentials in accordance with our values, our intellect and our emotions. (Judith S. Lee, "Joining In: A Personal Account," p. 15)

6. Is it valid to consider converting to Judaism because of the desire to be part of the same religion in which my spouse and I have chosen to raise our children?

Conversion into Judaism is a serious endeavor and ultimately must reflect a sincere commitment on the part of the convert.

However, to begin to explore Judaism as a statement of commitment to one's children's religious well-being is praiseworthy. Conservative Rabbi Michael Wasserman recounts the thoughts of a new Jew, Kathy, one of his students in his Introduction-to-Judaism course.

> Kathy [said] . . . that having grown up with parents of different faiths (Catholic and Lutheran), she considers it important to have a single religion in the home so that the children can get a consistent set of religious messages. She wants religion to play an important role in their family life, and is willing to accept Daniel's religion so that she will have Daniel's support in that area. She can take that step, she says, because she does not believe that any one religion has a monopoly on truth. (Michael Wasserman, "The Convert and the Rabbi as 'Stress Absorbers,' " p. 161)

Reflecting on a later stage of parenting, Francis Price concludes:

> My entrance into Judaism dates from the beginning of my small son's religious education. . . . When our son was five and had reached religious school age, I sent him to a synagogue near our home. My mind began to turn to Judaism, not only for him but for myself. I must admit it was purely an academic thing with me [initially]. What makes a Jew a Jew? How does a Jew think? What are his traditions? These and many other questions nagged at me and, for the sake of my child's religious training, I wanted to know the answers. My quest for Jewish knowledge began. (Maurice Lamm, *Becoming a Jew*, p. 15)

Similarly, one of my own students for conversion into Judaism, Diane Gerberg, recalls her own spiritual evolution.

> I started thinking about my family unit. We were thinking about the education of our son. And I was thinking in terms of all he had

to learn in Hebrew. And the thought came into my mind that maybe he should go to yeshiva. And because religion has always been extremely important to me – throughout my life it has always been my standard bearer in a sense, the thing that was very very important to me – I started looking at my family unit and feeling in a way not part of it. It was a strange sensation that came over me one day where I realized that my son and my husband were Jewish and I was this oddity in the house. . . . I wanted to make my family a unit. I wanted to be part of my family. And I really believed that this was the place to be. To me it was like coming home. (Stephen Weiss, "Interview with Jew by Choice")

7. Is it reasonable to begin the encounter with Jewish study and Jewish religious practice as a response to experiences I encountered within my Jewish spouse's extended family?

Whether for children or in-laws, no one should enter Jewish life solely in response to others. However, it is entirely commendable to begin to explore Judaism because of powerful feelings of family, whether with Jewish in-laws or with other new relatives.

In *A Certain People*, author Charles Silberman interviewed many Jews by Choice who had been drawn into Judaism after becoming comfortable with Jewish family settings. The Passover *seder*, Hanukkah celebrations, festive weddings, sensitive mourning customs, *bar/bat mitzvah* festivities, and similar memories evolved into a growing comfort with Jewish religion (Charles Silberman, *A Certain People: American Jews and Their Lives Today*, p. 308). Dolores, a convert to Judaism, tells writer Susan Weidman Schneider: "It probably sounds a little macabre, but it was going to Jewish funerals [of her husband's extended family] that first attracted me to Judaism. There was no open casket, which I liked, and the *shiva* [seven days of mourning] seemed very civilized and psychologically sensible" (Susan Weidman Schneider, *Intermarriage*, p. 201).

Also responding to in-laws, an English Jew by Choice writes about his own changing motivations:

> The project [of conversion into Judaism] . . . was one about which I had felt not the slightest tremor of religious or transcendental sentiment. . . . I had undertaken it with reluctance, only to meet the needs of my future wife's parents. . . . I approached the matter, therefore, with diffidence and embarassment. . . . Yet to my surprise, the nature of the experience itself was such that these feelings were changed into interest and respect.
>
> I began a modest course of study. . . . I learned by heart a number of prayers and she explained the significance of the Jewish festivals. . . . As Passover was due, I was taken through the Haggadah. . . . I was charmed by the way it [the Seder] involved children . . . [and] that for Jews, it is in domestic matters that religious and aesthetic feelings come together; for example in the Seder, or in the lighting of the Sabbath candles. (cited in *Commentary*, reprinted in Maurice Lamm, *Becoming a Jew*, pp. 45–46)

8. What about my spouse? Is it unreasonable to feel attracted to Judaism as a result of my love for my partner?

Here, too, it is perfectly understandable to become interested in Judaism through the eyes of a lover, a fiance(e), or a spouse. Perhaps ultimately this quest may lead to religious fulfillment and conversion into Judaism on its own terms. Lois Lederman, a Jew by Choice, shared with Lena Romanoff an assessment of her entry into Judaism in the context of intimacy with her husband, Hershel.

> When I fell in love with Hershel, I wanted to know everything about him—his interests, his ideas, beliefs and hopes. . . .
>
> It was Hershel's love for his heritage that influenced me to explore it for myself. Although it was my love and respect for him

that sparked my initial desire to discover Judaism, in the end it was my decision. . . . I know the entire process has brought us closer to each other. . . . (Lena Romanoff, *Your People, My People*, p. 54)

9. Am I justified in considering conversion because I am attracted to the positive qualities of the Jewish people throughout history, the State of Israel, and so on?

Judaism is more than simply a creed; it is also a religious communion to fellow Jews around the world and throughout time. Conservative Rabbi Simcha Kling writes in a (Conservative) Rabbinical Assembly primer for converts, *Embracing Judaism*:

> A convert to Judaism not only adopts a new theology and different ritual practices but also joins a different people. To be a Jew means belonging to a unique historical community. The community is neither racially nor genetically defined, since those born outside it may become fully accepted members. Yet it is a community in which history, culture and tradition have been transmitted through family. . . . People not born into the community need to learn its history, culture and traditions. (p. 6)

Elsa Rosenberg attributes part of her motivation for becoming a Jew to her encountering the reality of the Jewish historical community as a volunteer in Israel.

> One month stretched into eight months, working on a kibbutz [a collective farming community]. It was one of the most rewarding and memorable periods in my life. My consciousness was expanded about what being Jewish is all about. I learned more about the principles and moral values of the people for whom I felt an increasing affinity. (Elsa Rosenberg, "Why People Choose Judaism," p. 19)

In similar fashion, writer David C. Gross relates the testimony of an Afro-American convert, attracted to collective Jewish perseverance in the face of oppression:

Jews have become strong over a thousand years of oppression and I wanted to become part of that strength. . . . I wanted to become a Jew because it gave me a great strength. I wanted to become a Jew because I felt it gave me the answer to an inner peace in life. . . .

I wanted to become a Jew because it was the answer to a life filled with confusion and uncertainty. Judaism gave me security and understanding. (David C. Gross, *The Jewish People's Almanac*, pp. 511–512)

10. This comment by a Jew by Choice of African-American background leads to the question: Can you convert to Judaism if you're black, Asian, Hispanic, or of some other non-white ethnic or racial group?

Judaism offers a religious lifestyle and fellowship that bind together Jews around the world of countless racial and ethnic groups. The State of Israel has accepted and rescued Jews from Europe, from Ethiopia, from Arab lands, from Latin America, from the Orient, from India, from over 100 varied communities worldwide. Local synagogues should be equally color blind. Our tradition teaches: *"Kol Yisrael arevim zeh bazeh"* ("The fate of all Jewish people is intimately bound up with one another"). Someone of color who converts into Judaism is fully accorded all its honors and privileges. Demonstrating this acceptance into a Conservative congregation is the following anecdote recalled by Professor Julius Lester, an African-American convert to Judaism.

I knew that [after formal conversion] I could no longer stay at home on Shabbat morning and be happy studying [alone]. I needed to be in a synagogue, needed to be with other Jews, singing prayers to God. . . . So the following Saturday . . . I drove the ten miles to the [Conservative] synagogue in Northampton.

From the beginning of the preliminary service I knew that I had found my home.

If I had any doubts that B'nai Israel was truly my home, they were banished when the *gabbai,* the man who passes out the *aliyot* [ritual honors], whispered in my ear . . . *"Kohen* or *levi?"*

"Israel," I responded.

"Shlishi [third honor]," he responded. "What's your Hebrew name?"

"Yaakov ben Avraham."

He patted me on the shoulder and continued around the congregation. (Julius Lester, *Lovesong: Becoming a Jew,* p. 241)

11. Am I alone in feeling a desire to become Jewish as part of a search to reconnect with my Jewish ancestry?

In an age of openness, more and more cases are coming to the fore of persons with Jewish roots who are now reestablishing ties to their Jewish heritage. Rabbi Allen S. Maller has written about meeting many Jews by Choice "who have discovered Jewish ancestors—[sometimes as much as] three to five generations removed. . . . If converts really are the incarnated souls of lost Jews from previous generations, a great deal of their behavior is easily explained" (Allen S. Maller, "Jews by Choice," p. 23). As an example of this pattern, in the very same symposium in the *Reconstructionist,* Jew by Choice Elsa Rosenberg recollects that after her grandfather died, "Going through his books and papers, I discovered in a footnote to our family genealogy, that centuries ago in Austria there were Jews among my ancestors. This seemed an almost providential confirmation of my instinctive turning in this direction" (Elsa Rosenberg, "Why People Choose Judaism," p. 20).

Quite common today are households in which one parent is Jewish. The adult children may have been raised as Christians or with no religion. In her article evaluating the experiences of similar adult children of interfaith marriages who ultimately converted to Judaism, journalist Charlotte Anker reports a wide range of findings.

The *Shoah* [Holocaust] is clearly an impetus. . . . "I knew I could be killed because I was Jewish [said one such woman]. . . . I knew there was no getting away from being Jewish; it's always with you."

Other [adult children of mixed marriage] . . . are drawn by the spiritual elements of Judaism, observing that born Jews often take for granted the spiritual pull of Judaic rituals. . . .

[Or similarly representative of motivations for conversion into Judaism] a recent trip to Israel at the age of forty triggered in [one such person]. . . . It was "a question of finding what heritage to identify with . . . Israel blew me away. . . . It was an extremely emotional experience." (Charlotte Anker, "We Are the Children You Warned Our Parents About," pp. 34–39)

12. Should I be troubled that the stimulus to explore Judaism was sparked by Jewish friends whose religious lifestyle seems so appealing?

In a society in which many non-Jewish people have close friendships with Jews, such affinity is a wonderful way to see the strength and beauty of Jewish living.

Tom McHale was attracted to Judaism during his college years because of his friendship with some Jewish students. As Lena Romanoff, a therapist and committed Conservative Jew, assesses in *Your People, My People*, "Religion—or lack of it—was not a matter of priority for him [Tom], yet his increasing contact with Jewish students made him begin to wonder what it was about Judaism that inspired so much loyalty and pride among many of his friends." Tom reflected: "[I] envied them when the Jewish holidays came around. They really looked forward to going home for Passover and Rosh Hashanah. I guess they detected my envy, because I was often invited along. I liked what I experienced" (Lena Romanoff, *Your People, My People*, p. 3).

Ms. Romanoff concluded that "the more he experienced, the more Tom felt that Judaism could fill a spiritual and cultural void in his life. Eventually Tom decided that he wanted to become Jewish" (p. 3).

Among those he interviewed for a study on the motives of converts to Judaism, Professor Egon Mayer encountered one eloquent Jew by Choice who came to Judaism through a Jewish community. "I began to think about converting to Judaism a little bit, when by chance I had an apartment within an Orthodox community during one year of college. I saw that the people had something, a closeness, a bond between themselves as friends, as family, that most non-Jews I knew didn't have" (cited in Egon Mayer and Amy Avgar, *Conversion Among the Intermarried*, p. 12).

Alternatively, Anne Burg, a convert to Judaism in my Conservative congregation, related to me:

> We tremenduosly enjoy [the congregation]. . . . We are now coming every week to Sabbath services and are delighted that families with young children are so encouraged and provided for. The wonderful spirit in [the] . . . congregation is very "catchy" and in a few short months, we went from a family who lit Shabbos candles and went to High Holy Day services to a family who enjoys attending Sabbath services weekly, studying and learning more about the religion, and motivating me to finally convert. (Conservative Congregation Agudath Israel, Caldwell, New Jersey)

13. Is it either peculiar or unprecedented that my attraction to Judaism was ignited by reading books about the experiences of Jewish people in dramatic settings such as the Holocaust or the rise of the State of Israel?

As more and more written accounts of Jewish life become available, many Gentile Americans feel closer to Judaism because of what they read. Some Jews by Choice identify with the fate of Jews because of popular books, films, or their study of Jewish ideas in college courses. Nancy Wingerson, for instance, recalls that the beginning of her teenage interest in Judaism stemmed from *Exodus*. Other converts have been influenced by *Anne Frank* or by the writings of Eli Wiesel, Chaim Potok, and Leon Uris. Wingerson recalls:

> [Reading *Exodus*] was my first real exposure to the Holocaust. It haunted me. I kept reading and reading about it. Soon I found I was very pro-Israel. I kept taking Zionist positions in arguments with my friends.
>
> [Later on, at college, in Jewish studies courses, Wingerson] felt that . . . sense of being in one place but belonging to another. I felt a hunger to learn more about Judaism. (Paul and Rachel Cowan, "Our People: Nancy Wingerson's Story," p. 60)

In a related fashion, Shoshana Lev, a convert to Conservative Judaism, observes:

> I passed through Christianity, from the dogmatism of Catholicism to completely undogmatic Quakerism, through atheism and agnosticism, meditation and yoga, and still could not find a vehicle for religious expression. One day I picked up a copy of Leon Uris' *Mila 18* and made a shattering discovery: at age eighteen, I didn't know that Hitler had exterminated six million Jews. I had always assumed that concentration camps and prisoner-of-war camps were the same thing, and that Hitler was just another tyrant. I learned about anti-Semitism and genocide. I wanted to know what it was about the Jews and their beliefs that made others want to exterminate them. So I went to a Jewish bookstore and there found a little volume by Milton Steinberg called *Basic Judaism*. At last I felt I had found what I had been looking for: here was what I believed. (cited in Maurice Lamm, *Becoming a Jew*, p. 8)

Also affected profoundly by Uris' *Mila 18* was Jew by Choice Samantha Lindblad:

At age 28 I read a book that changed my life. The book was *Mila 18* by Leon Uris. It was about WWII, the Warsaw Ghetto, and it was about Jews.

Jews in the twentieth century? I am sure that somewhere in my subconscious I was aware that some Jews were still around. But outwardly they were always the people of the Bible, depicted by Catholicism and her off-shoots as the murderers of God.

But within the pages of this book, a novel incredibly based on a true incident, Jews were just like everyone else. . . .

I turned to books of Jewish belief. . . . I was surprised to find out how many things Christianity had taken from Judaism.

As I continued to study Judaism my sensitivity and awareness of the world around me grew. (Samantha Lindblad, "A Convert to Judaism Tells Her Story," pp. 3–4)

14. Is it really necessary to convert to Judaism if my father was Jewish? Doesn't Reform Judaism recognize patrilineal descent as adequate for Jewish status?

Yes, the Reform movement does recognize patrilineal descent. However, there are a few problems with this assumption: First, even within Reform Judaism, Jewish status is not automatically conferred upon the children of Jewish fathers and non-Jewish mothers. Reform requires that such sons and daughters be raised actively as Jews—*brit* (ritual circumcision) or baby naming at birth (and no baptism), synagogue membership, religious school, *bar/bat mitzvah*, and other basic Jewish experiences. Furthermore, even if these mainstream encounters do occur, Reform's patrilinealism is not universally accepted within Reform Judaism, and it is rejected by the other Jewish movements. It is a fundamental break with the two other major branches of American Judaism and with Jewish communities (Reform included) elsewhere throughout the centuries and throughout the world. That is why the Conservative movement's Committee on Jewish Law and Standards affirms:

> Jewishness is defined through either lineage or through conversion to Judaism. . . .
>   Matrilineal descent [being born to a Jewish mother] . . . has been authoritative in normative Judaism for many centuries as the sole determinant of Jewish lineage.

If you are sincerely interested in being part of the entire Jewish religious tradition and future, we welcome your involvement. Nevertheless, we do urge your entry into a conversion program so that you will appropriately become accepted as a Jewish person by the entire Jewish people.

15. Is it true that rituals such as immersion in the *mikvah* (ritual bath) and ritual circumcision are required for conversion?

Conversion into Judaism should be a profound experience. Rabbi Ismar Schorsch has stated, "[Conversion] is tied up with many factors of the personality, of the home, of the community, and it is a step not to be taken lightly, not without preparation and not without ritual celebration" (Ismar Schorsch, keynote speech to Conservative Movement Conference on Intermarriage and Conversion). Simply proclaiming that someone has become Jewish at the end of a process of study and religious observance and growth would be a cold, unfeeling transition. Rituals are necessary to mark critical rites of passage—birth, adolescence, marriage, death, and conversion. To enhance the power of the moment, traditional Judaism also requires ritual at conversion: the meaningful acts of immersion in the *mikvah* (a ritual pool) for men and for women, and ritual circumcision for uncircumcised males. Lena Romanoff, director of Philadelphia

Jewish Converts Network, writes: "Many who go to a mikvah as a part of their conversion find it to be a deeply meaningful experience—a spiritual cleansing and renewal; sometimes, even a mystical relief of tension" (Lena Romanoff, *Your People, My People*, p. 31).

In like fashion, Julius Lester writes about the powerful meaning of ritual circumcision for his entry into Judaism: "After the circumcision . . . this is how I feel. Now I am whole. . . . Only a small bit of skin was removed but it is as if something within me has been set free" (Julius Lester, *Lovesong: Becoming a Jew*, p. 215).

16. What other procedures are necessary for conversion?

The Rabbinical Assembly's *Rabbi's Manual* (1968) offers the following additional guidelines:

> A rabbi, approached by a prospective convert, should acquaint his/herself with the family background and present circumstances of the applicant, and with the motives that prompt him or her to seek conversion to the Jewish faith. . . .
>
> A minimum of six to eight months of intensive study of assigned material should be required for the average applicant for conversion. . . . A longer or shorter period may be required for a specific individual, at the discretion of the rabbi. . . .
>
> During this period of instruction and preparation he or she should be invited to attend synagogue services as often as possible. . . .
>
> [After the conclusion of adequate study and religious growth] two colleagues [rabbis or cantors], or, if that is infeasible, two qualified laymen in the community, should be acquainted with the particular case and invited to join the rabbi in constituting a Bet Din [traditional court of law]. The Bet Din examines the knowledge and attitude of the prospective convert and presides

over his or her admission into the Jewish faith. (Jules Harlow, *The Rabbi's Manual*, pp. 13–16)

17. What's the next step?

If any of these answers reflect your own frame of mind, then we invite you to consider a serious encounter with Jewish study and observance. Join an Introduction-to-Judaism course to learn more about Judaism and whether Judaism is right for you. To do so, you are welcome to contact your local Conservative congregational rabbi or the regional office of the United Synagogue for Conservative Judaism. In addition to study, the rabbi and synagogue can offer the opportunity to experience Jewish ritual and prayer observances in a communal setting, as well as providing "mentors"—people who have already converted to Judaism—as well as born Jews who can guide your religious growth as a Jew.

If you are interested in reading more on this subject, the following are recommended:

1. Lena Romanoff's *Your People, My People* (Jewish Publication Society) offers helpful insights from the perspective of a Jew by Choice who skillfully directs the Jewish Converts Network of hundreds of couples within the Philadelphia metropolitan area.
2. Rabbi Simcha Kling's *Embracing Judaism* (Rabbinical Assembly) is a Conservative primer for prospective converts.
3. Julius Lester's *Lovesong* is a sensitive and poetic personal testimony to his path from Christianity into conversion as a Jew.
4. Rabbi Joseph Tabachnik and Dr. Brenda Forster's *Choosing Judaism* (KTAV) is a study of the data collected from 400 questionnaires completed by graduates of the conversion training institute of the Chicago Board of Rabbis,

surveying the range of motivations, observances, and values that accompanied this process.

If you wish to begin your own initial exploration of "Basic Judaism," the following resources are recommended:

1. The Sabbath: *The Shabbat Seder* by Ronald Wolfson (New York: Federation of Jewish Men's Clubs, 1985).
2. Kosher food: *The Jewish Dietary Laws*, by Samuel Dresner and Seymour Siegel (New York: United Synagogue of Conservative Judaism, 1959).
3. Prayer: *Man's Quest for God*, by Abraham J. Heschel (New York: Charles Scribner, 1954).
4. Theology: *The Book of Jewish Belief*, by Louis Jacobs (West Orange, NJ: Behrman House, 1990).
5. Holidays: *The Jewish Holidays: A Guide and Commentary*, by Michael Strassfeld (New York: Harper & Row, 1985).
6. Jewish history and culture: *Jewish Literacy*, by Joseph Telushkin (New York: William Morrow, 1991).
7. Hebrew language: *Reading Hebrew (Sephardic)* (New York: Behrman House, 1982).

4

Dual-Faith Parenting: Second Thoughts about a Popular Trend

A re you an interfaith couple trying to raise or considering raising your children in two religions? Are you attempting to reconcile what you recognize are different backgrounds and heritages you have brought to the marriage? Are you also trying to respect the desires of, and maintain loyalty to, both of your families of origin? Are you seeking to move beyond the traditional parameters of organized religion, beyond barriers that seem to separate groups and individuals? Yet at the same time, do you each identify at some level with your birth religion, even while not considering yourself to be traditionally believing or practicing?

VOCABULARY OF VALUES

Raising your children as "both Christian and Jewish" may seem to you to be a reasonable solution for transmitting a religious identity to your sons and daughters. Perhaps you plan to organize, and may have already organized, joint ceremonies with newborn males consecrated both at a Jewish

97

ritual circumcision (a *bris*) and at a Christian baptism. Your goals may include celebrating both Hanukkah and Christmas, Passover and Easter with your youngsters.

Your motivation may be to provide the next generation with "the best of both" religions, to be at the vanguard of an idealistic and barrier-free society. If sometime during their teenage or adult years your children decide to choose one of the two faith communities, that would be satisfactory, since they would be making their own choices.

This approach may seem sensitive and feasible. It may reflect your appreciation of the importance of religion in life. Perhaps it acknowledges that the family, church, and synagogue, through their principles and rituals, are critical in teaching morality, especially in a society where schooling is often secular and "value-free."

In *The Intermarriage Handbook*, researchers Judy Petsonk and Jim Remsen have assessed: "For many children, and for many adults, religion is an important part of . . . self-definition. Religion gives people a common history, values, traditions, rituals, stories, jokes. This shared system gives them an anchor in the world—an identity" (p. 193).

Thus the avoidance of a religious dimension may create a void in a person's healthy emotional, psychological, and spiritual development. A typical reaction to such an environment is indicated by a young woman named Mary, a product of this type of interfaith home: "[My parents'] home was really not a religious home at all. Religion was avoided like the plague, and values never discussed because they would open up a Pandora's box and lead to religious discussion that was taboo. Thus I grew up confused over what I was supposed to do about religion" (Steven Carr Reuben, *Raising Jewish Children in a Contemporary World*, pp. 116–117). In a related fashion, Reform temple educator Susan Greenberg has shared the ambivalence reflected by questions posed from children being raised in "both" religions.

Which am I today?
   Did the Jewish God or the Christian God make me?
   Will God be angry if I have a Christmas tree?
   Who's stronger, Jesus or God?
   What prayers do I say today? (This from a child who attends catechism on Saturday and Hebrew school on Sunday)
   My Mommy says when I grow up I will get to choose Jewish or Christian, but will she be mad if I choose Daddy's religion?
   If I'm Jewish and Christian now, when do I get to be just me? (Susan Greenberg, Letter to Editor, p. 56)

A religious identity will be critical to most people, as children and throughout life. They need some rituals associated with birth, reaching adolescence, marriage, and coping with death. They require a concepts of religion in order to deal with faith concerns at moments of illness or crisis, of peak joy, of personal spiritual awareness, of medical/ethical issues ranging from abortion and birth control to organ donations and terminating life-support systems.

Religion is a fundamental *vocabulary of values* often necessary for a healthy life.

The question raised here is whether a viable religious identity is likely to be fostered in a child raised as "both a Christian and a Jew."

CONTRASTING JEWISH AND CHRISTIAN INPUT

While Judaism and Christianity both make vital contributions to spirituality, each has its own integrity and each possesses a distinct religious message. Therefore, raising children in both may present developmental problems.

By age 3 to 5, our children already become old enough to ask and to be sensitive to religious questions, and parents need to be prepared for and comfortable with consistent rather than contradictory answers. What happened to Grandpa, now that he has died? Do we believe that abortion is okay? Are we in favor of organ donations? Is it all right to disconnect life-support systems to a terminally ill patient? Where is God? What is my religion? How come there are different religions? What happens to good people who are not Christians or not Jews? Who created the world? What are miracles?

Therapist Lena Romanoff has pointed to the following sequence of questions as representative of this bewilderment: " 'If I'm Jewish, then how can I believe in Jesus?' he [Brendon Perez] asked his parents. 'And if I'm Catholic, how can I not believe in Jesus? Do I believe in him on Sunday but not on Saturday?' " (*Your People, My People*, p. 53). Under the best of circumstances, these are difficult questions to answer. Without a unified and confident response from parents, religious schools, or clergy, a child's inquisitiveness must be met with "Mom and Dad do not agree on this" (causing a loyalty conflict) or "there is no answer" (creating confusion).

Like Judaism (Reform. Conservative, Reconstructionist, Orthodox), Christianity includes an extraordinarily diverse range of faith groups (evangelical Protestants, mainline Protestants, Eastern Orthodox, Roman Catholics). Since Jewish, Catholic, and Protestant beliefs frequently disagree, artificially combined Jewish-Christian responses to inquiries will not be sufficient.

Our offspring cannot be instructed to believe both that God is One (the *Shema*) and that there is a divine Trinity (Father, Son, Holy Ghost). A son or daughter cannot be taught to believe that Jesus was the messiah and the son of God (Christianity) and that Jesus was neither (Judaism). A child cannot meaningfully be told that infants are born with original sin (Catholics, Lutherans, Eastern Orthodox, Methodists, and Presbyterians) and that babies are born totally without moral blemish (Judaism).

Boys and girls cannot handle reading Christian scriptural passages asserting that Jews killed Jesus while at the same time studying to be good Jews themselves.

We cannot effectively believe the claim of many Christian groups that Christianity (a *new* Testament) has superseded ancient Judaism (an *old* Testament) while simultaneously affirming the Torah (Hebrew Scripture) as central to Jewish life.

Moreover, a youngster should not be instructed that only members of one's own religious group can be "saved" in heaven when they die (Evangelicals), and at the same time be informed that all ethical persons of all religious groups will be rewarded by God in the hereafter (Judaism and some liberal Christian denominations). Eloise, a retired teacher who had been raised in two religions, related a painful incident: "I went home from (Baptist) Sunday school one day and cried as I told my mother that the teacher had said that the Jews—which I took to include my Jewish father—were going to hell because they didn't believe in Jesus" (Leslie Goodman-Malamuth and Robin Margolis, *Between Two Worlds*, p. 21).

School psychologist Dr. David Yammer observed:

> Children can be taught that different people or peoples believe contradictory Jewish vs. Christian statements. It is when they are taught that they are expected to feel comfortable "living the contradiction" that conflict and/or confusion arises. We have a natural tendency to avoid cognitive dissonance. Asking a child to live with ongoing dissonance is asking a lot.
>
> We cannot expect a child to be able to be serious about both religions at the same time.
>
> Children do better when parents have done the work necessary to present relatively consistent responses to "what our family believes."

JUDAISM AND CHRISTIANITY: MUTUALLY RESPECTFUL YET INCOMPATIBLE

In open societies, it is critical that all religions be mutually respectful of one another. Jewish, Catholic, and Protestant clergy can belong to the same local clergy association. Lay people should be encouraged to befriend neighbors and class-mates regardless of religious differences and affiliations. Political coalitions may join different denominations in public advocacy. Yet civil sharing and mutual respect should not be confused with theological incompatibility. Rabbi Harold Schulweis has pointed out:

> It is important that the differences in . . . birth traditions not be trivialized. The theological differences between Christianity and Judaism are likely to cast cultural and moral penumbra larger than the [two partners to an intermarriage] . . . may have imagined. They may come to understand that genuine tolerance does not entail indiscriminate adoption of all faiths and that openness does not mean to reduce all traditions to sameness. (Harold Schulweis, "Peering into the Limbo of Judeo-Christian Beliefs," pp. 244–245).

The integrity of any Jewish or Christian system demands that its adherents be devoted solely to that faith. One cannot be a Jew *and* a Christian. One cannot be a Catholic *and* a Protestant, or an Evangelical *and* a member of a mainline Christian denomination.

In particular, to be genuinely raised both as a Jew and as a Christian is an oxymoron. After all, Christianity arose as a conscious rejection of Judaism, and Judaism remained apart because of its nonacceptance of Christianity. To pretend other-wise is to trivialize both religions and relegates their rituals into meaningless rites or holidays devoid of any religious commitment.

Furthermore, this pretense tends to ignore serious unre-solved parental conflicts.

What are the parents' ties to their respective religions?
Is "we'll give the kids both" a subtle form of competition?
Does it mask other issues that have not yet come to the surface?

Ultimately, such questions will prey on parents' consciences later in life.

A *BRIS* AND A BAPTISM ARE DIFFERENT

Sometimes an interfaith couple seeks to placate both the Christian and the Jewish families by providing both a *bris* and a baptism for a newborn. Such a couple is giving little thought to the religious significance of these mutually contradictory acts.

For Catholics, Lutherans, Eastern Orthodox, Methodists, and Presbyterians, infant baptism is directly traceable to the teachings of Jesus. It is a *"sacrament* . . . [a] visible, tangible, effective sign through which [Jesus] God . . . enters [one's] life, and draws [a person] . . . to Himself through His grace" (Alan Schreck, *Your Catholic Faith: A Question and Answer Catechism*, p. 70). For these "Christians who believe that infants are born in the state of [original] sin [traceable to Adam and Eve] . . . through baptism God washes away this sin" (John C. McCollister [Lutheran], *The Christian Book of Why*, p. 51).

In addition, Roman Catholics as well as those Protestant denominations practicing infant baptism regard this as an act of "incorporation," of formal admission into the religious community. As is stated in the Episcopalian *Book of Common Prayer*, for example, "Baptism is the sacrament by which God adopts us as His children and makes us members of Christ's Body, the Church, and inheritors of the Kingdom of God" (Episcopal Church of America, *Book of Common Prayer*, p. 858).

Similarly, for Roman Catholics: "Through baptism, Catholics are delivered from original sin . . . [and given] entrance into the fellowship of the church" (Alan Schreck, *Your Catholic Faith: A Question and Answer Catechism*, pp. 72–73).

In a fashion similar to Christian baptism, a Jewish *bris* ceremony brings the child into a formal relationship with the Jewish faith community. In contrast to baptism, however, a *bris* is not a cleansing of inherited moral taint. It is simply a sign of a child's entry into a covenant with God, a God who judges each individual solely in accordance with his or her own deeds, not those of Adam and Eve, our ancestors, our parents, our children, our neighbors, or our coreligionists. Rabbi Harold Schulweis eloquently has observed:

> Circumcision is the initiation into the covenant with God and Abraham. The 8-day-old child carries no baggage of [original] sin with him into the world. He is no alien flung into the hands of demonic powers. . . . The Jewish child is born innocent, body and soul, created and sustained in God's image. He has no need to be saved because no Satan threatens him, no eternal damnation hovers over him. As a Jew he will be raised in a tradition that mandates him to save lives, not souls. (Harold Schulweis, "Peering into the Limbo of Judeo-Christian," p. 242)

Jewish *bris* and Christian baptism are both very special. They represent the beginning of incorporation, of formal entry into a specific local faith. Each brings youngsters into a separate and distinct religious community.

Thus, *bris* and baptism are totally incompatible with each other. Rabbi Harold Schulweis has pointed out, "Circumcision and baptism are not a knife-or-water option, dramas of values. They affect our relationships to God, world, neighbor and self" (Harold Schulweis, "The Hyphen Between the Cross and the Star," p. 173). Each marks the entry into a specific Christian or spiritual Jewish path. You cannot meaningfully be admitted into both belief systems.

HANUKKAH AND CHRISTMAS ARE DIFFERENT

During the December holiday season some families decide to celebrate both Hanukkah and Christmas. It is assumed that gift-giving should occur under both frameworks and that the households should partake in the display of both the Christmas tree and Hanukkah menorah.

Yet as with the *bris*/baptism duality, Hanukkah and Christmas are more than empty shells for justifying exchanging presents or convening an extended family meal. Each holiday is an expression of religious values fundamental to Christianity or to Judaism.

Christmas is the spiritual reexperiencing of the hope personified in the birth of Jesus, with the intent of having the spirit of Jesus enter anew into the faith, the very being of the believing Christian. "[Protestant] Christians around the world celebrate Christmas as the birthday of their Lord, Jesus Christ. The word 'Christmas' is a contraction of the phrase 'Christ's mass,' i.e., a service of worship honoring the Christ child." (John C. McCollister, *The Christian Book of Why*, p. 205). "[For Catholics] the Son of God came [to the world] in the flesh [at Christmas time] by being born of a young woman of Nazareth named Mary. . . . This [was] . . . the key to God's plan to redeem the human race from sin and rebellion and restore [human kind] . . . to His friendship" (Alan Schreck, *Your Catholic Faith: A Question and Answer Catechism*, p. 28).

This December festival is adorned with a wide array of religious imagery. For example, as Lutheran pastor and professor John C. McCollister has written:

> In many instances, a star is placed atop a Christmas tree as a symbol of the star that appeared at the time of Jesus' birth. The wreath represents the crown of thorns placed on the head of Jesus by the Roman soldiers just before his crucifixion. Some Christians equate Christmas gifts with the presents of gold, frankincense, and myrrh which the Wise Men brought to the Christ child. (*The Christian Book of Why*, pp. 210–212)

For Roman Catholics, even the popular Christmas carol "The Twelve Days of Christmas" has religious implications.

The partridge in the pear tree was Jesus Christ. The two turtle doves were the Old and New Testaments. Three French hens stood for faith, hope and charity. The four calling birds were the four gospels of Matthew, Mark, Luke and John.

The five golden rings recalled the Torah or Law, the first five books of the Old Testament. The six geese a-laying stood for the six days of creation. Seven swans a-swimming represented the sevenfold gifts of the Holy Spirit. The eight maids a-milking were the Eight Beautitudes.

Nine ladies dancing? These were the nine fruits of the Holy Spirit (Galatians 5). The ten lords a-leaping were the Ten Commandments. Eleven pipers piping stood for the eleven faithful disciples. Finally, the twelve drummers symbolized the twelve points of belief in the Apostles' Creed. (St. Pius School, "The Twelve Days of Christmas")

In contrast to this Jesus-centered festival of Christmas, Hanukkah is a Jewish festival rejoicing in the human victories of the dedicated few against the might of an oppressive majority. It is a reminder of the successful revolt of Mattathias and his sons in overturning religious persecution. The Maccabees reacted against the oppression of a Syrian Greek tyrant, Antiochus, who had tried to suppress the practice of Judaism and to impose his own pagan ritual practices.

Whereas Christmas replaces the Jewish understanding of Torah with Jesus, Hanukkah insists that no person or faith or even a king like Antiochus can ever replace Torah for us. Inspired by God's revelation of Torah, a small band of Maccabees defeated the mighty Syrian army, demonstrating the biblical adage, "Not by power or by might," but rather by God alone does true human success depend.

Hanukkah is the affirmation of Jewish peoplehood against the philosophy of assimilation. Dr. Ronald Brauner of Pittsburgh has observed: "[The real message of Hanukkah is that] if we are interested in the perpetuation of Judaism, then our focus, at some point, must [be the recognition that] . . . we are not like everybody else; we do hold distinctively different values and perceptions of truth . . . distinct from our non-Jewish fellow Americans (Ronald Brauner, "Hanukah," p. 2).

The Maccabees did not did seek a human embodiment of God to save them. Rather they acted decisively on behalf of their own unique form of religious freedom. Genuinely celebrating both Hanukkah and Christmas – the former representing the primacy of God's Torah and its *mitzvot* (commandments) and the latter representing the turning away from Torah Law (Christianity's turning instead to Jesus) – is unauthentic and misleading.

PASSOVER AND EASTER ARE DIFFERENT

Springtime religious celebrations may lead you to decide to raise your child with both Passover and Easter, with two sets of extended family meals, *matzah*, Easter eggs, and so on. Once again, to do so is to blur the profound and incompatible meanings of these two essential holy days and to retain only their cultural manifestations.

For Christians, Easter commemorates the death and resurrection of Jesus. For Catholics, Jesus' death is seen as a salvation experience for humankind. Jesus is viewed as the "Lamb of God" whose crucifixion serves to redeem all persons from their sins. Protestants stress the resurrection dimension of Easter. For Christianity, resurrection augurs a potential victory over death and moving on to eternal life. "Easter – the festival which commemorates the resurrection of Jesus from the dead . . . [is] the center of all [Protestant] Christian theology. [Protestant] Christians believe that Jesus' resurrection provided proof that he was the Son of God and has given to all of his followers eternal life" (John McCollister, *The Christian Book of Why*, p. 230). "The bodily resurrection of Jesus Christ from the dead is a central Catholic belief, perhaps *the* central Catholic belief. . . . The resurrection of Jesus is the act of God that reveals that death, sin [the punishments for original sin], and Satan have been conquered. Therefore, Easter, the feast of Jesus' resurrection, is the most important holy day for Catholics" (Alan Schreck, *Your Catholic Faith: A Question and Answer Catechism*, p. 36).

In contrast to Easter's profound religious meaning, which focuses on Jesus, Passover is focused exclusively upon the relationship of the Jewish people with God alone. Passover is Judaism's most popular and powerful home ritual. It celebrates human freedom, the Exodus, and the Israelites' recommitment to the God of their ancestors. Passover is the annual reenactment of God's intervention and the liberation of the Jews from slavery and bondage.

The Passover *Haggadah* does not mention the name of Moses, since by comparison to God's role in the Exodus, Moses, or even the future messiah is of limited consequence. Passover commemorates *God's* miracles, *God's* hearing the cry of the oppressed, *God's* fulfillment of His promise to redeem Abraham's descendants from Egypt, *God's* ability to subvert a king (Pharaoh), an army, and an array of pagan gods.

To transmit loyalty to both Easter and Passover is possible only if one omits the religious content of both holidays and relegates their significance to empty family meals, devoid of spiritual substance.

A SYNAGOGUE IS NOT A CHURCH

Perhaps, in another effort to be fair to both Judaism and Christianity, you plan to bring your child periodically to church and to synagogue. While this practice reflects a universal approach, it too is fraught with religious peril.

The Rev. Ronald Osbourne, a former chaplain at Iowa University, observed:

When Jews worship with Christians almost nothing is accessible, almost everything is problematic. . . . "Old Testament" readings are selected in the Christian lectionaries to interpret New Testament experience. Even the Psalms gather Christian meanings. . . . [In addition] 'New Testament' readings, creeds, prayers, trinitarian invocations, acclamations and doxologies are all utterly impossible to a Jewish participant, or at least one with theological sensitivity and integrity. (Ronald Osbourne, "Marriage of Christians and Jews," p. 11)

Moreover, the display of Christian symbols, the cross, and particularly the crucified body of Jesus serve as an irritating reminder to Jews of the thousands of coreligionists who have died in the past through misplaced religious zeal.

Jews also are ill at ease with references to the Trinity, the idea of Jesus as messiah, Catholic overtones of sin and forgiveness, the virgin birth, saints, celibacy for clergy, confession, kneeling, and a spiritual distance between the laity and the status of priests, nuns, and other people "of the cloth." Mainline Protestant churches share some of these features. In general, communion rites, collection of the offering, choir-led hymns, absence of male head coverings, and invoking the name of Jesus are awkward for Jews.

Similarly, Christians need a reorientation in order to become comfortable with the synagogue service. The use of Hebrew is new to them, as is a prayer book that is read from right to left on the page and from back to front within the volume. Ceremonial objects such as _kippot_ (skull caps), _tallit_ (prayer shawl), Torah scrolls, and private yet audible prayers are quite strange to the uninitiated. Newcomers may be surprised at a synagogue's informality, diminished reliance upon sermons, lengthy liturgy, and concentration upon the nuances of the sacred narratives in the Five Books of Moses.

It is incorrect to assume that a child can "own" both of these religious services, let alone either one if treated superficially.

BAR/BAT MITZVAH DIFFERS FROM CHRISTIAN
CONFIRMATION

During early adolescence both Judaism and Christianity have ceremonial milestones, such as *bar/bat mitzvah* and Catholic confirmation (not to be confused with Jewish confirmation in Reform and some Conservative congregations). Each of these ceremonies marks the formal entry of the child into a specific religious community. The rituals are laden with declarations of loyalty by the young adult to the particular church or synagogue tradition that sponsors the occasion.

For Catholics, the sacrament of confirmation, like baptism, is traceable to the life and teachings of Jesus. For mainline Protestants, while confirmation is not a sacrament, it does confirm the teenager's earlier baptismal vows. For both, confirmation represents a ceremony of "incorporation," of final acceptance into the religious community of faithful Christians. It is "the 'bestowal,' through prayer and anointing, of a fuller empowerment of the baptized person by the Holy Spirit so that he or she may lead a fuller Christian life" (Alan Schreck, *Your Catholic Faith: A Question and Answer Cathechism*, p. 75).

> [The sacrament of] confirmation is an affirmation of belief in a particular doctrine. The person is confirming the faith to which his [her] parents brought [him/her] at birth. The ceremony takes place during a Sunday service, with the individual making a personal statement or agreeing to a credal vow stated by the clergyperson. . . .
> The ceremony conveys full membership in the congregation. (Judy Petsonk and Jim Remsen, *The Intermarriage Handbook*, p. 251)

Bar/bat mitzvah, like confirmation, provides a ceremony of "incorporation," of formal entry into the Jewish faith community. This entry into Jewish adulthood, however, occurs during the reading of the Torah, Judaism's most sacred and self-defining possession. The 13-year-old boy or 12- or 13-year-old girl is reminded that he or she represents the newest link in a Jewish chain of tradition spanning centuries. Like Christian confirmation, this milestone is a public act of loyalty by a young adult to one specific religious community.

JUDAISM AND CHRISTIANITY RESPOND DIFFERENTLY TO DEATH

Inevitably your child will encounter the death of a loved one. It is important for a son or daughter reaching adulthood to have specific regimens of response to such times of emotional stress.

Offspring do best when they have witnessed parents considering and deciding upon "what we do." Separate and contradictory sets of rules or a family pattern of indecisiveness will add to a person's grief and disorientation.

For example, when faced with decisions upon the death of a sibling who was similarly raised in both religions, it is impossible for a child of intermarrieds to approve of mausoleum (above-ground) burial as in Christianity and simultaneously disapprove of it (Judaism). It is not possible to bury one's deceased relative almost immediately (Judaism) while at the same time delaying burial until after a vigil or a wake.

An open casket for viewing is common for many Christian groups, but it is forbidden for Jews. Kneeling in prayer and crossing oneself is proper etiquette in some Catholic or Protestant settings, yet it is totally foreign to Jews. At the grave site, some Christians place flowers in the grave, whereas Jews place shovels of earth.

A separate yet related dilemma occurs at the time of a tragic death of a child who has either no religious affiliation or dual affiliation. Here too the intermarried family has one more painful set of decisions to make.

Should the son or daughter be buried in a Christian cemetery or a Jewish cemetery?

Will the designated cemetery accept such an unaffiliated person?

Will burial among Jews alone imply that this deceased youngster will not receive heavenly rewards in the eyes of a Christian parent?

Will burial in a totally Christian setting be felt as an eternal betrayal of one's ancestors by a grieving Jewish parent?

These unresolved latent concerns add enormous layers of complexity to an already terribly traumatic situation. Moreover, life-and-death decisions may reawaken an intermarried parent's unresolved tensions regarding his or her religion of birth.

CHOICE IS NOT FOR CHILDREN

Some parents assume that if they expose children to both religions, their sons or daughters will be able to make educated choices at a later time. This passing of responsibility to the next generation is unfair. Adults raised in mixed-marriage settings stressed to interviewer Charlotte Anker the unnerving prospect of rejecting the heritage of either one parent or the other:

[As one woman said to Anker,] "No matter how prepared they think they are, parents often freak out when this happens. They become enraged to see their children become devout Jews or Christians." . . .

"Sometimes under the pressure, the children go off and become Buddhists—then both parents feel rejected." . . .

A significant number of [adult offspring of mixed marriage] . . . refuse to affiliate with any religion because they cannot bear to choose between parents. (Charlotte Anker, "We Are the Children You Warned Our Parents About," p. 37)

Other children who were raised to make their own choice of religious affiliation emulate their parents, pushing off this decision onto someone else. Many young women attempt to resolve the issue of divided loyalties to parents by planning to assume the religion of the man they marry.

As one offspring of such a home expressed to writers Judy Petsonk and Jim Remsen: "I had to actually say to myself, "What am I gonna choose? Am I gonna get mixed up with this Southerner and go live in the South and become a Southerner, or go with this Jew and become a Jew?" (Judy Petsonk and Jim Remsen, *The Intermarriage Handbook*, p. 200)

Moreover, adult sons and daughters of households that have deferred religious issues tend either to be uneasy about affiliating with any organized religion, or they consciously choose a religion distant from both parents.

"WHO AM I?"

Raising one's child to have only a passing familiarity with Judaism and with Christianity will not solve the problem; it will succeed in creating loyalty to neither and may result in the child's developing a superficial religious identity.

Here are several painful reflections offered by sons and daughters of interfaith households raised in this dual fashion.

"All my life I've been aware of being half and half. I feel like I'm on the fringes of things in a lot of ways. I'm half Jewish and half Christian. . . . I've wanted to know who I was ever since I was a teenager."

"You can't be both. You're neither and stuck and don't really know what you are. You are afraid if you say you are one or the other religion that you will offend someone, so you figure out ways to avoid the subject and not get into situations where you'll have to answer questions at all."

"It's not like being a Democrat or a Republican. The feelings are there all the time. Every day something arises that reminds me of the fact that I'm two things, split."

"I have felt like a schizophrenic for most of my life or perhaps like a giant piece of taffy, constantly being stretched and pulled to capacity in both directions. . . . For as long as I can remember, I have yearned to integrate, or magically fuse, my two halves, so I wouldn't have to choose one over the other." (Lydia Kukoff et al., *Working with Interfaith Couples: A Jewish Perspective—A Guide for Facilitators*, pp. 109–110)

Rev. Ronald Osbourne has written: "[Consequently] what happens [in such situations] is that the children are not exposed to either religious tradition sufficiently to feel religious meanings from the inside out. Since religion is caught, not taught, it is never caught. They, in fact, are raised as [nothing]" ("Marriage of Christians and Jews," p. 11).

In order to resolve these difficulties, Nancy Kelly Kleiman, a Christian woman married to a Jewish man and raising her children as Jews, writes:

[A person] can no more be religious without belonging to a particular religion any more than I can talk without using a particular language. It was a specific religion that [was] the vehicle my parents had to teach me about God matters of the spirit. [My children] will become fluent in the religious language of Judaism and heritage of its people because that is the vehicle which we [Nancy and her husband] chose to communicate with them about God and matters of the spirit. (Nancy Kleiman, "Religion as a Language," p. 157)

"WHERE DO I BELONG?"

Many parents choosing either no religion or two religions for their children underestimate the identity problems that are created for their sons and daughters when confronted by their peers.

Friends will inevitably ask one another:

What is your religion?
Where do you go to church or synagogue?
Do you go to Hebrew school, Catholic CCD (Confraternity of Christian Doctrine), or Protestant Sunday school?
Will you have a *bar/bat mitzvah* or Christian confirmation?

Religious school is the place where children develop a special peer group, find adult role models, build a framework of ethics, learn religious skills, and solidify their identity.

> It has been estimated that at least 90% of American children attend [one specific type of] religious school at some time during their pre-teen years. Going to religious school is a generally accepted privilege of American youngsters, even those whose parents seldom or never enter a house of worship and who are not dues paying members of any church or synagogue. To deny this privilege to a child is to deny . . . something that, in the United States, is considered as much a part of a normal child's upbringing as his [her] baby rattle or his [her] tricycle. (David Max Eichhorn, *Jewish Intermarriage: Fact and Fiction*, pp. 90–91)

AMERICAN SOCIETY IS A CHRISTIAN SOCIETY

Some Jewish parents assume that the best strategy in an interfaith marriage is the denial of any problems. Let us do nothing, ignore religious issues, and allow human nature to run its course.

Yet as Albert Memmi, a writer and intermarried Jew, has observed:

> But let's not pull the wool over our eyes: in this case, to do nothing is a decision with the probable consequence that the children will become part of the [Christian] majority. . . .

"Let society have its way—the school, the neighborhood, the surrounding culture. . . . The entire society will do the job" [ultimately leading one's heirs into Christianity. (cited in Louis A. Berman, *Jews and Intermarriage: A Study in Personality and Culture*, p. 195)

Intermarriage between Jews and Christians is not regarded as a serious long-term demographic problem by many Christian clergy. Unless the children of a marriage between Jew and Christian are consciously and substantively raised as Jews, these boys and girls and certainly their descendants most likely will become part of a vast Christendom. As priests and ministers have commented to me, Jewish-Christian marriage is not a problem but rather like a "blip on a computer screen" or a "ripple in the ocean" for Christianity.

For Judaism, however, as a tiny minority religion trying to preserve itself in the face of a Christian majority, intermarriage is perceived quite differently. It is a direct threat to our continuity.

TIME BOMBS

Parents who are contemplating the religion of their children and have not resolved their religious differences can be facing "time bombs." Often these unexpected problems surface as crises occur. In those times, we instinctively fall back on our religious and cultural backgrounds.

The surfacing of these disparate experiences might upend the raising of children as "both Christian and Jew" in unanticipated ways.

Examples of time bombs are discussed at length in Paul and Rachel Cowan's volume *Mixed Blessings: Marriage Between Jews and Christians*.

When Jews and Christians first fall in love, they usually regard themselves as individualists who will be able to transcend the specific cultural demands of the pasts that shaped their beliefs and laid claims on their loyalties. But that is a more difficult task than they imagine, for at some profound level of self and psyche, most will always be attached to the religious and ethnic tribes in which they were raised. . . .

[When] a struggle over religion does begin [later in the marriage], it often takes couples by surprise, thrusting them into confusing, seemingly endless discussions. For suddenly they discover that they are not interchangeable parts of the American whole, but two people whose different pasts have endowed them with a distinct set of feelings. . . .

The time bombs that explode are usually ignited by the stress that develops at the moments when interfaith couples are faced with important choices, or difficult lessons. (*Mixed Blessings*, pp. 128–131)

Time bombs are life-cycle events that release emotionally charged feelings into a seemingly calm family setting. For example, the birth of a baby or a child's reaching an age traditionally associated with religious school or *bar/bat mitzvah* may set off suppressed anxieties.

Given the latent power of Judaism's group identity, a Jewish mother or father may suddenly acknowledge discomfort with her or his failure to transmit Judaism to the next link in a chain of a tradition that spans millennia.

Similarly, the death of a parent or some other jolt in the sequence of family succession could unearth similarly deep-seated regrets. Albert Memmi has written:

Suddenly [with the birth of a child] all theoretical options which had been relegated to the background and left in a convenient and equivocal shadow require urgent attention and threaten to materialize by themselves and at random. . . . What upbringing should they be given? A religious upbringing or not? How do you present them with the fact of being Jewish? I still don't know what I should tell my children about Jewish history. Besides, is it exactly *their* history? Should I decide that it is and that they will be Jews? (cited in Louis A. Berman, *Jews and Intermarriage: A Study in Personality and Culture*, pp. 194–195).

Beyond life-cycle time bombs such as childbirth, even the normal course of confronting life's challenges can trigger one's unacknowledged conflicts and ambivalence. Rising to the surface may be hitherto submerged commitments to Jewish survival or to a person's sense of mortality, or laments about dying without Jewish heirs.

Arlene Miller concluded her research on mixed marrieds with this assessment:

> In some cases, Jews [make such decisions regarding marriage, family life, and child rearing] . . . and later want to retreat back. After years of marriage, priorities of needs may change considerably and the [transmission of] ethnic identity [to a next generation] which was not valued in young adulthood may take on special value as one [actually] becomes a parent, approaches old age, faces life crisis, etc. (Arlene A. Miller, "An Exploration of Ethnicity in Marriages Between White Anglo-Saxon Protestants and Jewish Americans," p. 9)

CONCLUSION

The religious identity of children constitutes a vital dimension of their self-image and emotional and spiritual maturation. Religious tutelage should not be left to chance. Neither should random aspects of Judaism and Christianity be thrust upon children. These two traditions are not merely two variations of the same theme. They represent fundamentally different lenses through which to view birth, adolescence, marriage, adulthood, and death. Each offers unique and distinctive practices, holidays, beliefs, symbols, and rituals. They represent incompatible views of God, sin, repentance, the messiah, and life after death.

Moreover, each provides a separate framework from which to deal with contemporary ethical dilemmas posed by medical science, ranging from abortion, fertility drugs, and surrogate motherhood to organ transplants, living wills, and disconnecting life-support systems from a comatose and brain-dead patient.

A Legacy of Confusion

Do not bequeath to children and perhaps grandchildren a legacy of confusion. Ambiquity in religious identity was expressed elegantly by Disraeli, the nineteenth-century British prime minister and offspring of a Christian and Jewish home. When Queen Victoria asked him about his own religious background, Disraeli lamented, "I am, dear Queen, the blank page between the Old and New Testament."

Parents owe their children a clear statement regarding their religious upbringing.

Having encountered a great deal of ambivalence among adult sons and daughters of intermarried parents, interfaith workshop leaders Paul and Rachel Cowan concluded:

Both those who praised their parents and those who criticized them conveyed the same message. They valued clarity and a sense of security. They felt parents should choose a religious identity for their children and not leave it up to them to choose. Furthermore, they thought parents should furnish an environment in which the children would feel comfortable living with that identity. (*Mixed Blessing*, p. 247)

Expert Advice

In offering advice to hundreds of interfaith couples with whom she has been in contact, therapist Lena Romanoff has become convinced of the need ultimately to resolve a specific religious identity for children. "My concern arises when [interfaith] couples tell me they plan to have a family [prior to resolving this child-rearing conflict]. Children . . . are ill equipped to absorb two conflicting religions and cultures into their lives. They often become confused and overwhelmed" (*Your People, My People*, p. 53).

Similar concerns are expressed time and again in the volume *Between Two Worlds*, in which Leslie Goodman-Malamuth and Robin Margolis elaborate on their extensive research among adults reared in interfaith homes.

> Growing up as an "outsider" who belongs to two worlds, but is not wholly part of either, can have a negative impact on our ability as adults to enjoy and nurture causes and groups. . . . A number of our respondents [to their questionnaires] directly attribute their propensity to walk alone [apart from organized groups and institutions] to their betwixt-and-between status as descendants of intermarriage. (p. 123)

Psychologist David Yammer observed: "While parents may think that they are giving their child 'both' religions rather than 'nothing,' children often perceive different messages given by parents as no message, as a confusing message, or as a 'loyalty trap' in which any religious behavior is seen as taking sides with one parent against the other.

Resolving Religious Issues

Just as parents decide where to live, what schools to attend, which medical group to visit, parents also should decide for their children which religion is most suitable. Neither two religions vaguely harmonized nor the absence of religion altogether will serve as a viable lifelong solution for a child.

5

Choosing Judaism for Your Child

The preceding chapter discussed the unfeasibility of trying to raise a child of an intermarriage with two religions. If you are contemplating raising your child within Judaism, or if you wish to know more before making such a choice, the following questions and answers will be of benefit to you.

1. Why would my child(ren) need religion at all?

In *Do Children Need Religion? How Parents Today Are Thinking About the Big Questions*, researcher Martha Fay describes a growing realization among her unchurched peers that religious issues unavoidably arise during parenting years.

As pediatric psychiatrist Dr. Sirgay Sanger observed to Ms. Fay: "[Even] children [of secularist parents] *invent* religion in order to explain the world, in order to explain sickness or loss, to explain why they don't have four grandparents or why a mother's pregnancy did not result in a brother or sister. Left to themselves, children come up with explanations that mimic every religion in the world" (cited in Martha Fay, *Do Children Need Religion?* pp. 20–21).

- "Mom, Sally next-door says that God makes babies."
- "Dad, on TV people who die always go to heaven."
- "My teacher taught us that God created the sky and the ground."

Being part of a specific religious tradition offers a context in which to respond to these childhood experiences.

Religion also assists mothers and fathers in reinforcing the ethical values they seek to impart to the next generation. One interviewee reflected to Martha Fay in assessing the benefit of sending a child to Sunday school: "It is not so much what they are learning as that they hear it *there*. We talk about all the same things at home, but just as when we talk about school things at home, they don't take it as seriously as they do in school. There is an added seriousness to these issues because they heard about it elsewhere as well" (Martha Fay, *Do Children Need Religion?* p. 83).

By linking right and wrong to a "higher authority," we impart a sense of conscience to our youngsters. Without God, without religion, in an age in which we are skeptical about the morality of government and of institutions of secular learning, "finding an acceptable surrogate, or backup, to one's exercise of parental authority turns out to be an immensely difficult task" (Martha Fay, *Do Children Need Religion?* p. 84).

In addition, a religious affiliation is important for the formation of personal identity. Religion gives people a common history, values, traditions, rituals, stories, jokes. It gives all of us an anchor in the world. The avoidance of religion may create a void in emotional, psychological, and spiritual development. Here are two painful reflections offered by sons and daughters of interfaith households lacking a clear religious identity.

Kids may feel alone in a certain social sense. . . . But I felt alone in a very basic sense. I never felt I belonged.

Don't make your kid feel like she is nothing. Everybody wants to be something [specific], to be called something [specific], and it isn't good to be nothing. (Lydia Kukoff et al., *Working with Interfaith Couples: A Jewish Perspective—A Guide for Facilitators*, pp. 109–110)

2. Does Judaism offer beliefs compatible with modern living?

Many of the unique attractions of Jewish beliefs are cited in published reflections of adult converts into Judaism. Having experienced both Christianity and Judaism, Jews by Choice are well qualified to offer comparisons. Ed, a Jew by Choice in one of Paul and Rachel Cowan's study groups, commented on how the Conservative Judaism he encountered had "made sense" for him. "The whole structure of Judaism makes more sense to me now than [previous experiences with organized religion]. I feel as if it has more tolerance for everything. It doesn't have the same sense of sin. Rather, the belief is that if you did something wrong this time, you can try again next time. Everything, from sexuality to death, is discussed" (Paul and Rachel Cowan, *Mixed Blessings*, p. 243).

NOT ALL OR NOTHING

Judaism is blessed with a large array of beliefs and observances. However, a person need not feel like a "bad Jew" if he or she does not do everything. Rabbis point out that no one is perfect. Only God can do "all" of Judaism. Similarly, not even the "least observant Jew" does "nothing." Human beings are perceived as trying to find their religious level on a continuum of commitments. Contemporary Jewish religion inspires individuals to increase involvement at their own pace. Jews add customs and ceremonies at moments when these practices become personally meaningful.

Thus, a Jew is not a hypocrite if, for example, he or she incorporates only part of Sabbath traditions. The Jewish notion of a continuum acknowledges the existence of gradations. Judaism insists: a little is better than nothing, a lot is better than a little. Paraphrasing Franz Rosenzweig, an early twentieth-century Jewish philosopher: "For the modern Jew, observance is no longer a matter of *all or nothing*. One only has to start. Nobody can tell where this beginning will lead." In Judaism of today, the issue is not one of "all or nothing" but rather one of ascending a ladder of commitments, one rung at a time. It is not how much of Judaism engages you at this point in time but rather in which direction you are headed—toward greater or lesser involvement.

AN EMPHASIS ON GOOD DEEDS: RELIGION IN ACTION, NOT JUST IN FAITH

Whereas most other groups insist upon the primacy of faith, Judaism concentrates on "religion in action," righteous actions toward other human beings. Rachel described why she felt more comfortable as a Jew than within previous religious affiliations. "Though I was taught [in Catholicism] that deeds were important, the stress was on having faith, on "believing in" something, even though or perhaps especially because it evaded all reason. In Judaism, by contrast, it is the emphasis on action, on righteous behavior that I find so attractive" (cited in Lydia Kukoff, *Choosing Judaism*, p. 20). Many converts to Judaism have expressed affection for this activism on behalf of a better world. "First and foremost among the features of Judaism which my studies taught me to admire . . . was its intense practicality. . . . Jews did not sit passive and wait for the Messiah to come, for if they did so he would not come" (Abraham Carmel, *So Strange My Path: A Spiritual Journey*, pp. 128–129).

AN OPENNESS TO QUESTIONING

Judaism remains open to questioning, to challenging, and to exploration. Pursuing truth is considered to be like searching for the signature of God. Judaism has never been harmed by challenges from scientific theories or secular ideas.

From the interaction of Judaic ideas with those of society, Jewry continues to derive new vitality. In the novels of Chaim Potok, for example, Judaism wrestles with modern psychology, with modern Bible scholarship, with contemporary mysticism, with the world of art. Potok's *Wanderings*, a history of the Jewish experience, portrays Judaism throughout the millennia as having the ability to acculturate, to encounter the best ideas within the world-at-large. Jewish religion has contributed in the style of a bee, going from flower to flower and producing spiritual honey for the world.

The Passover *seder*, Judaism's primary intergenerational holiday ritual, mandates asking questions and seeking new insights. The *seder* stresses the never-ending quest for religious meaning derived from sacred tradition. In the continuous striving for answers, ongoing inquiries are found in Jewish books, newspapers, and journals. Lydia Kukoff, a newcomer to Judaism, noted: "The allowance, sometimes encouragement, of questions concerning belief, God and truth is a welcome relief. One *can* be religious and question; in fact it is one's duty to question. Once I learned that *Israel* meant "to struggle with GOD," I felt my destiny at hand" (Lydia Kukoff, *Choosing Judaism*, p. 20).

SANCTIFICATION OF LIFE'S FULL RANGE OF EXPERIENCES

Some religions consciously segregate religious and secular aspects of life. The "sacred" moments are reserved for visits to the house of worship. In contrast, Judaism sees opportunities for holiness (*kiddushah*) in our everyday, mundane experiences. The simple act of eating at home can be elevated to sanctity via the dietary laws. Earning money and acquiring possessions can become blessed acts if they include *tzedakah*, righteously contributing a fair percentage of one's wealth to less fortunate persons. Marital sex for enjoyment, for human bonding, and for self-fulfillment is a *mitzvah*, a praiseworthy embodiment of God's will.

> For me, another attraction to Judaism is the principle of the sanctification of life. For years I have yearned for a lifestyle in which religion is integral, not peripheral. The concept of celebrating, and loving all of life, and making the ordinary holy, is supremely attractive; a constant devotion to God, which, rather than denying the earthly, the human and the complex, celebrates them. (Lydia Kukoff, *Choosing Judaism*, p. 20)

NO INSISTENCE ON ORIGINAL SIN

Judaism views the souls of newborn babies as totally pure and has never regarded sin as a difficult problem. Judaism does not believe in perfect people who are saints, but rather in flesh-and-blood human beings. All of us make mistakes. We then seek to change our ways through the divine gift of *teshuvah*, the innate human capacity to alter our behavior. Even Moses, Abraham, and the other biblical giants made moral errors. Jewish laws are not seen as a demand for perfect behavior. The system of *mitzvot* (commandments), affecting all times and arenas of existence, offers guidelines for human improvement and ethical growth. As Jew by Choice Gail Saville has commented: "When I was small, I often wondered how God could possibly think I was so terrible. . . . It is a comfort now to learn that God thought highly of me all along" (Gail Saville, "Why I Chose to Become a Jew," p. 20).

ALL MORAL PEOPLE REWARDED BY GOD IN THE HEREAFTER

Although there is no monolithic Jewish view of the hereafter, many rabbis teach that divine "rewards" are provided for *all* moral persons of *all* religious backgrounds. These Jewish views indicate that when the body (our physical self) dies and we leave this physical world, our soul (our spiritual self) passes on to God's eternal realm. The souls of all human beings (Jewish, Christian, Moslem, etc.) are treated equally in the world to come. If a man or woman has been moral during this life, his or her soul has been nurtured with the proper ethical fiber to thrive in God's presence. In the very same hereafter, a human being who has been immoral, whose soul has suffered spiritual impoverishment, will be eternally remorseful. For Judaism, if we are no longer within our bodies, separate locations of heaven and hell make no sense. Instead, all human souls, basking together in God's presence, will be spiritually suffering or "at rest" (blissful) in accordance with their righteousness during life in this world.

AN EMPHASIS ON THIS WORLD RATHER THAN AFTERLIFE

Although Judaism believes firmly in the spiritual life of the soul in the hereafter, the emphasis of Jews has always been upon concrete actions in this world. It is precisely via acts of righteousness toward other human beings that our soul matures and achieves the desired status of being a *"gitte neshumah"* (a good soul, deserving of God's presence in the world to come). Lydia Kukoff has written: "What I liked most about Judaism was that it was oriented toward *this* life and *this* world in a very real way . . . a system to live by, a system that at the same time had legal, spiritual . . . and ethical components that were inseparable from the religion itself. . . . Judaism emphasized living with my fellow people in *this* world" (Lydia Kukoff, *Choosing Judaism*, pp. 12–13).

DIRECT ACCESS TO GOD

In Judaism, no clergy or communal leaders are any closer to God than lay persons. No intermediary officiants are necessary for confession of one's sins or of beseeching God's presence. Everyone can lead services if capable, even a *bar mitzvah* or *bat mitzvah* young person. Nor will the Jewish messiah be God, Son of God, or a Savior. Gail Saville expressed with admiration:

> As a Jew, I don't have to go through an ecclesiastical switchboard . . . in charge of human affairs to reach God. . . .
>
> When I am in a car, I do not like riding in the passenger's seat, putting my life in someone else's hands. I prefer controlling my own destiny; I prefer to earn my own salvation. (Gail Saville, "Why I Chose to Become a Jew," p. 20)

PERSONAL RESPONSIBILITY FOR ONE'S ACTIONS

After sampling Eastern religions, secularism, Islam, and even the Catholic priesthood, Abraham Carmel found a spiritual home in Judaism. As a man whose energies focused primarily upon ethics and morality, Carmel was delighted that Judaism insisted that each man and woman is responsible for his/her own actions. Blame cannot be pushed aside, nor can forgiveness be offered indirectly.

> [In Judaism] there [is] . . . the splendid, robust principle of assuming undivided personal responsibility for one's actions. . . . The Jew must stand upright on his own two feet before the Judge of All. He has no patron saints to plead his cause, no Father Confessor to grant indulgences, absolutions or dispensations. . . .

Even on the great Day of Atonement . . . only the sins directed against God are thus forgiven. Sins committed against his neighbor are forgiven only after he has begged his neighbor's forgiveness. (Abraham Carmel, *So Strange My Path: A Spiritual Journey*, pp. 128–129)

A BALANCE BETWEEN TRADITIONAL ETHICS AND MODERN TECHNOLOGIES

Judaism has been able to incorporate the use of certain modern technologies in a way that is consistent with its system of beliefs.

Most of Judaism's respected rabbis and teachers permit abortion in certain circumstances, notably when the physical or emotional life of the mother is in jeopardy. Judaism does permit the disconnecting of life-support systems from a patient who has experienced brain-stem death.

The rabbis allow the transplanting of organs if they are immediately designated for a specific recipient.

Rabbis sanction the use of fertility medications, in vitro fertilization, and other therapeutic techniques if unassisted methods of reproduction have failed to bless a married couple with children.

Rabbis permit medically advised amnio-testing and other invasive procedures but caution against the potential abuses of genetic engineering.

Judaism remains steadfast in preserving religious limits in the use of modern technologies while simultaneously being open to new evidence and scientific breakthroughs for re-evaluation.

3. Does Judaism create a sense of community, of belonging?

When a Jewish person who is new to an area seeks affiliation with a congregation, the Jewish Community Center, United

Jewish Appeal, or chapters of national Jewish organizations, an immediate networking process begins. Friendships, a sense of belonging, a planting of roots, and the availability of assistance can be the benefits.

Judaism tells people who they are and from where they come. The memoirs of New York's former Mayor Ed Koch reflect the appeal of Jewish identity: "As a boy . . . my world ticked to the beat of the Sabbath and Jewish holidays. It was more than a religion, it was a way of life, a way of looking at the world. It invested me with an unshakable sense of who I was" (Edward I. Koch, *Citizen Koch*, p. 10). Being Jewish can be a great blessing to the individual, offering pride, interconnectedness, a sense of roots, a way of looking at the world, and familial nurturing.

In 1992 more dollars were contributed nationally to the United Jewish Appeal than to any other philanthropic cause (the Salvation Army, the United Way, Catholic Charities, etc.) even though Jews comprise less than 2.5 percent of the American population.

A South American Jew by Choice commented: "Rabbi, in my native country, everyone was Catholic, and I felt no particular bonds to anyone else as individuals in society at large. In contrast, now as a Jew, I feel an immediate bond to every Jewish person whom I meet." A Russian Jewish immigrant confided in one of my congregants: "In the U.S.S.R. we were told that religion is bad, a burden. Here in America I am amazed that, because of the ties which fellow Jews feel toward one another, I am being assisted in finding housing, employment, medical care, and friendships. Thank God for Judaism and Jewish community!"

4. Does Judaism teach helping *all* people in distress?

The Jewish religion is passionate about *tikkun* (mending) the world at large. Judaism affirms that humankind must not be content with imperfection in God's world. We are mandated to be God's partners in restoring the world to its initial state of perfection. Journalist Yosef Abramowitz wrote: "Why be Jewish? . . . Imagine what the world would look like if everyone valued human life. Imagine a time when justice prevails for all and there is peace. These are messianic images, and the Jewish system of life and mitzvot is a framework to bring us closer to this vision" (Yosef Abramowitz, "Why Be Jewish?" p. 47). In contemporary terms, author and Holocaust survivor Elie Wiesel has commented: "A Jew cannot remain indifferent to human suffering, whether in former Yugoslavia, in Somalia, or in our own cities and towns. The mission of the Jewish people has never been to make the world more Jewish, but to make it more human" (American Jewish Committee advertisement in the *New York Times*, September 27, 1992). Being motivated by a divine imperative for pursuing justice, it should be no surprise that American Jews have established an abundance of organizations to serve universal human needs. Although these groups have Jewish names, they provide assistance to the world at large. For example:

- Mazon: feeding the hungry in the United States and abroad
- American Jewish World Service: serving imperiled groups abroad
- The Jewish Fund for Justice: combatting poverty and discrimination in America
- Shomrey Adamah: advocating ecological responsibility
- Shalom Center: advocating peace
- ADL: combatting racial, religious, and ethnic bigotry

The Jew is called upon by our tradition to inspire the world by embodying the Torah command, "Love your neighbor as yourself."

The Torah does not say "Love the *world* as yourself": that commandment would be too easy to fulfill. It is easy to love "humanity," because such affection is so vague. "To love humanity" is simply a slogan. It leads to no practical results. However, to love your neighbor, your brother, your coreligionist, a specific person or group requires a commandment precisely because it is difficult. It forces you to act in very concrete ways and thereby sets into motion an example for others to follow.

By keeping alive the memory of our martyred six million ("our neighbors") in the Holocaust, Jews have become the world's conscience in human affairs. Because of the ethical dimensions of these Jewish teachings, we cry out against the "ethnic cleansing" aimed at defenseless minorities in the Balkans, against Iraqi barbarity toward the Kurds, and against a host of similar atrocities. Elie Wiesel has commented:

> By working for his own people a Jew does not renounce his loyalty to mankind. On the contrary, he makes his most valuable contribution. . . . By struggling on behalf of Russian, Arab or Polish Jews, I fight for human rights everywhere. By calling for peace in the Middle East, I take a stand against every aggression, every war. By protesting the fanatical exhortations to "holy wars" against my people, I protest against the stifling of freedom [elsewhere]. . . . By striving to keep alive the memory of the Holocaust, I denounce the massacres in Biafra [and similar ones] and the nuclear menace. Only by drawing on his unique experience can the Jew help others. A Jew fulfills his role as man only from inside his Jewishness. (Elie Wiesel, "Pride in Being Jewish," p. 19)

Abraham Joshua Heschel taught: "Judaism is the track of God in the wilderness of oblivion. By being what we are, namely Jews . . . we will aid humanity more than by any particular service we may render" (Abraham Joshua Heschel, *The Earth Is the Lord's*, cited in Sidney Greenberg, ed., *A Modern Treasury of Jewish Thoughts*, p. 34).

5. Does Jewish religion offer spiritual satisfaction?

More and more, Americans Jews and Christians alike are acknowledging that our needs extend beyond the limitations of our five senses. Many people have become aware that "there is more to reality than meets the eye. The everyday [physical] world is . . . real only in the way a dream is real. We see it and we hear it and indeed we live in it. We stake our lives on it. And in an instant it is gone" (Lawrence Kushner, *Honey from the Rock*, pp. 32–33).

Judaism is a pipeline into this pursuit of the spiritual side of life. Our religious experience teaches us that there is another dimension of reality that intersects with our ordinary existence. Rabbi Harold Kushner, observing the incredible success of spirituality literature and tapes sold in bookstores, has tried to define this spiritual thirst. "There is a kind of nourishment our souls crave, even as our bodies need the right foods, sunshine, and exercise. Without that spiritual nourishment, our souls remain stunted and underdeveloped" (Harold Kushner, *Who Needs God?* audiotape).

Judaism offers a legacy for spiritual meditation and fulfillment through meaningful involvement in private and public prayer.

> Prayer is first and foremost the experience of being in the presence of God. Whether or not we have our requests granted, whether or not we get anything to take home as a result of the encounter, we are changed by having come into the presence of God. A person who has spent an hour or two in the presence of God will be a different person for some time afterward. (Harold Kushner, *Who Needs God?* audiotape)

For some other converts to Judaism, entry into the Jewish faith community also has sparked spirituality, religious vitality. In *An Orphan in History*, Paul Cowan describes his wife

Rachel's spiritual rebirth via conversion. "She said that she had been thinking about the idea [of conversion] for months, ever since she discovered that worshipping as a Jew released something inside her which enabled her to think about God; to feel, at rare moments, a faith whose intensity startled her" (Paul Cowan, *An Orphan in History*, p. 217).

CONCLUSION

The Jewish community invites interfaith parents to consider choosing the Jewish religion for their children. Your offspring can find profound meaning in Judaism, whether intellectually, spiritually, or in terms of making a better world. They may become inspired by authentic claims upon them from the Jewish tradition, Jews throughout the globe, and the Jewish covenant with God. At different points in your son's or daughter's lifetimes, each of these contexts might become more important and inspiring. Judaism is a rich and compelling legacy, speaking powerfully to people today as it has to Jews throughout millennia.

Why choose Judaism for your children?

What's the gain?

In this age of innumerable choices, seriously consider passing the blessing of Jewishness to your sons and daughters. Make contact with your local congregation, rabbi, or United Synagogue regional office to begin the process. Also, investigate special "Gateways" programs intended for interfaith couples, sponsored by the Jewish Theological Seminary and the Rabbinical Assembly. The "Gateways" brochure states:

> There are a growing number of congregations and rabbis who are seeking the best way to address the role of non-Jewish spouses in life-cycle events, or to bring the non-Jewish spouse into Jewish literacy programs in a non-coercive way. Others have established

sensitive counseling programs and social settings to enable inter-married couples to cooperate in the maintenance of a Jewish home for the Jewish spouse and children. (*Gateways: An "Outreach" Program of the Jewish Theological Seminary*, promotional brochure) (For further details and locations of "Gateways" programs, contact Dr. Anne Lapidus Lerner at the Jewish Theological Seminary, [212] 678-8069, or Rabbi Stanley Kessler in West Hartford, CT, [203] 232-6348.)

Do not underestimate Judaism's precious legacy and ability to speak to your children's present and future needs. Let them study, savor, and explore Jewish religion. It will enrich their lives and the lives of those around them!

6

Raising a Jewish Child
in an Interfaith Home

Not all interfaith couples are the same. It should not be assumed that all are uninterested in meaningful involvement in Jewish life. A Rabbinical Assembly Task Force identified couples at distinct points on a continuum of Jewish involvement.

- The Secular Couple—These have chosen nonreligious solutions to family life-cycle events and ethical decision-making. They are usually uninterested in any efforts at Jewish community outreach.
- The Religiously Dual Couple—These are uncomfortable making a decision on behalf of either religion. They make choices that minimize conflicts by attempting to treat all religious ceremonies as "cultural" rather than as part of a belief system with theological implications. They often resist synagogue or church overtures.
- The Religiously Undecided Couple—These have not yet resolved their religious issues. They are frequently open to discussing new ideas, seeking information, and hearing the experiences of other couples. They may be receptive to

outreach from congregations. They are at an "entry level" of exploration.

- The Religiously Decided Couple—They have made a commitment that their family's religious practice and child-rearing intentions shall be exclusively Jewish. (Jewish Family Service [Metrowest, New Jersey], "Outreach to the Intermarried," p. 1)

If you are a religiously decided couple committed to raising your children as Jews, you have made a wonderful choice. However, Jewish identity will not be transmitted automatically. It will require careful nurturing and commitment by parents and grandparents.

Many Jewish adults coast along in their Jewishness. . . . They "feel Jewish" because they internalized certain attitudes or habits. Their "Jewishness" is often bottled up within their memory-banks. . . . The smell of fresh bread evokes memories of Shabbat *challah*. . . . Blintzes sizzling in a pan suddenly bring forth the mental picture of the lovely observance of Shavuot in the late spring.

For a child who has never, or rarely, experienced these observances, just talking about them means little or nothing. Hearing about how mommy and daddy used to sit around the Shabbat table as little children is nothing more than another piece of nostalgic story-telling. It is part of the *parents'* Jewishness. It does not make the *child* feel more Jewish. . . .

Although there are Jewish children who beat the odds, we cannot realistically expect children to internalize being Jewish unless they are surrounded [with Jewishness as a living experience]. . . .

Jewish identity is *not* hereditary. It is taught to a child, both formally and informally. (Jane Epstein, "Jewish Identity Is Not Hereditary," p. 3)

In a 1983 study of adults raised as Jews in interfaith homes, conducted by the American Jewish Committee, the writers concluded that many of these Jewish offspring have little if any Jewish identity. Not only are they personally unobservant of Jewish ritual and do they fail to affiliate with a synagogue, but they also feel no special ties either to Israel or to other Jews in need. In many cases, they do not regard being Jewish as important, nor would they choose to be Jewish if they had the choice of reentering the world.

Many of this Jewishly ambivalent group are children of mixed married who decided "to raise their sons and daughters as Jews" but who did *nothing* to make concrete the transmission of this heritage. I have a relative, for example, whose son was to be "raised as a Jew" but who was never enrolled in a synagogue, never attended religious school, and was never exposed to any Jewish home observances. Today that teenager is a nice young man but with no Jewish identity whatsoever.

Having made the praiseworthy decision of "choosing Judaism for your child," you must now take the next step: planning a concrete strategy for training this precious youngster as an authentic Jewish person.

The first step in this effort must be *affiliating with a synagogue*. As Barry Shrage, Executive Vice President of Boston's Jewish Federation, wrote:

> Congregations continue to be the primary gateway to Jewish life.
>
> They are [especially] the primary gateways for young Jewish families: their afternoon and weekday schools educate the vast majority of Jewish children; their camps, youth groups, and Israel experiences dominate the market. . . .
>
> Finally, only our synagogues can restore *kedushah*—holiness—to the center of Jewish life. Without it, there will be no Jewish future. (Barry Shrage, "Bringing Federations Closer to Synagogues," p. 13)

The following questions address some concerns intermarried families ask about affiliating with a synagogue and raising a child of an interfaith marriage within the Jewish community. The responses reflect the conservative rabbi's viewpoint.

1. Why should we bother to join a synagogue, when most rabbis refused to officiate at our interfaith wedding ceremony?

"Not infrequently, couples will harbor a lingering resentment at rabbinic refusal to officiate at their marriage. Some couples are truly shocked to discover that the Jewish partner is still welcomed as a member in our synagogues and that the non-Jewish partner can participate in our programs" (Avis Miller, "Reaching Out—Dealing with Intermarried Families," p. 9). It is true that all Conservative and Orthodox, and most Reform and Reconstructionist rabbis will refuse to officiate at interfaith wedding ceremonies. This refusal is based not on personal animosity or a desire to reject the persons involved, but rather upon religious principles. Reflecting upon a typical premarriage interview, Rabbi William Lebeau has written:

> I explained to Tom and Sarah why it was impossible for me to conduct their Jewish wedding by showing them . . . the wedding ceremony. . . .
>
> The second prayer [of the wedding ceremony] . . . thanks God for sanctifying *us* (those who are within the Jewish community) by giving us the commandments that govern our lives, including the commandment to marry as a Jewish couple. I explained to Tom that he could not be included in this blessing as long as he chose to remain outside the community bound by God's commandments as articulated in the Torah.
>
> We then studied the proclamation that the *hatan* (Jewish groom) makes to the *kallah* (Jewish bride), "*Harey at mekoodeshet lee b'taba-at zo k'dat Moshe ve-Yisrael*"—"Behold you are made sacred to me by this ring according to the religion of Moses and the people of Israel." Tom could not say this, because Jewish law requires that

a Jewish marriage include two Jews who feel compelled to live according to the law of Moses and the people of Israel.

Sarah and Tom listened carefully and reluctantly acknowledged the inappropriateness of the service for them. (William H. Lebeau, "The Interfaith Marriage Ceremony: A Time for Honesty—Not for Rabbis, Priests or Ministers")

Traditional rabbis also will refrain from participating in numerous other categories of marriage ceremonies. For example, they will turn down a wedding request if one of the parties has a civil divorce but does not have a Jewish (religious) divorce as well.

In none of these instances does a rabbinic refusal to officiate imply lack of interest in assisting people to raise children as Jews, or to help with a personal quest for Jewish involvement. Rabbi Barry Baron has written:

Rabbinic authority to officiate at marriages derives from rabbinic responsibilities to administer Jewish law. The title "rabbi" implies the bearer's allegiance to that law. Jewish law sanctions the marriage of Jews to each other, and as a rabbi, I feel that I can only officiate at marriages which Jewish law sanctions. . . .

My love for Judaism stops me from officiating at interfaith marriages even as it leads me to embrace interfaith couples. . . .

I can only say that the force of tradition which leads me that way is the same force for deeper spirituality and meaning in my life and the lives of others, including many who are in interfaith marriages. (Barry Baron, "Interfaith Marriages: Rabbis Respond," p. 2)

It is time for you to consider any residual resentments that stem from your wedding ceremony and, if necessary, talk about these resentments with a rabbi.

While most . . . rabbis decline to participate in intermarriage ceremonies . . . [many rabbis] have been most willing to meet with couples and their families to discuss their concerns. Rabbis regularly volunteer many hours to co-lead intermarriage groups for couples, their parents, and Jews by Choice. Thus, while couples, parents, and rabbis may at times view the wedding ceremony differently, there are open lines of communication and a commitment to outreach. (James Rosen and Roslyn Zinner, Letter to the Editor on behalf of the Baltimore Board of Rabbis, p. 9)

The interfaith wedding ceremony lasted for only one day. In contrast, your relationship with your children is eternal. In order to raise them as Jewish children, it is important that you cross over the threshold of a local congregation and join.

2. Are intermarried couples and their children welcome to become involved in Conservative synagogues?

Many mixed marrieds are under the mistaken impression that only Reform temples welcome intermarried couples who seek to raise their children as Jews. Nothing could be further from the truth. In fact, in Conservative Judaism, bringing an intermarried family closer to the congregation not only is permitted but it is defined as a *mitzvah* (commandment), the *mitzvah* of *keruv* (bringing people closer). *Keruv* connotes the attempt to bring Jews and their non-Jewish spouses closer to us and to our established communal standards. As past president of the International Rabbinical Assembly, Rabbi Gerald Zelizer has taught:

A key objective should be the raising and education of the children [of mixed marrieds] as Jews. We can only meet that crucial objective if we are more receptive to what we call *keruv*, "bringing closer" actively the interfaith family so that the children can be salvaged as Jews, even where one spouse remains non-Jewish. . . .

The image that we project outside of the walls of our synagogue should be more welcoming of interfaith couples—making them feel comfortable . . . assisting the education and raising of their children as Jews. (Gerald Zelizer, Rosh Hashanah Sermon, 1991)

On behalf of Conservative Judaism's Committee on Jewish Law and Standards, its chairman, Rabbi Kassel Abelson, also has written: "The higher interests of the Jewish people call for us to make such "reyim" (non-Jews married to Jews) welcome in the synagogue and in the Jewish community. We have to make every effort to save intermarried families for Judaism, and to help these families provide Jewish homes (Kassel Abelson, "The Non-Jewish Spouse and Children of a Mixed Marriage in the Synagogue," p. 132).

3. Is it not true that unlike Reform temples, Conservative synagogues permit only the Jewish persons of the household to become congregation members?

It is correct that Reform temples allow non-Jewish relatives to be "members," but generally this membership is restricted to certain functions. It applies to paying dues, voting in annual congregational meetings, and other technical activities. In many communities, it does not apply to any leadership positions involving policy decisions. This ambiguity of second-class membership is criticized even by many within the Reform movement.

> Lydia Kukoff, Reform's Former Director of Outreach, [has said,] "We need to consider the feelings of the non-Jews in our midst. . . . We should offer them every opportunity to have Jewish experiences. But," Kukoff emphasizes, "at the same time we must maintain Jewish integrity. We should not be tentative in our message. We are Jews. This is a Jewish place, and we welcome you." (cited by Stephen Fuchs, "Reach Out—But Also Bring In," p. 69)

The creating of different levels of members, granting full rights to Jewish members and limited rights to non-Jews, is unacceptable for Conservative Judaism. Rather than creating the illusion of total acceptance via an unequal category of membership, Conservative synagogues adopt the approach prevalent within America's Catholic and Protestant churches, offering "membership" in a theological institution only to persons who are born into or converted into that faith group. Other persons in the household are not "members," but they are welcome to attend every religious service, adult education program, and social function.

In other words, Judaism is a faith community, as is Catholicism and each denomination of Protestantism. Faith communities are not simply social settings in which all fine, decent human beings can participate fully and equally. Just as certain civic privileges are available only to American citizens, so too are certain religious sacred rites made available only to members of the faith. Relatives of faith community members should be made welcome in both synagogues and churches, but religious distinctions still remain. A non-Christian does not receive communion rites or come to be regarded as a formal member of a church, even though he or she may attend services, adult education, social functions, and other church gatherings.

Similar principles apply to synagogues. To act otherwise is to redefine a synagogue as a social club, equally accessible to all regardless of faith commitments, and not as an American-style faith community. To involve Christian spouses and children in Jewish services, adult education lectures, family social gatherings, and the like is praiseworthy. However, to enable practicing Christians or other non-Jews to participate as if they were Jews in Jewish ritual settings or in leadership levels within the synagogue is to create confusion in the minds of all concerned.

Conservative rabbis and congregations not only welcome the intermarried, but recognize and appreciate the praiseworthy nature of mixed couples who consciously seek out a traditional Jewish movement. Rabbi Avis Miller, the chairperson of the Rabbinical Assembly's *Keruv* Committee, wrote: "Intermarried families who choose to attend a Conservative congregation are making a strong statement about their Jewish commitment. . . . By joining a Conservative congregation, they are choosing a non-minimalist option" (Avis Miller, "Reaching Out—Dealing with Intermarried Families," p. 8).

4. What types of programs do Conservative congregations offer for the intermarried?

Many of us in the Conservative rabbinate have been privileged to have intermarried couples integrate meaningfully into aspects of our congregational life in an authentic Jewish fashion. Numerous conservative synagogues offer a range of options:

- Introduction-to-Judaism courses
- Holiday workshops
- Hebrew literacy classes
- Learners' *minyan* (religious service)
- Family service
- Special *keruv* to the intermarried

Several years ago, for example, I was privileged to supervise Project Link, a *keruv* program tied to our synagogue's religious services and staffed by Rabbi Sam Weintraub. The following are representative reflections shared by the participants:

There were 8 or 9 of us, and we were studying with Rabbi Weintraub. He taught us all about the religion, from the most important holiday to the least important holiday, all ritual. We sat every week and talked and asked questions again and I just felt that at that point that's what I wanted to do. I wanted to make my family a unit. I wanted to be part of my family. And I really believed that this was the place to be. To me it was like coming home. (Diane Gerberg, cited in Stephen Weiss, "Interview with Jew by Choice")

The wonderful spirit in the congregation is very "catchy" and in a few short months we went from a family who lit Shabbat candles and went to High Holy Day services to a family who enjoys attending Sabbath services weekly, studying and learning more about the religion. . . . The congregation has really added to our feeling we have a part in this new community . . . we are delighted and grateful to have the congregation be such an important part of our lives. (Anne Burg, Membership Application, Congregation Agudath Israel, Caldwell, New Jersey)

In order to categorize and encourage the wide array of *keruv* programs available in Conservative congregations, the Jewish Theological Seminary established a Gateways program, creating a competition for grants to further this outreach. The following list of grant winners is indicative of some of the array of offerings.

Berkeley, CA
Congregation Netivot Shalom
Rabbi Stuart Kelman

> A mentoring program that links an intermarried couple with a caring Jewish couple that will serve as a resource and a guide. In addition are monthly sessions in which the entire group assembles for lectures, discussions, and joint activities. Mentors deepen their own understanding of Judaism in formal study.

Miami, FL
Temple Samu-El Or Olom
Rabbi Larry G. Kaplan

> In a community attracting young families of Hispanic origin, including a significant number of interfaith couples, this synagogue has undertaken a bilingual basic Judaism course and activities [conducted in English and Spanish] tied to ritual

observances, such as Passover *seders*, Sukkot meals, Sabbath observances and the like. The activities component would be trilingual, including Hebrew.

Northampton, MA
Congregation B'nai Israel
Rabbi Philip Graubart

This program is called "Stepping Stones to a Jewish Family" and is geared toward the unaffiliated. One teacher is hired for every six or seven interfaith families in the program. These teachers guide the families through the program, including an education component, synagogue attendance, visits with rabbis and other field trips, and communal dinners and celebrations. A Committee on Jewish Living, consisting of individuals committed to a Jewish way of life, serves as a cadre of role models and acts as the sponsoring body of the program.

Ridgefield Park, NJ
Temple Emanuel
Rabbi Stephen C. Lerner

"Pairing Couples" is a program in which intermarried couples are paired with "host" couples in which one partner has converted into Judaism. The host couples accompany their intermarried partners to synagogue services, join them for ritual observances and Sabbath meals, and act as support for them.

Potomac, MD
Congregation Har Shalom
Rabbi Leonard S. Cahan
Rabbi David Kaye

The congregation offers three types of *havurot* [couples clusters]. One focuses on a family education program for families with a non-Jewish parent. Another is for childless couples who are intermarried. The third is for Jews who have issues to explore concerning intermarriage.

Winnepeg, Canada
Congregation Shaarey Zedek
Rabbi Henry Balser

"Project Link" involves a series of informal gatherings, with couples meeting in homes to explore and learn about Judaism, its rituals and practices. The goal is to help the intermarried make informed choices about religious affiliation. There is a yearlong follow-up program of hands-on classes and activities. In addition, couples in the program will be linked to a family. There also is a one-day program devoted to discussing such topics as "Choosing a Faith," "What Does Religion Mean to Me," and "Relating to Family and Friends as an Intermarried Couple."

Chicago, IL
Anshe Emet Synagogue
Rabbi Michael Siegel

A basic Jewish literacy program focuses on intermarried families, including the synagogue's publication, *From Our House to Yours*. The program includes yearlong courses in Jewish heritage and spirituality, beginning Hebrew, holiday and life-cycle "teach-ins," beginners' services, and communal activities.

Lexington, MA
Temple Emunah
Rabbi Bernard Eisenman

This synagogue has launched "The Kesher Project." It consists of six components: a three-session introductory course on basic Judaism, a structured and narrated *Shabbat* dinner, a linking of intermarried couples with Jewish families for joint Sabbath observances, a social group made up of the intermarried couples in the program, and outreach programs to the parents and children of the intermarried.

Raleigh, NC
Beth Meyer Synagogue

Rabbi Daniel A. Ornstein

The congregation offers a program called "Jewish Ties." At its core are a series of monthly meetings in homes, at which intermarried couples can learn about Jewish practices and concepts in a nonthreatening environment. The goal is to offer intermarried couples an opportunity to enhance their family life for themselves and the raising of their children through Judaism. Among its features is a monthly program called *B'Yachad*, for the intermarried with children. Also *Shabbat* and festival workshops are provided.

Kansas City, MO
The Beth Shalom Congregation
Rabbi Raphael Kanter
Prairie Village, KN
Congregation Ohev Shalom
Rabbi Daniel M. Horowitz

The two synagogues have created The Heartland Center for Jewish Outreach. The program provides basic Judaism courses to interested non-Jews, and it increases community awareness of Jewish beliefs and practices. It reaches out via university and/or college affiliation, computer networking through bulletin boards of a major online service, expanded multimedia films and audiotape materials, collaboration with educators and agencies devoted to outreach, and identification of successful outreach models used elsewhere that are adaptable to the Heartland Center.

Columbus, OH
Congregation Tifereth Israel
Rabbi Harold J. Berman

This program targets both the intermarried and the marginally Jewish. A featured component is a number of subject oriented study sessions covering such topics as "Starting to Learn Judaism," "Starting to Learn about Jewish Holidays," "Starting to Read Our Special Books," and "Jewish Life-cycle Revisited."

South Orange, NJ
Oheb Shalom Congregation
Rabbi Lawrence Troster
Rabbi John S. Schechter

A committee of four Jews married to Jews and four Jews married to non-Jews meets regularly to discuss issues and to plan a program of interest to intermarried families, as well as additional training of teachers in the synagogue school and staff on how to deal with children of intermarried families. This is supplemented by a rich Jewish family education series and a variety of learning experiences that are replete with spirituality and meaning for the intermarried who are open to exploring Judaism in a welcoming atmosphere.

Des Plaines, IL
Maine Township Jewish Congregation Shaare Emet
Rabbi Edmund Winter

A support group program is offered for the parents of the intermarried. Also a separate support group for the intermarried themselves allows them to consider issues related to intermarriage in depth, over time, and in a Jewish setting. This aspect of the program is spearheaded by an outreach committee involving members of the parent support group.

Norwood, MA
Temple Shaare Tefilah
Rabbi Pamela Barmash

"Project Shaare Beit Knesset" is an outreach program to the intermarried and the marginally Jewish who have children ages 2 to 4. Subscribing to the view that the age of the children is what influences a parent's response to the synagogue, the educational programs developed are all family oriented. In addition, specialists in Jewish life and culture lead discussions and workshops on the Jewish home, prayer, *Shabbat* and festival observances. Tot *Shabbat* (for children aged 3 to 5) and

Mini-*Minyan* (ages 5 to 8) are a part of the program, as is an effort to integrate family education into the synagogue's lower school.

Jewish literacy courses are offered in dozens of locations. The literacy program is chaired nationally by Rabbi Avis Miller, Adas Israel Congregation, Washington, DC, who describes the project as follows:

Many Conservative synagogues around the country are offering entry-level courses in Jewish living. . . . Wherever the courses in Jewish literacy are offered, they have a number of features in common.

The outreach to intermarrieds is explicit but not exclusive. Intermarried couples are welcomed along with others who are in the orbit of the Jewish community. . . .

The courses provide not just information, but affect and social contact with Jews as well. Teachers are encouraged to share their own personal enthusiasm for Judaism. Other committed members of the community join the classes to socialize with those hesitating on the fringes of Jewish life.

Documentation is kept concerning who joins these classes and why, and what kinds of Jewish opportunities they are seeking.

Follow-up courses are offered in areas of interest to the participants. The idea is to encourage not just entrance but long-term participation in an ongoing Jewish community. (Avis Miller, "Outreach to Intermarrieds: Parameters and Outlines," p. 3)

Who comes into these *keruv* programs? According to Rabbi Samuel Weintraub, the former supervisor of *keruv* efforts in New Jersey:

Couples . . . present significant differences in family development and specific Jewish interests. However, in their underlying attitudes to Judaism, and to the experience of being intermarried, they show certain commonalities:

1. First, they were eager . . . to find other people in similar circumstances. . . .
2. Generally, there was a desire, of one or both partners, for some meaningful association with Jewish traditions and communities . . . including interests in Jewish study, Jewish celebration . . . and synagogue affiliation. . . .
3. Virtually all couples wanted religion in the home and rejected the idea of a bireligious or blended home, particularly because of its effects on children. (Samuel Weintraub, "Project Link: Principled, Sensitive, Conservative Outreach," p. 42)

5. Isn't it true that children of a Jewish father and a non-Jewish mother cannot be raised as Jews?

This harmful myth dissuades many intermarried couples from raising their offspring as Jews. It is important to remember *one caution* and *two facts*:

Caution: Beware of the patrilineal descent confusion.

The Reform movement does recognize patrilineal descent (i.e., even if the mother is not Jewish, the child may be considered as a Jew without benefit of conversion so long as the child publicly identifies as a Jew). Unfortunately, there are a few problems with this approach. First, even within Reform Judaism, Jewish status is *not* automatically conferred upon the children of Jewish fathers and Gentile mothers. The Reform movement requires that such sons and daughters be raised actively as Jews, including *bris* (ritual circumcision) or baby naming at birth (and no baptism), synagogue membership, religious school education, *bar/bat mitzvah*, and other basic Jewish experiences.

Furthermore, even if these requirements are met, Reform's patrilinealism is not universally accepted within Reform Judaism, and it is rejected by the Orthodox and Conservative movements. Thus, it represents a fundamental break with the

other two major branches of Judaism, and even with the
Reform movement in many parts of the world. That is why the
Conservative movement's Committee on Jewish Law and
Standards affirms:

> Jewishness is defined through either lineage or through
> conversion to Judaism.
> Matrilineal descent [being born to a Jewish mother] . . . has
> been authoritative in normative Judaism for many cen-
> turies as the sole determinant of Jewish lineage.

Nevertheless, without patrilineal descent, you *can* raise
your children as Jews!

Fact: All children born to a Jewish mother are Jewish in the
eyes of Judaism, whether or not the father is Jewish. Rabbi
Perry Rank, president of the New Jersey Region of the Rabbinical Assembly, noted: "Most distressing to me are those who
would see her children as only half Jews. Accordingly to Hala-
cha, they are full Jews and should be treated accordingly"
(Perry Rank, "Keruv, Covenant and Understanding Conservative Judaism," p. 13).

Fact: Children born to a non-Jewish mother and a Jewish
father *can* be raised as Jews in a Conservative congregation as
long as they are converted to Judaism. The conversion process
may begin at the time of birth, at some point during a child's
toddler or elementary years, or even commence at the point of
preparation for *bar/bat mitzvah* (note: ask your rabbis for a
description of the range of viable options).

> Rabbi Morris Shapiro in a Law Committee Responsa (1980) entitled
> "Who is a Jewish Child?" comes to the conclusion that we should
> maintain the generally accepted halachah, for Halachah itself offers
> an easy solution to the problem of the offspring of a Jewish father and
> a non-Jewish mother, and that is conversion. . . . When there is
> agreement on the part of mother and father to have their children

converted and raise them as Jews, every possible aid and encouragement should be given to them. If they are already young children
then the process of conversion should begin immediately. (Kassel
Abelson, "The Non-Jewish Spouse and Children of a Mixed Marriage in the Synagogue," pp. 138–139)

We are anxious to work with you in raising your children as
Jewish children! Please consult your local Conservative rabbi
for more information.

6. What is the impact of enrolling my child in a program of formal Jewish education and of informal Jewish settings?

We have already noted that the first step is synagogue affiliation. The second step is formal education. It is important to
seek suitable Jewish formal education for children from the age
of 5 to 17. You should begin with a Jewish nursery school.
Rabbi William Lebeau, dean of the Rabbinical School of the
Jewish Theological Seminary, noted:

> One of the earliest contacts with the Jewish community for fami-
> lies in which one marriage partner was not born a Jew will occur
> when the child of that marriage enters into a pre-school program
> in a synagogue or Jewish community center. . . . Pre-school
> teachers have an important responsibility in encouraging those
> families to deepen their Jewish commitment.
>
> The nursery school teacher [will] . . . be especially sensitive to
> the children from these families, whose regular contacts will be
> with Christian grandparents, aunts, uncles and cousins. Every
> attempt should be made to encourage the family of the pre-school
> children to create a strong Jewish home and to provide love and
> security which will enable these children to feel secure in their
> Jewish identification. (William H. Lebeau, "Ways to Express
> Ahavat Yisrael: Through Keruv," p. 6)

Formal Jewish education should continue with kindergarten and elementary school years in a Solomon Schechter or other Jewish day school, or in a sequence of synagogue Sunday and religious schools, followed by Hebrew high school.

Some parents complain about their own days in Hebrew school or Jewish day school. However, they begrudgingly come to realize that, without years of formal Jewish education, they would never have acquired the religious knowledge to function as a Jewish adult. One of the parents of youngsters in a local synagogue Sunday school, for example, reflected to a study group:

> I never fully appreciated my Hebrew school education until I went off to college. In my program there were very few Jewish students and the Christian kids constantly asked me questions about Jewish rituals, holidays and beliefs. Because I knew the answers, I felt proud and reaffirmed in my Jewishness. God forbid, how I would have felt if my knowledge had not been so strong.

Furthermore, in terms of quality, current-day Jewish education is light years ahead of Jewish classrooms in the 1950s and 1960s. Indeed, the 1985 demographic and attitudinal survey of the UJA/Federation of MetroWest, New Jersey, Jewish community revealed that nearly 80 percent of parents regard the quality of their children's Jewish day school or synagogue school experiences as either "good" or "excellent." Only 1 percent find these settings "poor" or "unacceptable."

We *know* that formal Jewish education is critically important for our children. Do not fall into the trap of asking your children whether they want to attend formal Jewish studies, any more than you would offer them choices about secular education. In this context, I think of the many adults who were forced to take music lessons as children and today are grateful for that parental decision.

Similarly, do not leave to a child's whims the critical decisions of participating in Jewish communal and group activities such as Jewish day camps and overnight camps, youth groups, *tzedakah* projects, Jewish Community Center activities, and others. I cannot overestimate the importance of giving your children, who are raised as a minority in a non-Jewish society, the opportunity to feel the warmth and comfort, the self-esteem and the pride of being part of Jewish endeavors with boys and girls their own age. The informal education transmitted in this fashion should become an indispensable part of your Jewish family life agenda.

A note of caution: Keep in mind that Jewish schools, whether Conservative, Reform, or Orthodox, all teach commitment to Judaism!

> When we accept . . . children [of the intermarried] into religious school, it is with the hope that [like all their classmates,] they will seek a marriage partner who will transmit a love for Jewish practice, Jewish learning and Jewish living to their children.
>
> We . . . find a way, lovingly, sensitively, and caringly to tell the student with a non-Jewish mother or father that we do not cast aspersions on his parents' marriage, but that we hope his or her love for Judaism will grow so strong that he/she will want to share life with one who shares that love. (Stephen Fuchs, "Outreach: Parameters and Prospects," audiotape)

7. What is meant by Jewish family education? Is this something that would be important for my family?

Recent data indicate that Jewish identity will best be developed among children whose entire nuclear family is part of the educational process. In other words, Jewish family education must be structured not as a luxury, but as a necessity. The client for Jewish learning and Jewish experiences must be *the entire family.* "If children see and hear their parents 'doing Jewish,' they will both sense its significance and consider exploring it seriously with a model for doing so. Planning only child-centered activities makes Judaism seem childish" (Shoshanna Silberman, "Developing Jewish Rituals for Your Family," p. 67).

In the immigrant Jewish family during the early decades of the century, Jewish family education did not have to be structured. "The home itself was the parents' classroom. The content of Jewish education offered therein revolved around the telling of family, tribal and national histories. . . . Each religious festival was imbued with [its own] special home ritual. Even the central life-cycle experiences—birth, *bris*, wedding, death—usually took place in the home" (Ron Wolfson, *Jewish Family Education*, p. 2).

As the immigrants and their children pursued integration into American life, however, they adopted the cultural model of the United States, in which religious messages were transmitted primarily via the congregational school. This segmented approach was viable for Jews as long as children lived close to extended family and in a heavily Jewish neighborhood. Today, for most Jewish families neither of these conditions exists. As a result, Jewish children are learning Jewish content in settings that are divorced from their home lives. Judaism is not being reinforced by parents, siblings, or the household. "Children pick up parental convictions and beliefs, and where there are none, a vacuum is created that is readily filled by gurus and sects and cults [or by secularism]. . . . The school can teach dates, history, and geography, but not the language that penetrates the soul" (Harold Schulweis, *In God's Mirror*, pp. 195–196).

Working as a family and a community, we must develop for our children a strategy of meaningful encounters with Judaism. Both formal and informal opportunities abound. "Live Judaism passionately . . . the philosophical, mystical, liturgical, ritual or national; learn it, do it, live it passionately. Let the children see you. Whenever possible, do not segregate the generations. . . .

Judaism . . . cannot be taught, it must be caught. Do it in front of the children. Make it contagious" (Nina Beth Cardin, cited in Jonathan Woocher, "Jewish Survival Tactics," p. 12).

Educator Susan Werk suggests that you continually point out what is Jewish about your community: Go to the kosher butcher and bakery. Visit the Jewish bookstore and Jewish Community Center. Go on a hunt for kosher symbols on products in the local supermarket.

Create a network of families pursuing similar goals of promoting Jewish continuity. Join a *havurah*, a cluster of eight to twelve households who share your beliefs and interest. Invite families who seem receptive to this agenda to share *Shabbat* or Holiday meals with your family. "We formed a *havurah* [fellowship or community] with other families and came together, with our children, in our celebrations. In this informal and close-knit community, we were able to affirm Jewish traditions as well as create new modes of expression without being hindered by ideological labels" (Shoshanna Silberman, "Developing Jewish Rituals for your Family," p. 67).

Following is a suggested checklist of hands-on activities (also recommended by Susan Werk, educational director of Congregation Agudath Israel, Caldwell, New Jersey):

- Have a "Jewish Object" treasure hunt in your home. Go to each room and see how many objects in your home deal with being Jewish. Examples: books, *menorahs*, candleholders, pictures, Jewish calendars, *tzedakah* boxes, *kippot, tallit, tefillin, seder* plate, *kiddush* cups, *mezuzah*. . . .
- A car ride can be a wonderful opportunity to sing Hebrew songs together (playing a cassette tape or CD of Jewish melodies), to share family memories of Jewish occasions, or to play a Jewish category game.
- Share with your sons and daughters pictures of Jewish events during your childhood: Hanukkah candlelighting, Purim costumes, Passover family gatherings, *bar/bat mitz-*

vah ceremonies and receptions, Jewish wedding ceremonies of relatives. . . . Create new photos of their childhood Jewish "Kodak moments."

- Share with your youngsters why you decided to live in your neighborhood with all of its Jewish content.
- Create a family recipe book with your favorite Jewish foods. It might include Grandma's honey cake for holidays, Aunt Sarah's kugel, or Dad's Sunday lox and eggs. Decorate and illustrate your book with the assistance of the younger generation.
- Initiate "God Talk" with your child. There are wonderful books that can serve as resources: *Teaching Your Children About God* by David J. Wolpe, *God's Paintbrush* by Sandy Eisenberg Sasso, *Old Turtle* by Douglas Wood. Keep a diary of their questions and your answers.
- Be a Jewish role model for the next generation. Show them that you care about local and national Jewish issues. Demonstrate by your involvement in Jewish rituals, holidays, and synagogue life that Judaism is not "just for kids," but for all stages of life.
- Read Jewish bedtime stories, welcoming interaction with the children. Discuss movies, television shows, and news reports that have a Jewish theme, as well as newspaper articles about Israel or other Jewish topics.
- Involve your children in selecting which charities (Jewish and general) will be the recipients of the family *tzedakah* box collections.
- Educate your offspring to the concept of being a *mensch* (a morally good person) and structure opportunities for doing *mensch*-like deeds: volunteering at a senior citizens home, sending get-well cards, visiting a recuperating patient, welcoming newcomers to your area, writing thank-you notes.
- Build a Jewish home library of children's books, adult books, and reference books, as well as Judaic videotapes,

audio-cassette, or compact disc recordings, and subscribe
to magazines. Of particular value are: *One-Minute Bible
Stories* by Shari Lewis, *The Jewish Kids Catalog* by Chaya
Burstein, *A Kid's Catalog of Israel* by Chaya Burstein, and
biographies of Jewish heroes.

• Begin an Israel travel fund for your family, and also plan
family vacations to other sites that have Jewish significance (e.g., Holocaust Museum when age appropriate,
Jewish Museum in Manhattan, historic synagogues such
as Philadelphia's Mikvah Israel).

Judaica enhancements should be implemented with the
intent of establishing a Jewish "rhythm" for our young.

What it comes down to for parents is to ask ourselves how much
we care. If we care very much, our challenge is to try to build a
critical mass of Judaism in our children's lives. . . .

Where we come out in level of observance is less important
than that—by the choices we make—we show our children that we
value, that we learn with and alongside them, that we bring
Judaism into our homes, that we educate them Jewishly and that
together we experience Shabbat and other festivals in the cycle of
the Jewish year—the framework on which is hung the more than
3,000-year-old history of our people. (Suzanne Singer, "A 'Critical
Mass' of Judaism May Prevent Intermarriage," p. 4)

8. Rabbi, what is the value of Jewish ritual for my family's life?

After synagogue affiliation and formal Jewish education, the
third step in raising a Jewish child is family practices. Holidays,
especially Passover and Christmas, are times when families,
both immediate and extended, gather together in celebration.
For interfaith families, these occasions may be particularly criti-

cal because they elicit and exacerbate emotions that do not always find expression in day-to-day life. Sensitivities are greatest because precious childhood memories and associations are evoked.

> Recently, the media and psychological literature have begun to pay more attention to the importance of rituals for the emotional well-being of the individual, the family, and the community. . . . The "strong family" research . . . has highlighted the importance of home-centered rituals and traditions in fostering spiritual and emotional wellness as well as family cohesion. . . .
>
> When a family shares Jewish rituals . . . they forge links, not only among themselves but also to a larger community and to an ancient and ongoing heritage. . . . (Julie Hilton Danan, *The Jewish Parents' Almanac*, p. 11)

Keep in mind that parents should expose their offspring not just to a view of solemn, stern occasions such as Yom Kippur, but also to the joyous aspects in the rich texture of the Jewish calendar year.

> Yom Kippur symbolizes for many Jews quintessential religious experience. As a result, God is stern and demanding, with a contrite fast as the most typical expression of His service.
>
> Not only does this conclusion discount the dizzy joyousness of Purim, the profound ecstasy of Simhat Torah, the ritual celebration of the three major festivals and the familial happiness of the Sabbath table, it also does not give adequate due to the real significance of Yom Kippur.
>
> Indeed, Yom Kippur demonstrates the very essence of Judaism, a vision of a world with law and love in balance. (Shlomo Riskin, "With Law and Love," p. 23)

Many mixed-married couples are surprised when they encounter the powerful enhancement of family ties forged by Jewish ritual life.

I did not expect that the cycle of Jewish holidays and rituals would become so ingrained in our family life. Even though we stay up until midnight on December 31, it is on Rosh Hashanah that we take stock of our lives and make our resolutions. Each Passover, we measure Nathan's growth by his increasing proficiency in Hebrew. We begin our weekend time together by lighting Shabbat candles on Friday night. . . . Even more than we thought they would, Jewish holidays and rituals regularly bring us together and strengthen our family ties. (Andrea King, _If I'm Jewish and You're Christian, What Are the Kids?_ p. 140)

Parents must be willing to incorporate these observances slowly, step by step. This is not an all-or-nothing dimension of life. Be prepared for partial involvement, for making mistakes, and for future growth.

1. Learning . . . Sometimes a friend or relative can show you how. Sometimes a professional, like a nursery-school teacher . . . is happy to help. . . .
2. Getting support—Jews enjoy celebrating together. . . .
4. Going slowly . . . taking a step at a time and not being overwhelmed by too much too soon. . . .
5. . . . A visit to a good synagogue library or Jewish book store may yield treasures of helpful material—from Jewish books and games to records and tapes of Shabbat songs. (Sharon Strassfeld and Kathy Green, eds., _The Jewish Family Book_, pp. 59–61)

9. What should be done about the December Dilemma (Christmas/Hanukkah)?

In confronting this unavoidable annual period of cultural and religious tension, keep in mind your goal of raising children with a healthy Jewish identity. In this sense, your objectives are similar to any other adult who seeks to rear their son or daughter as a Jew, whether or not the parents are intermarried. For this reason, mixed marrieds intending to nurture their youngsters' Judaism are best served by celebrating only Hanukkah within the confines of the home. A Christian mother or father may choose to supplement the household's observances with his or her private attendance at a church service or other communal Christmas ritual.

Although it may be difficult to explain to very young children, tell them that both America and Judaism encourage people both to be involved with one's *own* religious traditions and to be respectful of the holidays of other family members and friends as well. A valuable resource in this sensitive parenting process is "The December Dilemma" section in Ron Wolfson's book, *The Art of Jewish Living: Hanukkah.* "If we are strong in our Jewish commitments, there is little danger that approaching the warmth and beauty of another's holiday will threaten our fundamental identity. But appreciation does not mean appropriation. Because appropriation leads to confusion, loss of identity and, ultimately, assimilation" (Ron Wolfson, *The Art of Jewish Living: Hanukkah,* p. 173).

Although Christmas is powerfully present in malls, television ads and programming, and other areas, a valuable lesson for Jewish children to learn is the message of Hanukkah—that Maccabees were unwilling to relinquish their unique religious way of life even though the vast majority of other people celebrated in a Greek cultural fashion. "There is a great value [like the Maccabees] in being unique, different, valuable in your own right. . . . Is this not the very same struggle that we Jews living in a predominantly Christian society must also wage?" (Ron Wolfson, *The Art of Jewish Living: Hanukkah,* p. 173).

This is also a perfect occasion to teach the perils of peer pressure and the importance of standing up for one's personal principles, whether or not this behavior will be popular. Jewish educator Joel Grishaver tells a story about a child who was upset about being different in school and trying to explain Hanukkah to peers:

His father hugs him and says: "Jews are different from other people. We don't do everything that everybody else does. We have our own important things. Our holiday is Chanukah and Chanukah is a holiday about being different. When Antiochus wanted the Jews to do everything that everyone else did and not be different, the Maccabees had to fight to get their freedom. Chanukah teaches us to remember that Jews are different. . . .

"I want you to be special and different from everyone else. I love you. When you get older and everyone else does things like smoke or drink or take drugs, I want you to know that you can be different. When everyone else you know forgets to be kind to other people, I want you to be kind. When everyone else is afraid to stand up for what is right, I want you to be the one who leads people to do the right thing. Never forget, you are different and special." (Joel Grishaver, "December Dilemma," p. 3)

An intermarried Jewish acquaintance told me that when his son reached age 3, the child asked the inevitable question, "Dad, how come we don't celebrate Christmas in our home?" "Sam," the father answered him, "Christmas is a great holiday for Christian people, such as your mother and your grandparents. However, if you celebrated Christmas, you would be a Christian, and so you would not have our great holidays—Rosh Hashanah, Sukkot, Simchat Torah, Hanukkah, Tu B'Shvat, Purim, Passover, Israeli Independence Day." Or, as one of my congregants told her child: "Danny, it is like a birthday party. Sometimes, you go to someone else's party and say, 'This is great.' But it is not *your* party. But don't worry, your party will come. Christmas is not our holiday, but our holidays [*Shabbat*, High Holy Days, Passover, Shavuot, Hanukkah, Purim, Simchat Torah, and so forth] are great and we have them all year long!" Ron Wolfson concludes:

> The child who has experienced the building of a *sukkah* will not feel deprived of trimming a tree. The child who had participated in a meaningful Passover Seder will not feel deprived of Christmas dinner. The child who has paraded with the Torah on Simchat Torah, planted trees at Tu b'Shvat, brought first fruits at Shavuot, given *mishloah manot* at Purim, and welcomed the Shabbat weekly with candles and wine and challah, by the time s/he is 3 years old will understand that to be Jewish is to be enriched by a calendar brimming with joyous celebration. (Ron Wolfson, *The Art of Jewish Living: Hanukkah*, p. 173)

CONCLUSION: THE PARENTAL ROLE IS DECISIVE

As parents of Jewish children being raised in an interfaith home, it is particularly necessary to be sensitive to today's issues of Jewish continuity. These concerns motivate all concerned parents of Jewish youngsters, whether or not the mother and father are part of an intermarried couple.

Much more so than in previous generations, young parents concerned with the long-term Jewish future of their children and grandchildren must create a personal strategy that maximizes the prospect of Jewish continuity. At ages 3 to 6 when youngsters begin to be presented with all other valued aspects of living, parents must also systematically promote Jewish identity.

> [Parents] are the only ones with the ability to make clear to your own children what you consider to be the values by which your family lives. When they become teenagers, and even before, they will rebel against your values, and they will test the limits that you set. That's the job of the teenager, that is, to rebel against your values. But if you choose [from toddler years onward] not to articulate these values, not to set these limits, in order to avoid the

inevitable confrontations that are going to come — do not recoil in horror and surprise if they make choices of which you disapprove. . . . Your children will choose their values when they become mature, with or without your permission. What choices they make and, more importantly, how they make those choices, will depend more than anything upon the direction they receive from you in their younger years. (Jack Moline, "Ten Things We Do Not Say Often Enough to Our Children," audiotape)

Values

Judaism has a great deal of wisdom and guidance for every aspect of our life. It is not confined within the walls of the synagogue but is easily available to help parents reinforce the ethical values they seek to impart to the next generation.

Parents framing their moral guidance in a Jewish mold will have a deep impact on the Jewish identity of their children. For example, one profoundly effective way in which my wife's deep commitment to Jewishness was transmitted by her parents was their constant reference to *baalabatish* (what a *mensch* would do in a similar situation). Rita even wrote a paper in a college child-development course assessing the influence this moral compass had upon her view of ethics and of Jewish identity.

In addition to speaking about Jewish values to children, to truly educate a *mensch*, parents must also act in a *menschlich* fashion. If you want your child to be a *mensch*, you must love others and show them compassion, caring, and concern. Your children will emulate what you do. They will not pay attention to what you say unless your words are consistent with your behavior.

Spirituality

Jewish children benefit greatly if their family enables them to go beyond books alone and into the world of religious encounter.

To do so, first of all, it is vitally important to include spiritual practices in your home life. Simply saying a blessing—*barukh attah Adonai*—before you eat, or upon reaching a holiday or milestone, or on seeing a gorgeous sight in nature, is an act that takes only seconds but instills in a youngster "an attitude of gratitude," an indispensable ingredient for happiness in life. As our sages reflected: "Who is truly wealthy? People who find happiness in their lot in life." Moreover, saying a simple blessing invokes God's presence in the life of the family. As the *hasidim* teach: "Where is God? Wherever we allow Him to come into our lives."

> If people would realize that Judaism is not a matter of obeying or pleasing God, it is a matter of changing the world by investing ordinary moments with holiness and making our lives matter in the process, then living Jewishly would no longer be an obligation. It would be an irresistible answer to one of life's most pressing questions. (Harold Kushner, cited in Jonathan Woocher, "Jewish Survival Tactics," p. 13)

Pride

Children must learn that being Jewish is not merely "okay" but is *special*. The child's pride in being a Jew needs to be nurtured with specific content relating to the full range of Jewish experiences and priorities.

As I learned very graphically in sessions with families in my own congregation, parents and student feel proud when they experience the following:

- Learn that Judaism was the first religion to believe in one God and that Judaism created a setting in which Christianity and Islam were able to rise.
- Are taught about the Jewish basis for praiseworthy values: primacy of learning, centrality of family, tolerance, *tzedakah*, comforting the bereaved, etc.

Witness multigenerational or communal ritual experiences such as candlelighting, the Passover *seder*, Yom Kippur service, and holiday meals.

Realize that the Jews were chosen by God to fulfill a special mission. We are commanded to keep alive the truth of God's existence and of God's standards of right and wrong. Being a *chosen people* with a mission does not mean we are "better" than others, but it does mean that we are unique and blessed with this divine responsibility.

As parents have indicated to me during Jewish awareness workshops, many facets of Judaism are sources not only of pride but of joy as well. They point to aspects of *Yiddishkeit* as diverse as Jewish foods, music, museums, ritual objects, games, and vacations to Jewish sites in the United States and Israel.

Knowledge and Experience

Parents say that they do not want to impose religion upon their children. In order for the child to be able to make informed choices about doing Jewish things, you need to give them the maximum of rituals, Jewish education, holiday celebrations, and synagogue experiences. Only when they have such knowledge and experience can they really choose. How can children who have never experienced a traditional *Shabbat*, never built a *sukkah*, never sung *Dayenu*, decide whether they want it in their lives? Give your child as much as possible. A little Judaism is better than none. A lot of Judaism is better than a little. There are infinite gradations.

At her *bat mitzvah*, a 13-year-old at my synagogue, raised with these building blocks to Jewish self-esteem in her toddler and elementary-school years, reflected about taking such memories into Jewish adulthood:

Why are people teaching their children to be Jewish and keeping the chain of Judaism alive? I know I will, because being Jewish is and always has been a big and wonderful part of my life. . . . I remember when I was younger, I loved getting dressed up and going to shul on Shabbat. When it was time in the service for *Adon Olam*, my friends and I all ran up to the *bima* and led the prayer. . . .

When I get older and have children, I'm going to teach them about being Jewish and let my children have magnificent Jewish happenings in their lives too. For I love being a Jew, and I'm going to keep *my* covenant with God and extend the chain of our Jewish heritage.

Why Be Jewish?

An important part of a conscious strategy of Jewish child-rearing is to be able to feel and project a sense of why being Jewish is joyous, fulfilling, exciting!

Spiritually, for children ages 3 to 6, Judaism's rich legacy includes ritual circumcision (*bris*), baby naming, nursery school, commencing Jewish education, *Shabbat*, Simchat Torah, Hanukkah, Purim, and a host of other experiences in our quest of God's presence.

Intellectually, Jewish sacred texts are distilled as bedtime stories, age-appropriate books, magazines, videos, computer programs, and music.

Ethically, Jewish social action offers youngsters the chance to join their parents in visiting the sick, welcoming the newcomer (immigrant, guest) to their home, placing coins in the *tzedakah* box to aid the hungry and the homeless, and witnessing family members' voluntarism in Jewish and civic institutions.

Judaism also offers personal meaning to us by connecting each Jew with profound commitments to the age-old Jewish tradition, to Jews throughout the world, and to God. (See chapter 1 for a full discussion of "Why Be Jewish?")

When children see both their peers and parents involved in aspects of Jewish life, they realize that Judaism is important to them at all stages. Author Dennis Prager said in a speech on "Raising a Jewish Child in a Christian Society":

> Adults shape children's lives. If adults take Judaism seriously, children take Judaism seriously.
>
> Do you know one of the main reasons that people leave Judaism? It is because [often] it is associated [solely] with being a child, and everything associated solely with childhood we leave. . . .
>
> If you stop Jewish education at age 13, a child will always identify Judaism with being a child. They will feel that sophisticated people study anthropology, political science, psychology . . . [in contrast] children watch cartoons and study Judaism. . . .
>
> If a parent takes Judaism seriously, it is a powerful message to a child. (Dennis Prager, "Raising a Jewish Child in a Christian Society," audiotape)

Keep in mind this chapter's *three crucial steps* in parenting a child in an interfaith home: (1) affiliation with a synagogue, (2) formal Jewish education for the child, and (3) family practices of Jewish holidays, life-cycle events, and other religious ceremonies.

We in the Conservative rabbinate and Conservative congregational world welcome intermarried couples to become involved in our religious services, our educational and cultural and social programs, our social justice activism. We invite you to enroll your youngsters in our pre-schools and our learning opportunities for ages 5 through 17. We urge you to come closer to traditional Judaism. It will enrich your life and the lifetime of your children.

7

Grandparents of Jewish Children Being Raised in Interfaith Homes

B ecoming a grandmother or grandfather of a Jewish child living in an interfaith home leaves Jews a mixture of feelings. On the one hand, there is the obvious bless- ings of being a grandparent: "To become aware of the possi- bilities of hoping for and peering into the intangible but real future . . . beyond my death" (Max Ticktin, "The Blessings of Being a Grandfather," pp. 382–383). On the other hand, there are challenges posed by the fact that the child will be raised in the setting of an intermarriage:

> For the parents of intermarried couples, the birth of their first grandchild is sometimes a bittersweet experience. Like all grand- parents, they see the grandchild as their link with the future. But many of them also feel that the future of their religious group is at risk. Although they welcome the child, they worry about how firmly rooted she will be in their heritage and whether she will carry on their cultural legacy. (Andrea King, *If I'm Jewish and You're Christian, What Are the Kids?* p. 86)

These mixed emotions derive from the realities of the threat intermarriage poses to the Jewish future of your family. Over

72 percent of the children in interfaith households (without conversion) are raised in a fashion other than Judaism. At least half of the other 28 percent of these youngsters are only nominally "Jewish" (no religious school education, *bar/bat mitzvah*, etc.). Having these children grow into adults who identify with Jewish religion, marry Jews, set up their own Jewish homes, and raise Jewish children is a challenge, but it's a goal that merits our utmost efforts. In a demographic study conducted several years ago in Philadelphia's Jewish community (only a small random sample of several hundred families, however), researchers had difficulty locating examples of Judaism surviving intermarriage for more than two generations. In other words, within three generations the descendants of today's intermarried probably will be absorbed within the undifferentiated mass of American Christendom unless the grandparents intervene. Do not remain silent. Silence will be interpreted as your assent or at least accommodation to assimilation. This chapter is intended to assist you in advocating Jewish continuity for your grandchildren, even though their parents are an intermarried couple!

1. How shall I effect the Jewish continuity of my extended family as a Jewish grandparent, that is, one step removed from my grandchildren?

Grandparents of Jewish children being raised in an interfaith home have added responsibilities for transmitting Judaism in a caring, nurturing fashion. Whatever the level of Jewishness of your household up to this point, your home now must become the type of Jewish setting that you wish your son's or daughter's home had become. Whether or not you previously have been observant of Jewish customs and ceremonies, the prospect of Jewish continuity for your descendants depends upon your becoming Jewishly affirming role models. In fact, grandparents often are the best vehicles for this transmission.

Grandparents [can] transmit religious faith and values. Grandchildren tend to see grandparents as being "closer to God" because of their age. In many of the families we visited [even
endogamous ones], the grandparents were the ones who took the
children to church or temple. Although research has shown that
religious behavior in children is affected most by their parents'
beliefs and behavior, grandparents who take religious commitment seriously put a brake on parental indifference to questions of
ultimate concern. (Arthur Kornhaber and Kenneth L. Woodward,
Grandparents and Grandchildren: The Vital Connection, p. 170)

During my childhood, I witnessed a wide range of lessons
from the elders within my family. From my great-grandmother
and great-grandfather, my Bubba and Zayda, I learned a love
for my Eastern European Jewish heritage, Yiddish language,
and the blessing of extended family clustered around the
matriarch and patriarch. From my mother's mother, my Nanny,
I learned about all kinds of tasty foods, family memories, and
stories. From my mother' father, my Pops, by example I was
taught the lesson of being a *mensch*, not only at home but in the
wider world. Every businessperson who had ever met him
told me of his *menschlichkeit*. These experiences accord with
the research described in Professor Robert Coles' *The Spirituality of the Child*. Coles notes how often children refer to the
ways their grandparents have influenced them. Like me, children remember the prayers, the parables, and the admoni-
tions shared with them by another generation.

The potentially deep and unique spiritual bond between
grandchildren and their parents' parents applies just as signif-
icantly when there is an intermarriage:

In interfaith families, when parents are trying to share with their
children different or multiple faith perspectives, the cementing of
the intergenerational bond requires extra attention and sensitivity. . . . [Yet] interfaith grandparents still serve as very important spiritual mentors, building relationships on a foundation of

unconditional love and emphasizing their similarities with their grandchild rather than their differences. (Robert Aldrich and Glenn Austin, *Grandparenting for the 90s*, p. 22)

Research has shown that "a great many [adult] offspring of intermarriage have reported quite movingly that the greatest spiritual influence in their lives came from their grandparents" (Leslie Goodman-Malamuth, book review of *Mingled Roots: A Guide for Jewish Grandparents of Interfaith Grandchildren*, p. 7).

Intermarriage has posed a special challenge for Elaine Friedman. As a grandparent to three young boys, Elaine sees herself as an important role model since the boys are "nonaffiliated." "What I relate to them about Judaism," she says, "should not only be gastronomical, but that often seems the case. When we talk, we talk about school, Little League, their hobbies. Religion is not first on their list, but I realize that it has to be. Time is precious, and I have the power to instill the true meaning of Judaism. If I don't, it will be lost."(Cherly Rubin, "Grandparenting," *Your Child*, p. 4)

One recommendation for providing a Jewish connection to these Jewish grandchildren in interfaith settings is to be called Bubbie and Zayde. As members of my congregation have verified to me, this simple act creates ongoing identification with *Yiddishkeit*, our Jewish heritage. As modern-style grandparents, we must overcome an initial reluctance to submit to "Old World" terminology. This is not what we had planned, but given the circumstances, this strategy is most meaningful. Zell Schulman wrote:

[Even] as a modern Jewish woman, living in today's busy world, I wanted my grandchildren to call me Bubbie. With intermarriage in the family, being called "Bubbie" is important. It has a good old-fashioned, traditional Jewish ring to it.

Most people think of a Bubbie as elderly, with white hair, and a small frame who talks with an accent. The only thing close to this image that this modern "bubbie" has would be my gray hair.

Being a "bubbie" in today's modern world may be different
[than in the past], but I wouldn't change it for anything. (Zell
Schulman, "A Modern Bubbie," p. 9)

**2. I recognize that my goal of transmitting Judaism to my
grandchildren would be aided immensely if my non-Jewish
son-in-law/daughter-in-law converted to Judaism. How should
I open up this discussion?**

A valuable description of techniques for engaging in this discussion is provided by Dr. Lawrence Epstein in a useful brochure entitled, *How to Discuss Conversion to Judaism* (Suffolk
Jewish Community Planning Council, [516] 462-5826). Keep in
mind that this discussion is *not proselytizing*. However, we are
acknowledging that many non-Jewish spouses are prevented
from considering conversion into Judaism by the misconception that Jews do not accept converts. Therefore the invitation
to enter the Jewish religion contains information that must not
be taken for granted. You are being unfair to a non-Jewish
relative in not clarifying these important issues and opportunities for religious fulfillment. Dr. Epstein writes:

Don't be afraid to discuss the subject. Most non-Jews are never
even asked if they would consider learning about Judaism. Many
would do so if they were simply asked to explore the subject. . . .
There are several steps for you to take.

1. Consider why you think being Jewish is important. Different
   people will have very different answers to this question.
   [See chapter 1]. . . .
2. Consider why you wish the person you care about to become
   Jewish. How will becoming Jewish help that person? What
   positive contributions to the person's life, marriage and family relationships will be made by becoming Jewish? The answers to these, of course, will depend on the person. . . .

4. There isn't a single correct way to ask someone to consider becoming Jewish. . . . After explaining why being Jewish is important, you might say something like, "Would you consider learning more about becoming Jewish?" The question could be followed by a discussion of the benefits of becoming Jewish for the person. . . .

5. Be willing to answer questions, give help when it is requested, and provide constant support. For example, it is important to reassure people that conversion does not mean that they must lose touch with their parents, brothers and sisters. Nor does it mean that happy memories of childhood need to be forgotten. . . .

There are about 200,000 people in the United States who have chosen to become Jewish. They did so because they found Judaism to be a wonderful way of life and because they found Jewish people, like you, who welcomed them. (Lawrence J. Epstein, *How to Discuss Conversion to Judaism*)

If your non-Jewish in-law responds affirmatively, direct him or her to chapter 3 of this book, "Considering Conversion to Judaism." It is also available as a separate booklet (from the Rabbinical Assembly, [212] 678-8060). And if your son-in-law or daughter-in-law does decide to convert, applaud and support his or her praiseworthy effort. Buy Judaica home ritual objects as gifts. Give appealing Jewish books. Invite the person to join with you in compelling Jewish experiences—building and decorating a *sukkah*, helping to plan an expanded family *seder* for Passover, preparing and distributing food baskets (*mishloah manot*) for Purim, dancing with family and friends on Simchat Torah, joining you in preparing for the Friday night *Shabbat* meal, attending suitable religious services, and so on. You must verbalize your affirmation and demonstrate commitment with your actions. You also should actively enlist the support of your son or daughter, who may be reluctant at first to express partiality for fear of later accusations of "coercion." Nevertheless, the official approval of the Jewish partner is a necessary prerequisite to a successful conversionary home.

3. Since I am not "religious," wouldn't it be hypocritical to begin to stress to my children and grandchildren that being Jewish is important to me?

It is true that by being involved in Jewish religious practices at home and in private prayer and synagogue prayer, a grandparent is provided with a natural framework to advocate Jewishness. Keep in mind that it is never too late to adopt such commitments! They will have a cumulative effect upon your extended family, building memories and shaping Judaism's relevance in your lives. And do not be intimidated by the prospect that your son or daughter will question you: "How come you are doing these Jewish things now, when you didn't do them when we were growing up?"

Feel empowered to answer honestly: "I have grown as a Jewish person. I now realize more than before just how important Jewish content is to my life. Furthermore, I want you to be aware that it is not by coincidence that our family and other families have changed in this way. One generation ago American synagogue life was dominated by decorum. Small children were not encouraged to come to services. We fell into that pattern in raising you, just as did our peers with their offspring. Today many synagogues have been reconstituted to be 'user friendly' for youngsters. Many congregations provide family services, Torah-for-tots, mini-*minyan*, and a whole range of similar programs. Also, unlike in the past, in the 1990s gift shops offer an incredibly wide selection of child-centered Judaica—videos, tapes, crafts, games, books."

There are many things we do in a particular way because we wish to transmit values to future generations. For example, when we go as a family to the movies, we do not take our youngsters to an "R"-rated film that we might normally see. Does that makes us a hypocrite? No! Similarly, when we talk in their presence, we are more careful with our language and what details about people we divulge. Does that make us hypocrites? No!

So too with regard to religious practices. Attending family-oriented religious services or engaging in other Jewish-oriented activities that you previously had ignored is not hypocritical. Rather, it is acting in the best interests of your grandchild. And what if you are not religiously observant when your grand-children are not present? That does not mean that your genuine concern for preserving the blessings and joys of Judaism within your family line is hypocritical. Do not allow this false logic to intimidate you into submission! Commitment to Judaism manifests itself in many nonreligious ways as well.

- Do you care about the fate of the State of Israel?
- Are you concerned when anti-Semitic acts occur?
- Are you proud of the incredible number of Jews who have received Nobel prizes and in other ways have contributed to society at large in disproportionate numbers?
- Do you value Judaism's age-old emphasis upon learning, questioning, searching for truth?
- Are you appreciative of the unique response of Jews when coreligionists are in trouble, either abroad via United Jewish Appeal or in localities through Jewish Federated agencies?
- Do you cherish being a link in a chain of Jewish tradition that spans over 150 generations and several millennia?
- Do you have high regard for Jewish family values and closeness?
- Does the memory of the Holocaust pierce the inner being of your soul?
- Have you felt the psychological, emotional, and spiritual value of Jewish ritual while coping with transitional mo-ments in your lifecycle—birth (*bris*, baby naming), adoles-

cence (*bar/bat mitzvah*), marriage (*huppah* ceremony), and death (Jewish funeral, burial, and *shivah*)?

- Have you felt closeness in a Jewish setting—while watching your mother or grandmother light Sabbath or holiday candles, while participating in a Passover *seder*, when you were sick and prayed for recovery, when a loved one died and you sought not to be alone, when you rejoiced at the birth of your own child?

If any of these questions are answered in the affirmative, then Judaism and its transmission to future generations mean a great deal to you, whether or not you consistently involve yourself in prayer, ritual observance, or holiday celebrations. Professor Arnold Eisen of Stanford reminds us:

> American Jews are more Jewish than they themselves realize. . . . The Jewishness of American Jews lies in all sorts of unexpected places. . . . [For example] a person's profession can also be a source of Jewish meaning. Several years ago . . . Jewish doctors across the United States founded the Maimonides Society, which is thriving because . . . [many] Jewish doctors are not coincidentally Jewish and physicians; Jewishness is wrapped up in their professional life. Friendship, family, public activity and politics are sources of Jewish meaning [for many Jewish people]. (Arnold Eisen, "The Role of a Jewish Research Institute," p. 8)
>
> There is a lot more God out there in people than we often are given credit for. I find that when I speak in the American Jewish community . . . largely secular segments of the American Jewish community, people are having experiences of God, not every day, but in their lives they are having them. (Arnold Eisen, "Abraham Joshua Heschel," audiotape)

For any of these or other reasons, being Jewish is very important to you! You recognize Judaism's vast array of blessings, different for each and every unique Jewish individual. This realization should empower you to express continually to your grandchildren that being Jewish is very important!

4. How powerful are rituals in the transmission process?

Jewish ritual practices have enormous spiritual power, not only on the grandchildren but also on all other family members. For my own children, each Jewish holiday is intimately associated with the distinctive tastes of their Nanny's traditional Jewish recipes, whether blintzes for Shavuot, hamantaschen for Purim, or *haroset* for the Passover *seder*, or with the memories of their Zayde's building of our *sukkah*, chopping our gefilte fish for Rosh Hashanah, setting up our oil Hanukkah *menorah*, leading the search for the *hametz* prior to Passover, and bargaining for regaining the *afikoman*.

Given the latent power of ritual activity, it is crucial that Jewish extended families regain ownership of Jewish ritual objects in their own homes. This ownership empowers us to transmit a visceral feeling of closeness to Judaism for grandchildren. It is the smells, sights, sounds, touch, hands-on experiences of Jewishness that will last, not merely intellectual arguments.

In earlier generations, our Bubbies' and Zaydes' homes inspired us as Jews, because they contained all types of Jewish ritual objects—family Bibles, prayer books, *tallis*, *tefillin*, *yarmulkas*, candlesticks, *mezuzahs*, *hallah* board and knife, *Kiddush* cups, Passover *seder* plate, and so much else. Today, we have often surrendered ownership of these magical tools to the synagogue. Rabbi Harold Schulweis has lamented: "Even among those Jews who are Jewishly affiliated, a growing chasm exists between the synagogue and school on the one hand, and the home on the other hand. . . . The Siddur, Machzor, Bible, prayer-shawl and skullcap are public property. Nothing is privately owned" (Harold Schulweis, "My Zeyda, His Grandchildren, and the Synagogue," p. 1).

Acquire these potent ritual tools and learn how to use them meaningfully in your home, both with and without your grandchildren present. Doing this will greatly enrich your personal spiritual life and also create superb role modeling for the youngsters.

A shared Shabbat dinner speaks volumes about the beauty of Jewish life and observance. A Hanukah party, Pesach seder, Purim seudah, building a Sukkah—all of these are concrete and vivid examples of the richness of Jewish life. If we take the time to make hallah with our grandchildren, we need give them no lectures on the beauty of the Sabbath. The activity itself tells them all they need to know. The more involved the grandparent is, the greater the storehouse of memories grandchildren carry into their future lives. (Hadassah Ribalow Nadich, "The Art of Grandparenting," pp. 22–23)

Don't limit the Jewish rituals imparted to your grandchildren to December and April, as competition to Christmas and Easter. Such a diminution of the riches of the Jewish ritual calendar is doomed to fail, since this twice-a-year technique places isolated Jewish holidays such as Hanukkah and Passover as a contrast to the public hype that the media and even our civic society give to Christianity's two primary celebrations. Social worker Karen Oleon Wagener cautions:

Don't try to create elaborate Chanuka festivities simply to compete with Christmas, advises Linda Fife [United Synagogue for Conservative Judaism]. . . . Instead, she advises that they emphasize all of the Jewish holidays throughout the year. . . .

"I call it Santa Claus-trophobia," concurs Rabbi Harold Schulweis. . . . "The whole world is into Christmas. But it's an artificial issue—you can't pin your whole religious identity on one holiday."

Grandparents, he suggests, should help provide their grandchildren with a solid Jewish base by making holiday celebrations a part of their life. "The Christmas Dilemma must start with the

Rosh Hashanah Solution," he counsels. "If a kid can sleep in a succa, he won't want to sleep in a creche."

Year-round Jewish observance may pose a challenge for some grandparents, but, ultimately, it may be the only response to inter-marriage. (Deborah Kaye, "Grandma Wrestles with Santa," p. 39)

Many useful publications are available, as are resource people who are Jewish educators, to help you creatively introduce the full range of Jewish ritual into your grandchild's life. For example, here is an excerpt from the wonderful journal, *Jewish Family*, issued for High Holiday season:

"Start A Rosh Hashanah Growth Chart"
   It is very important to keep track . . . track of growth, achievements, happy and sad times. One of the ways . . . is to use Rosh Hashanah to measure [grandchildren] . . . and record the results [along all sorts of parameters—growth in height, growth in knowledge of prayers for the holiday, etc].

"M'hillah: Asking for Forgiveness"
   Sometimes it's easier to ask for forgiveness or to say "I'm sorry" when someone gives you a formula or the words. . . .
   I am sorry if I hurt you by what I have done or have failed to do, by what I have said or not said to you since last Yom Kippur.
   I will strive to improve my ways, and I ask you for your understanding and forgiveness.

"Remembering to Remember"
   Traditionally, families visit the cemetery before the High Holidays. It is a significant way to remember that we are ambassadors for the generations that came before us. If this is not possible due to distance and mobility, this is an excellent opportunity to set aside some time to look at old photo albums, videos and the like. It is a chance to remember as a family and to tell stories about relatives and heirlooms that have been passed down. Share the stories that come with the

recipes you are using to make the holiday special. (Harlene Appelman, "Teaching Our Kids to Say I'm Sorry," pp. 2–3)

A valuable collection of other holiday activities can be found in Joel Grishaver's *40 Things You Can Do to Save the Jewish People* as well as in his *Activities for Jewish Grandparenting* (forthcoming).

5. What do I say if they accept my newfound Jewish lifestyle for my home but refuse to encourage Jewish activities within their own domain?

If that is the case, then clarify the following game plan with your son or daughter and non-Jewish spouse: "We are delighted that you have chosen to raise your children as Jews. Although disappointed, we recognize at this point in time your reluctance or unwillingness to intensify the Jewish content of your home. As grandparents, we intend to assume a significant role in transmitting our Jewish heritage to our grandchildren. We will do so whenever they visit our home. We will be taking them to services with us, since that is our current practice on *Shabbat* and holidays. We will be sending them gifts of Judaica toys, games, tapes, and books that will help make Judaism enjoyable for them. We remain ever ready to help you introduce Jewish ritual and practice into your household, but we will respect and abide by whatever decisions you make concerning your household, just as we are certain that you will honor our choices inside our house."

In order to follow through on this strategy, be prepared to acknowledge gaps in your own Jewish knowledge and show a willingness to learn along with your grandchildren. Author Sunie Levin has observed:

In your concern for imparting Jewish values to your grandchild, you will probably discover great gaps in your own knowledge. . . .

[Until now] not-particularly observant Jews are often startled by the depth of feeling aroused in them when their children marry outside Judaism. They want to perpetuate a Jewish identity in their grandchildren, but they are not sure how to bring this about—or even, for them, what a "Jewish identity" really means. (Sunie Levin, *Mingled Roots: A Guide for Jewish Grandparents of Interfaith Grandchildren*, p. 149)

Also be clear about the wide range of subjects that are part of our Jewish heritage, which you seek to impart. Whether you live closeby or engage in long-distance grandparenting, be creative in your Jewish endeavors. The following is a checklist of suggested strategies for Jewish grandparenting:

- Subscribing to Judaic book clubs and magazines for grandchildren to help keep them abreast of Jewish issues and to build a Jewish library
- Making regular phone calls before holidays, *Shabbat*, and family occasions to keep the relationship between parents, grandparents, and children fresh and alive
- Writing letters and cards for special occasions, especially at the Jewish holiday times, enclosing special items as a basis for future communication and connection
- Purchasing gifts of Judaica objects, such as a personalized Jewish calendar each Rosh Hashanah, stuffed Torah (similar to a stuffed animal), *menorah*, etc.
- Helping your grandchild collect and use audio- and videotapes and CDs with *Shabbat* and holiday songs, games, stories, plays, activities; also coloring books with similar themes
- Cooking and baking Jewish foods, such as *hallah*, hamantaschen, gefilte fish, Passover *haroset*, etc., while sharing the stories behind each recipe
- Engaging in traditional child-oriented Jewish rituals: Friday evening *Shabbat* blessing of children, searching for

the *hametz* the night before Passover, playing *dreidel*, dressing in costume for Purim, marching with flags and receiving candy on Simchat Torah, lighting the Hanukkah *menorah*, placing coins in the *tzedakah* box prior to *Shabbat* candlelighting.

- Participating in Jewish communal experiences: marching in the Israel Day parade, joining in UJA/Federation Super Sunday
- Doing Judaica arts and crafts: decorating a family or synagogue *sukkah*, creating *Shabbat* table laminated placemats, drawing pictures of Jewish heroes of the past and present who can symbolically be invited guests on *Shabbat* and holidays, knitting a *kippah*, helping to choose the patterns for a *bar/bat Mitzvah tallit*.
- Creating a family video and photograph record of significant Jewish moments and milestones in your family; you might also develop a Jewish family tree, tracing the origins of Judaism on both sides of the family, including the circumstances for being born into or choosing Judaism
- Compiling a memory drawer or trunk for items you used on past Jewish holidays or other observances, or establishing "time capsules" from your past (to be opened on special occasions)
- Scheduling systematic Family reunions, cousins club, or other gatherings, linked to the Jewish year, such as Hanukkah, Sukkot, Purim, Passover, Israel Independence Day—with appropriate games, gifts (where suitable), tasty foods, songs, and contests; also create a family newsletter

Keep in mind that even simple acts, such as the above, mean a great deal cumulatively to your grandchildren. Hands-on activities in tandem with *Shabbat* and holidays, life-cycle events, and ongoing Jewish celebrations will create a Jewish rhythm for your family. Children will not learn by words alone. They will not be convinced by mere abstractions. They need specific, hands-on role modeling to forge serious bonds with Judaism.

A strong Jewish self-identity is not achieved by merely telling the [grand]child "you are Jewish" and then letting him wonder in what way he is different from people who are not Jewish.

[It requires] seeing and doing those things that are decidedly Jewish in character. . . . [Concrete] Jewish associations must provide warm and happy memories, to which there must later be added feeling about the worth and importance of Jewish life. (Hayim Halevy Donin, *To Raise a Jewish Child*, cited in Lena Romanoff, *Your People, My People*, pp. 121–122)

These activities will build lasting Jewish memories, memories that will perpetuate within the soul of the grandchild a warm affection for the joys of being Jewish. Gradually, as our sons and daughters mature, these associations may be joined by additional, age-appropriate connections, to best create a positive sense of Jewish belonging.

6. Are grandparents who visit or are visited only periodically really important role models for the transmission of Judaism to their offspring?

MAXIMIZE VISITS

Do not underestimate the potential laden in visits with your grandchild. Grandparenting expert Sunie Levin has written:

Your visit is a golden opportunity to build strong family bonds. Grandparent visits with shared experiences can bind the extended family members together. As your grandchild grows older, the rituals of family visits become part of their heritage. Like great-grandmother's old family recipe, a fondness for certain customs is often passed down through the generations. As a grand-child becomes an adult, singing special songs and enjoying family jokes will become cherished and wonderful memories. (Sunie Levin, "When You Visit Your Grandchildren," p. 20)

Keep in mind the emotional power of kinship ties and person-alized traditions. Don't underestimate the powerful influence your words and actions have upon the psyche of your children.

Much of our education is unintended. Much of it is also unantici-pated. . . . Education happens in the margins of life, in the casual remark and in the small incident. We are teaching [our children] at every moment, whether we want to or not. The only question is what we will teach. What children remember is often quite differ-ent from what we planned.

That is why teaching religion must be done not in careful, specified settings [by formal teachers alone], but all the time [i.e., by parents or grandparents]. Faith must be lived. (David J. Wolpe, _Explaining God to Children: A Jewish Perspective_, p. 25)

OFFER GUIDANCE

We are commanded to tell youngsters what is Jewishly correct, even if they give us a hard time. "Even if the child argues and objects, for a while, at least, an answer carries an almost unimaginable weight of persuasive power" (David Wolpe, _Explaining God to Children_, p. 51). Recently, members of my synagogue shared with me their amazement at overhearing their 5-year-old child playing "house" with a neighbor's daughter. As the two youngsters discussed their imaginary households, my friend's daughter proudly described the Fri-day night _Shabbat_ dinner and ritualized Saturday morning family outing to the local synagogue, as well as a range of holiday moments including building a _sukkah_, lighting Hanuk-kah candles, and partaking in Passover _seders_. Although this young lady frequently objects to her relatives' insistence upon Jewish ritual practices and synagogue attendance, clearly she was internalizing the value of the enterprise.

BE A ROLE MODEL IN WORD AND DEED

Grandparents can *teach* not only by words but also by *deeds*. The following recommendations for enhancing Jewish identity are provided by UJA/Federation of New York City's Rabbinic Advisory Council. Choose several from this list.

- Invest yourself. Make the time and commitment to enhance yourself Jewishly and add meaning to your life and home.
- Share your journey with friends in a community context.
- Seek opportunities for serious study to increase your knowledge and to gain intellectual awareness and historical perspective.
- Seek a religious-spiritual component to your life with all your heart and soul.
- Make the Sabbath day and holidays holy. Enhance them with ritual and delight at home and at the synagogue.
- Be aware and involved in Jewish causes. Be supportive in action. Don't separate yourself from the community.
- Make a pilgrimage to Israel.

When children watch grandparents seriously involved in aspects of Jewish life, they realize that Judaism is important to all stages of life.

7. How shall we pursue the goal of making our grandchild into a good Jew, a *mensch*?

Judaism has a great deal of wisdom and guidance for every aspect of our life. It is not confined to the walls of synagogue. It also helps reinforce the ethical values that parents at home seek to impart to the next generation.

There are many ways in which grandparents too can impart certain values to their grandchildren. Here is an example of how *tzedakah* became part of the home life of Shimon Paskow:

> To my Bubbe, righteousness meant charity, and Bubbe was a very chairtable woman. She had *pushkes*, charity boxes, in the kitchen and her bedroom. There were round charity boxes, square ones and rectangular ones. . . .
>
> The pushkes came not only in different shapes, sizes and colors, but also with attractive pictures and inscriptions. Some had sketches of stone buildings with domes, others with impressive pictures of eminent rabbis with long beards and different hats. One wore a very large yarmulka; another, a big black hat with a wide brim; and one even had a fur hat, called a streimel. . . .
>
> The monies collected in the pushkes went to yeshivas, orphanages, soup kitchens, the poor, revered rabbis, homes for the aged, sanitariums, Eretz Yisrael, etc. . . . I, too, sometimes deposited a few pennies into the slots. . . .
>
> Physically, Bubbe is gone, but her memory lives on in me. . . .
>
> (Shimon Paskow, "I Remember Bubbe: The Receipts of Righteousness," p. 3)

In the realm of values, grandparents should rely upon the large corpus of Jewish "value concepts," which should guide explanations in interpersonal settings.

For example, Jonathan might object to joining the family in going to visit elderly Aunt Sadie, who is recuperating from hip surgery. He might claim it will be "boring." As an answer, you should say: "Judaism teaches us to act like a *mensch*. One way we do this is *bikkur holim*; we visit people who are sick. We believe that such visits are like medicine in helping the patient to recover."

Or, when Rachel complains about your inviting a new Russian Jewish family to *Shabbat* dinner because "they are hard to understand, and they don't have kids my age," you should take this opportunity to say: "Judaism teaches us how to be a *mensch*, and part of that teaching includes *hahnasat orhim*, greeting newcomers and guests to our home and community, helping them to feel comfortable in their new surroundings."

Similarly, grandmothers and grandfathers might prominently display a family *tzedakah* box and insist that each family member deposit something each week from their earnings or their allowance. If a child is unenthusiastic, remind them: "According to Judaism, a *mensch* always shares at least a portion of his or her possessions with people less fortunate."

And if a child finds a lost object and wants to keep this unexpected treasure, it is a superb moment to introduce the Jewish notion of *hashavat avedah* (returning lost objects to their rightful owner). Here too, being a good Jew, a *mensch*, offers specific guidance as to how to respond to a morally challenging situation.

Likewise, if you become aware that your grandchild and his or her friends are teasing or making fun of another youngster, explain the Jewish prohibition against *malbim p'nei haverav* (causing embarrassment to someone else). A *mensch* should never behave in such fashion.

Here are other values that can be taught in the same way:

- *Tikkun olam* — make a better world
- *Kibbud av ve'eim* — honor and respect parents and grand-parents
- *Hiddur p'nei z'kenim* — show respect for the elderly
- *Rodef shalom* — pursue peace among individuals and nations
- *Lashon hara* — do not gossip or spread slander
- *Zakhor* — remember the Holocaust to prevent any repetition
- *Mishpakhah* — keep the centrality of family
- *Pikuah nefesh* — saving a life takes precedence above all
- *Tzorkei tzibbur* — assist in meeting communal needs
- *Dan lekaf zekhut* — give others the benefit of the doubt

If grandparents frequently frame their moral guidance in a Jewish mold, they will have a profound impact upon the Jewish identity of their grandchildren. One profoundly effective way in which my wife's deep commitment to Jewishness was transmitted by her parents was via their constant reference to that which is *baalabatish* (that which a *mensch* would do in a similar situation). She even wrote a paper in a college child development course assessing the influence this moral compass had upon her view of ethics and of Jewish identity.

Keep in mind that in addition to speaking about Jewish values to grandchildren, to truly educate a *mensch* one must also act in a *menschlich* fashion. "If you want to teach your [grand]child that [to be a *mensch*] . . . you must love others and show them compassion, caring and concern; you must live those values yourself. Your [grand]child will emulate what you do, and won't pay much attention to what you say unless it is consistent with your own behavior" (Steven Carr Reuben, *Raising Jewish Children in a Contemporary World*, p. 42).

8. How shall I answer my son or daughter if he or she begins to ask questions about Jewish views of God or reasons for Jewish pride?

In terms of God, I recommend Rabbi David J. Wolpe's excellent volume entitled *Explaining God to Children: A Jewish Perspective*. Rabbi Wolpe offers discussions and exercises to empower parents (and grandparents) to instill within children a sense of awe, of mystery, of God's presence, of the miraculous in the world. In addition, *Explaining God to Children* discusses the painful reality of death, of illness, of bad things happening in the world of children (grandchildren) and their families. A religious framework gives boys and girls the spiritual strength to encounter life and continue to grow, to mature, to cope.

We want to create a family atmosphere that has sacred moments and a feeling of warmth. We want to encourage our [grand]children to question and to search. We want to make sure they learn how important it is to be good and to feel that they matter.

Religion can help in all these critical areas of growth. Belief in God affects self-esteem, and searching for God together can help draw a family close. (David Wolpe, *Explaining God to Children: A Jewish Perspective*, p. 2)

To those grandparents who express reluctance for God-talk with children due to their own theological doubts, Wolpe cautions that they may be inadvertently diminishing your offsprings' ability to cultivate their spiritual selves:

[Grand]children have very sensitive antennae. They pick up the discomfort of adults no matter how skillfully hidden. In time, children [grandchildren] learn that to ask about God does not help; their parents do not know how to answer. They will themselves grow up without the vocabulary to talk about God to their own children.

A spiritual education is as important to a full life as an intellectual and emotional education. . . . We need an attitude toward the ineffable, the world beyond what can be seen . . . forces in the world that are over and above us, and even within us. . . . What we believe about God greatly affects how we view ourselves, other people and our world. (David Wolpe, *Explaining God to Children: A Jewish Perspective*, pp. 3–4)

JEWISH PRIDE

Many facets of Judaism are sources of pride and also of joy. These include aspects of *Yiddishkeit* as diverse as the following:

- Jewish foods: latkes, chicken soup, chopped liver, hamantaschen, felafel, blintzes, stuffed cabbage, bagels and lox,

Simhat Torah candy apples, *hallah*, Hanukkah cookies, kasha varnishkas, stuffed derma
- Jewish music and dance: Fran Avni, Israeli music, *Hatik-vah*, Sephardic songs, Jewish-music radio show, the *horah* at Jewish weddings
- Jewish museums/art/ritual objects: Chagall windows, Meisler's sculpture, interesting *menorahs*, diverse *hag-gadot*, Star of David, synagogue stained glass
- Jewish group activity and games: *dreidel*, Jewish youth groups, Jewish summer camp activities, Purim carnival
- Jewish vacationing and touring: Manhattan's Lower East Side, Jewish sites in American cities (such as Touro Syna-gogue, in Newport, Rhode Island), family visits to Israel

With regard to the State of Israel, the following are examples of additional sources of Jewish pride:

- We can be proud of the remarkable achievements of the Jewish State of Israel. In less than 50 years, Israel has made its desert bloom. People from all over the world are being taught by Israelis how to grow crops on dry soil, how to conserve water, and how to take the salt and harmful chemicals out of water as well.
- We can be proud that Israel uniquely has rescued and welcomed hundreds of thousands of Jewish and non-Jewish refugees, including some survivors of crisis among Vietnam's "boat people," Jews from Ethiopia and Russia, Moslems from Bosnia, etc.
- Israel has produced remarkable discoveries in medical technology and health care. Hadassah Hospital in Jerusa-lem is a source of healing to the entire Third World.
- Israel has preserved and offered safe access to holy sites sacred to Judaism, Christianity, and Islam, enhanced by amazing archaeological excavations.
- Furthermore, Israeli scholars have produced an unprece-dented flowering of religious scholarship, with Israelis

setting a world-leading pace in the per capita reading of books.

Jewish grandchildren can also share parental pride in the disproportionate number of Jews who have contributed to science, culture, and social welfare for the world at large.

When Elie Wiesel wins the Nobel Peace Prize, or Isaac Bashevis Singer receives the Nobel for literature, or Betty Friedan is honored as the 'founding mother' of modern feminism, or Natan Scharansky becomes the international symbol of the struggle for human rights and resistance to the oppression of totalitarian regimes, or Paul Simon brings 750,000 ecstatic fans to their feet singing with one voice "Bridge Over Troubled Water,"—I am proud to be a Jew like them. (Steven Carr Reuben, *Raising Jewish Children in a Contemporary World*, p. 170)

Jewish pride and joy should be transmitted to our youth via carefully selected Bible stories, rabbinic parables, tales of Jewish heroes, Judaica videos, and other age-appropriate descriptions of our unique, exciting Jewish heritage. Creating a passion for Jewish life will likely forge a desire in youngsters to re-create Jewishness in the homes they will someday establish as adults.

9. Should I offer to finance the Jewish experiences of my grandchildren?

Many grandparents put away zero coupon bonds for college as an investment in the grandchild's professional future. Grandparents of Jewish children in interfaith homes have an even greater cause for concern about the youngsters' Jewish future. At birth, why not begin to put away dollars to help fund the necessary albeit expensive ingredients for imparting Jewishness to children:

- Synagogue affiliation
- Jewish education
- Informal experiences (Jewish camping, Jewish youth groups, Israel trips)
- Jewish friendship networks during college and beyond (single years)

SYNAGOGUE AFFILIATION

A Jewish youngster's healthy religious identity benefits immeasurably by your family's affiliation with a specific congregation, enabling the children to identify with a particular rabbi, cantor, religious educator, and the like. Make sure that you are affiliated with a specific congregation, and urge your daughter or son and family to join their local synagogue as early as possible in your grandchild's life.

> [People join synagogues] because they are searching for a place to discover God and spirituality. They seek a common community of faith . . . a sense of spiritual rootedness, inspiration and peace. . . .
>
> [Some others] want to feel that they belong, to develop and nurture friendships and relationships with [coreligionists]. . . .
>
> Others join . . . to have a place that will assist them in passing down the important values of Jewish life to their children. (Steven Carr Reuben, *Raising Jewish Children in a Contemporary World*, pp. 153–154)

This is a very important step. It defines an American family as serious or lacking seriousness about their religion. If financial considerations are a barrier to affiliation by your children, it would be wise to provide monetary assistance.

Once they have joined a synagogue, encourage your children to plug their youngsters into the expanding array of children's religious services offered by synagogues, and you should become involved in similar offerings in your congregation as well:

Seek user-friendly settings for youngsters. Do not be fearful that your grandchild will resist this commitment on your part.

> Parents [grandparents] say if I insist upon my child [grandchild] going to services, or to partake in Jewish rituals, they will become alienated. . . .
>
> Rather than fearing the response of children [grandchildren], parents [grandparents] must provide clear values. And yes, kids will rebel, that is what they do. But they need something to rebel against. A family's value system is like a pier. You must have something to push off against. (Dennis Prager, "Raising a Jewish Child in a Christian Society," audiotape)

In many congregations across North America, programs (with a variety of names) are structured to encourage young children to be in *shul* either Friday night or *Shabbat* morning via:

- Torah for tots (ages 1–4)
- Mini-*minyan* (ages 5–8)
- Family service (parents and youngsters)

Synagogues frequently also provide some of the following: children's Simchat Torah, Purim, Hanukkah services, as well as Rosh Hashanah, and Yom Kippur "Family Services."

These religious moments build a sense of comfort for the grandchildren as they encounter sacred spaces in synagogues and interact with the Torah and with religious leaders. Moreover, a grandparent's validating of religious experiences helps reinforce the staying power of these skills and memories for boys and girls in their formative years. "The importance to the child of an adult sharing a moment of strange and magical words cannot be overestimated. . . . Our actions may speak more loudly to our [grand]children than our words. . . . [After all, in this fashion] we are exposing our [grand]children to our Jewish selves (Sharon Strassfeld and Kathy Green, eds., *The Jewish Family Book*, p. 59).

JEWISH EDUCATION

All recent studies have confirmed the positive impact that formal Jewish education can have in transmitting Jewishness to one's offspring. Clearly, the earlier a child is enrolled and the more consecutive years of Jewish learning, the more positive attitudes toward Jewish continuity will be created. The latest research is a 1993 effort by Sylvia Barack Fishman and Alice Goldstein at Brandeis University entitled *When They Are Grown They Will Not Depart: Jewish Education and the Jewish Behavior of American Adults*. Fishman and Goldstein conclude that formal Jewish education is positively related to:

- ritual observance in the home
- membership in Jewish organizations
- giving to Jewish philanthropies
- seeking out a Jewish milieu

It is important to encourage your son or daughter to seek suitable Jewish formal education for your grandchildren, beginning with a Jewish nursery school and continuing at either Solomon Schechter or some other Jewish day school from ages 5 to 17, or a sequence of synagogue Sunday school (ages 5–7) followed by synagogue religious school (ages 8–13) and then to Hebrew high school (14–17).

INFORMAL EXPERIENCES

Parallel to formal education, we must advocate the Jewish communal and peer group memories that accrue from Jewish day camp, overnight camp, youth groups, a teen group experience in Israel, *tzedakah* projects, JCC activities, and others. For youngsters who are raised as a minority in a non-Jewish general society, the opportunity to feel the warmth and comfort, the self-esteem, the pride of being part of collective

Jewish endeavors of boys and girls their own age cannot be overestimated. The informal education transmitted in this fashion should become an indispensable part of the Jewish family life agenda. As with synagogue affiliation or religious school, do not allow finances to be a barrier to your grandchild's participation. If necessary, provide subsidies for these critically important investments in your family's Jewish future, or seek the intervention of the rabbi in discreetly reducing the fees. You will never regret the dollars nor the effort spent!

COLLEGE AND BEYOND

The forming of a Jewish identity does not conclude with the twelfth grade. If possible, offer to contribute to the financing of a grandchild's college if a suitable environment is selected. Grandparents should advocate that their grandchildren explore college options that include viable Jewish student populations, a Hillel Foundation, and nearby synagogue communities. Only college populations with substantial percentages of Jewish students will provide adequate peer group experiences. The B'nai B'rith Hillel Foundation evaluated Jewish student life on almost every campus your high schooler might consider. Consult their guide when the college search begins, usually during the junior year of high school.

And after graduation do whatever is possible to link single grandchildren to singles programs, networks, dating services, adult education, community service projects, and social justice activism offered under Jewish sponsorship. Most young people will select a marital partner not on the basis of ideology but rather because of propinquity, that is, they will marry the people they meet. Increasing opportunities are arising for single Jewish young adults to meet one another in nonthreatening settings.

CONCLUSION

Grandparents can no longer leave the Jewish future of their grandchildren to chance. Instead, they must develop a strategy of meaningful encounters for their grandsons and granddaughters with Judaism's joys, spiritual fulfillment, communal enhancement, intellectual stimulation, cultural aesthetics, social action imperatives, and institutional settings.

In addition to the numerous recommendations already provided in this chapter, consider some of the following, adapted from recommendations by Jewish educator Susan Werk:

- Train youngsters to regard money in terms of Jewish values. Collect coins if possible at *Shabbat* and *Yom Tov* candlelighting times and at special moments of joy or sadness to be placed into a family *tzedakah* box. Confer with your grandchild to decide where the *tzedakah* box coins and other contributions to worthy causes will be expended.
- Emphasize Jewish heroes and role models. Distinguish between a person being a celebrity (well known for sports, popular music, television, or film) and being a hero/role model (worthy of imitating his or her lifestyle). Read stories to grandchildren stressing the Jewish values embodied in the deeds of persons selected for emulation — biblical heroes (Abraham, Moses, Deborah), famous rabbinic scholars (Akiva, Maimonides, Heschel), leaders of Israel's courageous survival (David Ben-Gurion, Golda Meir), Jewish Nobel prize winners (Albert Einstein, Elie Wiesel, Menahem Begin).
- Create a network of grandparents pursuing similar goals of promoting Jewish continuity. Join a *havurah* (cluster of several households) through your synagogue. Invite families who seem receptive to this agenda to share *Shabbat* or Holiday meals with your family, and be receptive to reciprocal invitations.

- Collect a Jewish library, so that when your grandchildren visit you they can learn from and be influenced by the presence of Judaica books. Some excellent resources for youngsters are *One-Minute Bible Stories* by Shari Lewis, *The Jewish Kids Catalog* by Chaya Burstein, *A Kid's Catalogue of Israel* by Chaya Burstein, and *God's Paintbrush* by Sandy Eisenberg Sasso.
- Turn Jewish ceremonies into enjoyable, fun-filled occasions. For example, when grandchildren visit with you have a wheel of opportunities that are rotated on Friday in advance of *Shabbat*, for example, choosing which objects from an array of suitable items should appear on the *Shabbat* table; select from an approved menu for *Shabbat* dinner, and so forth.

Given current threats to Jewish continuity, and to the Jewish future of your family, you should be prepared to make new Jewish demands upon yourself and new Jewish opportunities for your grandchildren:

- You should be committed to be a Jewish role model in word and deed for your grandchildren.
- You should seek out and affiliate with a suitable synagogue.
- You should engage in hands-on Jewish activities with your grandsons and granddaughters.
- You should articulate Jewish values for being a *mensch*, and identify suitable Jewish role models and heroes.
- You should cultivate heart (spiritual), head (intellectual), and hand (social action) aspects of Judaism, making clear that being Jewish is important to you.

All of the above require effort and determination, but they will enhance your life and that of your household. They will transmit substantive Judaism to your future generations.

8

Preserving Jewishness
for Your Family

This volume is intended to convey an important message to intermarried Jews: Do not believe those who would mislead you into assuming that synagogues and rabbis of Conservative Judaism have written you off. On the contrary, within the broad range of principles provided by our tradition, we encourage you and your family to become more and more involved within the rich heritage of Jewish religion.

- For the intermarried Jew, we urge you to remain committed to participating in the chain of faith commitments and Jewish enhancements spanning centuries, of which you are a crucial link to our collective future.
- For non-Jewish family members, keep in mind that Judaism welcomes sincere inquiries about conversion and the unifying of the household as a full and equal member of the Jewish faith community.
- For intermarried parents, please avoid the misguided trend of dual-faith parenting. Your children deserve a clear message with regard to their own religious identity.

- If you make the choice of raising your offspring as Jews, please connect with a synagogue, with formal Jewish education for your children, with family interactions around Jewish holidays, and with available Jewish youth programming.
- To Jewish grandparents, we implore you to take an active part in this process of transmission of Jewish memories, values, and practices.
- To Jewish relatives of the intermarried, don't despair if your son or daughter, brother or sister, mother or father, grandson or granddaughter seems to be uninterested in reconnecting with our heritage. I am frequently asked, "Rabbi, is my intermarried relative and his/her family irretrievably lost to Judaism?"

The answer, indicated throughout this volume, is: Do not give up on any Jew! So many in our history have experienced an unanticipated resurgence of their suppressed Jewish identity. This process of return is not rational. It cannot be predicted. But at some point, as with Moses, a young adult living in Pharaoh's palace, or with many *marranos* who fled from Christian Spain, some impulse, some influence, rekindles Jewish identity. There is what Judaism calls the *pintele yid*, an aspect within all of us that never dies but at times flickers in a diminished fashion. The process of reconnecting with Judaism by persons seemingly on the periphery of Jewish existence, who had appeared lost to our people, is a process occurring again and again in our day.

A well-known example of this *pintele yid* return is the saga of Paul Cowan, recorded in his spiritual autobiography, *An Orphan in History*. Cowan was raised in the most assimilated Jewish family imaginable. He did not attend Hebrew school or synagogue, did not have a *bar mitzvah*, had few Jewish friends, and married Rachel, of Protestant background. The story of Paul's return to Judaism is the story—not stressed often enough—of many young people in our time who are slowly beginning to experience a reawakening of their Jewish identity. Paul was influenced by a series of experiences:

- His mother's two-sided interpretation of the Holocaust as a command to work for social justice toward all people, plus a recognition that no matter how successful or assimilated a Jew might be, anti-Semites will always remind us of our Jewish identity.
- His father's fascination with memories gained during his childhood on the Lower East Side of Manhattan, and the insistence that family outings frequently be made to this Jewish ethnic enclave.
- Paul Cowan's personal encounters with anti-Semitism during his student days at the preppie school world of Choate.
- During his collegiate years at Harvard, a momentous visit to Israel, where he encountered firsthand the vitality of Jewish existence.
- The questions posed by friends, family, and new in-laws upon his intermarriage to Rachel, forcing Paul more and more to confront the reality of his Jewishness.
- The sudden death of his parents, creating a rude awakening of his being either the last in 100 generations of Jews or the next generation in a continuing chain of tradition.
- The existential challenge posed by the birth and rearing of children.
- The process of saying *kaddish* for his parents in neighborhood synagogues, for the first time touching a living Jewish prayer experience.
- Long walks on the Lower East Side with Rabbi Singer, an Orthodox rabbi and social worker who was willing to answer patiently Cowan's growing list of questions and concerns.
- Finally, the recognition that many other young people were experiencing the same process of return, and the

willingness to institutionalize that commitment by affiliating with a synagogue (Anshe Chesed, United Synagogue congregation), establishing a relationship with a local rabbi (Rabbi Wolfe Kelman of the Rabbinical Assembly), and experiencing the conversion to Judaism of his wife and children.

Many Jews throughout the ages, and especially many today, may seem temporarily lost to Judaism, yet, as with Paul Cowan, their Jewish identity may suddenly be rekindled. The _pintele yid_, the spark of Jewishness, remains alive, awaiting the moment of return. Ethnotherapist Joel Crohn has seen in his group sessions with intermarried couples that "Jewish identity seems to surface in places where we don't expect it. . . . Jewish identity is tremendously powerful and persistent. . . . Strong feelings are often conveyed, even in the absence of religious practice. . . . I am continuing to see the Jewish identity appear in all kinds of places. . . . It is there, and it is waiting to be rekindled" (Joel Crohn, "Ethnotherapy: What It Is, How It Works and Applies to Programming for the Intermarried," p. 220).

Do not give up on your children or grandchildren as potential recipients of your Jewish heritage!

- Remember that conversion can make an enormous difference by unifying the mixed-married family as a unified Jewish home.
- Remember that raising a child as a Jew is possible even if the mother or the father is not Jewish.
- Remember that Jewish grandparenting of the children of the intermarried is crucial to the transmission of Jewish identity.

For all of the reasons stated in this book, do not surrender your goal of preserving Jewishness in your family!

—————— Appendix I ——————

Resource Guide

PUBLICATIONS

The following materials produced by Conservative Judaism's institutions may be ordered through the United Synagogue Book Service.

Am Kadosh: Celebrating Our Uniqueness, by Daniel H. Gordis. New York: Department of Youth Activities, United Synagogue of Conservative Judaism, 1992.

"Are You Considering Conversion into Judaism?" (pamphlet) by Alan Silverstein. New York: Rabbinical Assembly, 1993.

The Art of Jewish Living: Hanukkah, by Ron Wolfson. New York: Federation of Jewish Men's Clubs, 1990. See especially pp. 152–191.

Becoming Jewish: A Handbook for Conversion, by Ronald H. Isaacs. New York: Rabbinical Assembly, 1993.

"Choosing Judaism for Your Child" (pamphlet), by Alan Silverstein. New York: Jewish Theological Seminary, 1995.

"Communal Programming: A Constructive Response to Intermarriage," by Frayda Rembaum, in *Jewish Intermarriage, Conversion and Outreach*, ed. Egon Mayer. New York: Graduate School of CUNY, 1990.

"Conversion to Judaism in Historical Perspective: A Symposium," in *Conservative Judaism* 36:4 (Summer 1983): 27–73.

"Convert: Genuine Jew" (pamphlet), by Morton K. Siegel. New York: United Synagogue of Conservative Judaism, 1981.

Dual Faith Parenting: Second Thoughts about a Popular Trend, by Alan Silverstein. New York: Federation of Jewish Men's Clubs, 1993.

Embracing Judaism (A Manual for Conversion), by Simcha Kling. New York: Rabbinical Assembly, 1987.

"Grandparenting Jewish Children Raised in Interfaith Homes," by Alan Silverstein. Caldwell, NJ: Congregation Agudath Israel, 1995.

"Intermarriage: A Policy Statement." New York: Leadership Council of Conservative Judaism, 1995.

Intermarriage: What Can We Do? What Should We Do? New York: Program Department, United Synagogue of Conservative Judaism, 1992.

"Making Conversion a Priority," by Alan Silverstein. Caldwell, NJ: Congregation Agudath Israel, 1995.

"On Working with the Intermarried," by Jonah Layman, in *Proceedings of the 1991 Rabbinical Assembly Convention*. New York: Rabbinical Assembly, 1991.

"Outreach to Intermarried: Parameters and Outlines," by Avis Miller, in *Approaches to Intermarriage*, ed. Steven Bayme. New York: American Jewish Committee, 1993.

Principles and Compassion: Guidelines and Casebook for Teaching with Children of Intermarried Parents in Our Synagogue Schools, by Shelley Kniaz Melzer. New York: United Synagogue of Conservative Judaism, 1993.

Proceedings of the Committee on Jewish Law and Standards of the Conservative Movement, 1980–1985. New York: Rabbinical Assembly, 1988, section on *keruv*.

Program Guide for Outreach to Converts, compiled by Linda Schein Fife. Los Angeles: Pacific SouthWest Region, United Synagogue of Conservative Judaism, 1990.

"Project Joseph: Responding to Intermarriage," by Alan Silverstein, in *United Synagogue Review* 40:1 (Fall 1987): 10.

"Project Link: Principled, Sensitive Conservative Outreach," by Samuel Weintraub, in *Conservative Judaism* 42:1 (Fall 1990): 39–50.

"Raising Jewish Children in an Interfaith Home," by Alan Silverstein. New York: Congregation Agudath Israel, 1995.

Suggested Models for Introduction to Judaism Programs, prepared by Linda Schein Fife. New York: Rabbinical Assembly, 1992.

Suggested Models for Introduction to Judaism Programs: Update, prepared by Neil Weinberg. New York: Rabbinical Assembly, 1995.

Syllabus for the Teacher of Choosing Jews, by James S. Rosen and Joel H. Zaiman. New York: United Synagogue of Conservative Judaism, 1992.

"A Threefold Response to Intermarriage," by Alan Silverstein, in *The Intermarriage Crisis: Jewish Communal Perspectives and Responses.* New York: American Jewish Committee, 1992.

"Why Be Jewish? What's the Gain, the Pride, the Joy?" (pamphlet), by Alan Silverstein. New York: United Synagogue of Conservative Judaism, 1994. Teachers' and students' guide has been prepared by Susan Werk and Shelley Kniaz for use with pre-*bar/bat mitzvah* families.

OTHER RECOMMENDED READING

"Children of the Intermarried" (pamphlet), by Egon Mayer. New York: American Jewish Committee, 1983.

Choosing Judaism, by Lydia Kukoff. New York: Union of American Hebrew Congregations, 1981.

"Choosing Judaism: Issues Relating to Conversion," by Stephen C. Lerner, in *Celebration and Renewal,* ed. Rela M. Geffen. Philadelphia: Jewish Publication Society, 1993, pp. 71–89.

"Conversion among the Intermarried: Choosing to Become Jewish" (pamphlet), by Egon Mayer and Amy Avgar. New York: American Jewish Committee, 1987.

Conversion to Judaism: A Guidebook, by Lawrence J. Epstein. Northvale, NJ: Jason Aronson, 1994.

Ethnic Identity and Marital Conflict, by Joel Crohn. New York: American Jewish Committee, 1985.

40 Things You Can Do to Save the Jewish People, by Joel Lurie Grishaver. Northvale, NJ: Jason Aronson, 1994.

The Hadassah Magazine Parenting Book, by Roslyn Bell. New York: Free Press, 1989.

Hawking God: A Young Jewish Woman's Ordeal in Jews for Jesus, by Ellen Kamentsky. Medford, MA: Sapphire Press, 1992.

"The Hyphen Between the Cross and the Star," in Harold Schulweis, *God's Mirror*. New York: KTAV, 1990, pp. 168–177.

"Intermarriage and the Jewish Future" (pamphlet), by Egon Mayer and Carl Shengold. New York: American Jewish Committee, 1979.

Jewish Identity and Self-Esteem: Healing Wounds through Ethnotherapy, by Judith Weinstein Klein. New York: American Jewish Committee, 1989.

Jews by Choice: A Study of Converts to Reform and Conservative Judaism, by Brenda Forster and Joseph Tabachnik. Hoboken, NJ: KTAV, 1991.

Jews for Nothing: On Cults, Intermarriage and Assimilation, by Dov Aharoni Fisch. New York: Feldheim, 1984.

Love and Tradition, by Egon Mayer. New York: Plenum, 1985.

Questions Jewish Parents Ask about Intermarriage, by Mark L. Winer and Aryeh Meir. New York: American Jewish Committee, 1992.

Reflections: A Jewish Grandparent's Gift of Memories, by Ron and Leora Isaacs. Northvale, NJ: Jason Aronson, 1987.

To Raise a Jewish Child: A Guide for Parents, by Hayim Halevy Donin. New York: Basic Books, 1977.

"When One Parent Is Not Jewish," by Sharon Strassfeld and Kathy Green, in *The Jewish Family Book*, edited by Sharon Strassfeld and Kathy Green. New York: Bantam Books, 1981.

When Your Child Asks: A Handbook for Jewish Parents, by Simon Glustrom. New York: Bloch Publishing, 1991.

"Why Be Jewish?" (pamphlet), by Barry Holtz and Steven Bayme. New York: American Jewish Committee, 1994.

"Why Be Jewish," symposium in *Moment* 17:6 (September 1992): 36–51.

Your People, My People: Finding Acceptance and Fulfillment as a Jew by Choice, by Lena Romanoff with Lisa Holstein. Philadelphia: Jewish Publication Society, 1990.

VIDEOTAPES AND FILMS

"Choosing Judaism: Some Personal Perspectives." 30 minutes. Four Jews by Choice discuss their reasons for choosing Judaism, as well as a range of their Jewish experiences. Union of American Hebrew Congregations, New York.

"Ethnotherapy with Jews." 42 minutes. A videocassette and discussion guide, based on group-counter dialogues and research findings, on positive and negative feelings toward Judaism and Jewishness. American Jewish Committee, New York.

"Gefilte Fish." 15 minutes. Three generations of Jewish women express how they look at Jewish tradition. Ergo Media, Teaneck, NJ.

"The Myth of the Melting Pot Marriage: Ethnotherapy with Jewish–Gentile Couples." 30 minutes. Maps the terrain of interpersonal and identity issues in Jewish/non-Jewish marriages. American Jewish Committee, New York.

"Project Link." 60 minutes. A videocassette containing two separate filmed interviews with couples and staff during *keruv* (outreach) by Conservative rabbis to interfaith couples. Department of Public Affairs, Jewish Theological Seminary, New York.

"Where Judaism Differed." Five hour-long videocassettes exploring Judaism's relationship to paganism, Hellenism, Christianity, Islam, and modernity. American Jewish Committee, New York.

"Who Am I?" 35 minutes. A video by Lena Romanoff intended to give "the child's answer to the question Why be Jewish?" Jewish Converts and Interfaith Network, 1112 Hagy's Ford Road, Narbeth, PA 19072.

Appendix II

Promoting Jewish Community:
Apportunities Available
within Conservative Judaism

CONVERSION INSTITUTES

The Conservative movement in Judaism offers Introduction-to-Judaism courses in many regional locations throughout the world. Sponsoring rabbis from nearby congregations offer guidance as well as a connection to a supportive Conservative synagogue. For further information:

- contact the Rabbinical Assembly office—(212) 678-8060
- or contact Rabbinical Assembly Conversion Chairperson, Rabbi Neil Weinberg—(310) 476-9777
- or contact the Rabbinical Assembly 800 number for Conversion and Outreach—(800)-WELCOME.

In addition, here is a list of other significant resource people:

Rabbi Robert Abramson—United Synagogue of Conservative Judaism, New York. Consultant on Related Educational Materials—(212) 533-7800

Rabbi Moshe Edelman—United Synagogue of Conservative Judaism, New York. Consultant on Related Programming—(212) 533-7800

Dr. Lawrence J. Epstein—New York. Consultant on conversion—(516) 751-5013

Rabbi William Lebeau—Jewish Theological Seminary, New York. Consultant on conversion—(212) 678-8068

Lena Romanoff—Jewish Converts Network, Philadelphia—(215) 664-8112

Dr. Ronald Wolfson—University of Judaism, Los Angeles. Consultant on Jewish continuity issues facing Jewish families—(310) 476-9777

KERUV (OUTREACH) TO THE INTERMARRIED

The center for *keruv* programs offered by Conservative Judaism's institutions is the Gateways Program of the Jewish Theological Seminary in cooperation with the Rabbinical Assembly. For information on the wide range and diverse locations of Hebrew and Jewish literacy programs, holiday workshops, special *Shabbat* and *Yom Tov* experiences, and other *keruv* efforts, you may contact any of the following:

Dr. Anne Lapidus Lerner—Jewish Theological Seminary, New York—(212) 678-8069

Rabbi Stanley Kessler—Gateways Director, West Hartford, CT—(203) 232-6348

Rabbi Shelley Kniaz—United Synagogue of Conservative Judaism, New York. Consultant on children of the intermarried in synagogue religious schools—(212) 533-7800

Rabbi Avis Miller—Rabbinical Assembly Keruv Chairperson, Washington, DC—(202) 362-4433

Kay Pomerantz—United Synagogue of Conservative Judaism, New York. Consultant on parenting and grandparenting of young children—(212) 533-7800

Rabbi Robert Rubin—Project Joseph, New Jersey Region of the United Synagogue and Rabbinical Assembly. Consultant on regional *keruv* programs—(908) 925-3114

For ongoing information call the Rabbinical Assembly's hotline for Conservative Judaism's Conversion and *Keruv* (Outreach) Programs—800-WELCOME.

EARLY CHILDHOOD

Enrollment in early childhood programs under Jewish institutional auspices has skyrocketed to record highs. For more than a decade, pre-school has represented the major growth area in the spectrum of Jewish schooling experience.

Two hundred and fifty of our Conservative congregations currently have nursery school two to five days a week for children 2 to 5 years old. Many more run Sunday morning or one-day-a-week programs for children 5 to 7 years old as part of the synagogue school. The increasing demand by parents for quality nursery school education in our Conservative congregations provides a challenging educational opportunity. Nursery schools serve as an essential gateway for early Jewish education for both children and parents, encourage synagogue membership, and help expand communal involvement.

SYNAGOGUE SCHOOLS

In 1987–1988, the last years for which we have data, 43 percent of supplementary schools were under Conservative sponsorship. This constituted some 800 schools with about 108,000 students, according to the report of the Division on Jewish Demography of the Institute of Contemporary Jewry at the Hebrew University of Jerusalem.

There are effective, exciting synagogue schools in North America that produce knowledgeable, committed, and caring Jewish adults. Some of the characteristics of a quality school are:

- A "holistic" approach to learning, where there is an integration of the school program with all aspects of Jewish life – inside and outside of synagogue. The synagogue school experience begins in nursery school and extends into adulthood. It is multidimensional and extends to

youth groups (Kadima and United Synagogue Youth [USY]), camp experiences (Ramah and USY on Wheels), and Israel trips (Ramah and USY). The professionals and lay leadership of all these areas work together so that education extends beyond the four walls of the classroom.
- A vision that informs the style and direction of the curriculum, methodologies, and feel of the school. This vision matches both the ideology of the Conservative movement and the goals of the community.
- A constant desire to improve that entails attending to problems and challenges, frequent self-evaluation, discussion, and a willingness to try new things.
- The retention of students through the high-school years.
- A high level of participation in rich and frequent family programs.
- Careful attention to the environment—how the physical setting, rules, policies, and personal interactions teach our students.
- Experiences that both form and transform, that create a lasting effect on individuals.
- A significant professional development program.
- An understanding that the education of the next generation is a raison d'être of the synagogue.

SOLOMON SCHECHTER DAY SCHOOLS

Founded in 1956–1957 and nurtured by the United Synagogue of Conservative Judaism, the Solomon Schechter Day School movement has grown to 65 schools with more than 16,000 students and employing more than 2,000 educators in general and Jewish studies. There has been consistent growth in the Schechter schools over the last few years, in spite of a period of economic recession, and they have achieved great credibility throughout America. The schools attract a broad segment of the

Jewish population, and students think of the dual program as a natural environment.

CAMPS RAMAH

Ramah is a system of six regional overnight camps, a day camp, and year-round Israel programs. We service, at present, 4,500 youth each summer, 1,200 college-age staff, 500 units in our family camps, and another 2,000 children in synagogue and day-school weekends.

It is the experience of intensive immersion in a total environment of Jewish learning practices, arts, sports, and the tasks of daily living that lead toward personal commitment. One becomes a "Ramah-nik" forever. Over the years, involvement with Ramah has led to a committed population of Jews who, more often than not, affiliate with and support the Conservative movement.

The Camp Ramah experience is clearly a denominational one, and it is among the most powerful tools for imparting Jewish values, identity, and practical knowledge consistent with the Conservative movement. It is crucial to create a level field of opportunity for people to attend Ramah so that denominational camping can compete with other camping opportunities and enrich congregational life.

YOUTH MOVEMENTS

Youth programs under the sponsorship of the United Synagogue of Conservative Judaism include close to 25,000 members of Kadima and USY in more than 750 local affiliates throughout North America.

USY, founded in 1951, is for high-school-age participants, while Kadima, founded in 1968, is for those in grades 6 through 8. Affiliated chapters are divided into 17 regions, each with a director and well-established infrastructure.

Our synagogue youth movement is an integral component in the Jewish educational process and should be regarded as more than a social outlet. It provides our youth with an opportunity for a serious exploration of Jewish identity and nurtures their involvement in adult Jewish life.

Most Kadima programs focus on the local chapter, with some regional programs held on an occasional basis. Kadima publishes its own quarterly magazine, which is distributed to all members. Programming and educational materials for advisers are produced on a regular basis.

USY offers programs on the local, regional, and national levels. Locally there is a broad variety of balanced programming including religious, educational, and recreational components. Most regional and national programs focus on the educational and religious components. Regions sponsor several weekend *kinnusim* (retreats), some of which are home-hospitality weekends, while others are held at hotels or camp-sites. Most regions sponsor a weeklong camp program at the conclusion of the regular camping season. All weekend and encampment programs include an educational component based around a central theme. Regions also run training programs for advisers and often issue their own publications and materials.

The national office sponsors an annual convention over the winter recess, held in a different city each year. Depending upon locations, the convention attracts between 1,000 and 1,200 participants each year. A new theme is studied annually and an educational text exploring the annual theme through classical Jewish texts and experiential activities is produced.

USY sponsors the USY Israel Pilgrimage, a six-week summer Israel program that attracts about 600 participants. It also sponsors USY on Wheels, the only cross-country bus tour for high-school students that is kosher and *shomer Shabbat*. Both programs include an organized educational structure. USY also sponsors the Nativ Year program in Israel for entering college freshmen, with the Hebrew University, and USY High, an eight-week academic program for high-school students in cooperation with the Alexander Muss High School in Israel.

In addition, USY produces a broad array of educational materials for its members and staff.

The synagogue youth movement must be seen as a critical ingredient in fostering Jewish continuity. Kadima and USY can provide the opportunity for a serious exploration of one's identity in a nonthreatening environment.

ISRAEL EXPERIENCE

The Conservative movement sponsors 12 different Israel experience programs through Ramah and USY. Given the statistics that indicate the positive impact of an Israel experience in shaping a young person's Jewish identity, there must be a more concerted effort to attract greater numbers while continuing to increase the quality of the programs. At the present time, more than 1,000 people visit Israel through Ramah and USY.

The advantage of Israel programs affiliated with synagogue movements is that each participant returns home to a specific context and has the opportunity to process the experience with a circle of young people and adults who share a common frame of reference. This ensures that the Israel experience is part of a continuum, not an isolated experience.

COLLEGE LIFE

Hillel is the "Jewish address" on campus, and the Conservative Jewish presence is KOACH. We cooperate with Hillel on a variety of levels: KOACH professionals participate in Hillel student leadership conferences, attend the Hillel professional conference, and develop contacts with Hillel directors across the continent.

We are able to enhance the Hillel program in a number of different ways. The KOACH Creative Grants Program awards campuses up to $2,000 a year to develop programming for Conservative Jewish students. Activities have varied, from *Shabbatonim* to social action projects, to *kosher l'Pesah* kitchens to egalitarian *minyanim*, to social activities to academic presentations.

Our KOACH publications have increased in quality and quantity. A newsletter is published three times a year (distributed via direct mail and through Hillel Foundations), and special pamphlets are issued on different topics. These include Rabbi Neil Gillman's *Guide for the New Jewish College Student*, which is distributed to all college freshmen who were registered members of USY.

An annual KOACH *kallah* is held every February, bringing together students from campuses throughout North America. Regional weekends are also held in various parts of the country, enabling students to network with other like-minded young people who are interested in creating a vibrant Conservative community during their college years and beyond.

Coordination of efforts with our Center on Campus in Jerusalem has increased our activity in Israel for students spending time abroad. Assistance to congregations who serve college-age populations (both home and away) have also increased.

For general information, see *The Hillel Guide to Jewish Life on Campus*, available from the Hillel Foundation, 1640 Rhode Island Avenue N.W., Washington, DC 20036.

ADULT EDUCATION

Conservative Judaism has the resources to meet the challenges posed by adult education. We have a long history of translating

Judaism into a modern idiom. Indeed, adult education represents a critical vehicle for intensifying Jewish continuity.

- It can provide meaningful adult role-modeling for children enrolled in formal Jewish education.
- It can upgrade the quality of Jewish institutional leadership.
- It can stimulate non-Jewish relatives of Jews to contemplate sincere conversion to Judaism.
- It can temper the alienation of many Jewish students during their campus years.

In the words of Rabbi William Lebeau, dean of the rabbinical school of the Jewish Theological Seminary, we need adult education "[as a mode of action] when a Jew cries out for God, community or spiritual guidance. . . . To inspire . . . [uninvolved] Jews to commit to serious Jewish study and observance. . . . To find ways to challenge [knowledgeable Jews] to climb higher on the ladder of learning and commitment" (William H. Lebeau, "To Learn, to Teach, and to Observe: The Critical Role of Adult Education for Our Jewish Future," pp. 14–15).

Effective adult Jewish education has frequently been identified with large lecture hall and scholar-in-residence settings in which single-occasion gatherings of a passive nature can involve hundreds of Jewish men and women.

Given today's complex social climate, we need diverse formats and locations serving a growing variety of needs, lifestyles, ages, and interest groups. The following represent examples of this necessary diversity of adult learning venues:

- Hebrew literacy courses
- Holiday workshops—Passover, Hanukkah, etc.
- Introduction to Judaism and Jewish literacy courses
- Adult *bar/bat mitzvah*

- Parent education and family education programs
- Synagogue study *havurot*
- Community-wide public lectures
- Study groups at law firms, health care centers, financial institutions, etc.
- Senior citizens' "life-long learning" courses
- Talmud study circles
- Congregational adult education courses
- Radio interviews
- Audiocassette tapes of lectures and classes
- Retreats at Camps Ramah and other locations
- Learners' *minyan* programs at synagogues

The Conservative movement—our local synagogues, our United Synagogue Regional Programs, our educational outreach efforts by the Jewish Theological Seminary—has the materials as well as available personnel to meet these educational challenges.

Contact Headquarters for Conservative Judaism

Call any of these international offices to obtain information about regional sites as well:

United Synagogue of Conservative Judaism—(212) 533-7800 —representing over 800 Conservative synagogues

Jewish Theological Seminary—(212) 678-8000 and the University of Judaism—(310) 476-9777—training institutions for rabbis, cantors, educators, communal workers, executive directors, knowledgeable future laity

Rabbinical Assembly—(212) 678-8060—representing 1,400 Conservative rabbis

Women's League for Conservative Judaism—(212) 628-1600— representing hundreds of synagogue sisterhoods

Federation of Jewish Men's Clubs—(212) 749-8100—representing hundreds of synagogue men's clubs

National (Camp) Ramah Commission—(212) 678-8881—
headquarters of the various Ramah camp programs

Solomon Schechter Day School Association—(212) 533-7800—
central office for dozens of Solomon Schechter day schools

United Synagogue Youth—(212) 533-7800—main office for
the hundreds of USY and Kadimah chapters

Koach College Campus Activities—(212) 533-7800—headquarters for college programs under Conservative Jewish
sponsorship

Bibliography

Abelson, Kassel. "The Non-Jewish Spouse and Children of a Mixed Marriage in the Synagogue." In Joel Roth, ed., *Proceedings of the Committee on Jewish Law and Standards of the Conservative Movement 1980–1985*. New York: Rabbinical Assembly, 1988, pp. 129–142.

Abramowitz, Yosef. "Why be Jewish?" *Moment* 17:6 (December 1992): 45–48.

Aldrich, Robert, and Austin, Glenn. *Grandparenting for the 90s*. Escondido, CA: Robert Erdmann, 1991.

Anker, Charlotte. "We Are the Children You Warned Our Parents About." *Moment* 16:1 (February 1991): 34–39.

Appleman, Harlene Winnick. "Teaching Our Kids to Say 'I'm Sorry.' " *Jewish Family* 1:5 (September 1993): 2–3.

Baron, Barry. "Interfaith Marriages: Rabbis Respond." *Dovetail* 1:4 (February/March 1993): 2.

Bayne, Steven. "Communal Policy and Program Direction." In Aryeh Meir, ed., *The Intermarriage Crisis: Jewish Communal Perspectives and Responses*. New York: American Jewish Committee, 1991, pp. 59–60.

Bellah, Robert, et al. *Habits of the Heart*. New York: Harper & Row, 1985.

Berman, Louis A. *Jews and Intermarriage: A Study in Personality and Culture*. New York: Thomas Yoseloff, 1968.

Bloom, Harold. *The American Religion*. New York: Simon & Schuster, 1992.

Brauner, Ronald. "Hanukah." *Straightalk* 1:5 (December 1992): 2.

Burg, Anne. Membership Application. Caldwell, New Jersey: Congregation Agudath Israel, 1985.

Carmel, Abraham. *So Strange My Path: A Spiritual Journey*. New York: Bloch, 1964.

Coles, Robert. *The Spirituality of the Child*. Boston: Houghton Mifflin, 1990.

Cowan, Paul. *An Orphan in History*. Garden City, NY: Doubleday, 1982.

Cowan, Paul, and Cowan, Rachel. *Mixed Blessings: Marriage Between Jews and Christians*. New York: Doubleday, 1987.

——. "Our People: Nancy Wingerson's Story." *Moment* 8:10 (April 1983): 59–61.

Crohn, Joel. "Ethnotherapy: What It Is, How It Works and Applies to Programming for the Intermarried." *Journal of Jewish Communal Service* 65:3 (Spring 1989): 215–230.

Danan, Julie Hilton. *The Jewish Parents' Almanac*. Northvale, NJ: Jason Aronson, 1994.

Dershowitz, Alan. *Chutzpah*. New York: Simon & Schuster, 1992.

Donin, Hayim Halevy. *To Raise a Jewish Child*. New York: Basic Books, 1977.

Eichhorn, David Max. *Jewish Intermarriage: Fact and Fiction*. Satellite Beach, FL: Satellite Books, 1974.

Eisen, Arnold. "Abraham Joshua Heschel." New York: Jewish Theological Seminary, Fall 1992, audiotape.

——. "The Role of a Jewish Research Institute." *The Wilstein Institute Newsletter*, Spring 1993, p. 1.

Elkins, Dov Peretz. *Loving My Jewishness*. Rochester, NY: Growth Associates, 1975.

Episcopal Church of America. *Book of Common Prayer*. New York: Episcopal Church of America, 1989.

Epstein, Jane. "Jewish Identity Is Not Hereditary." *Your Child* 24:1 (Fall 1992): 3.

Epstein, Lawrence J. *Conversion to Judaism: A Guidebook*. Northvale, NJ: Jason Aronson, 1994.

——. *How to Discuss Conversion to Judaism*. Suffolk County, NY: Suffolk Jewish Community Planning Council, 1993, flier.

——. "Setting the Stage to Discuss Conversion." *Baltimore Jewish Times*, May 21,1993.

Fay, Martha. *Do Children Need Religion?* New York: Pantheon Books, 1993.

Fife, Linda. "Welcoming Converts into Synagogue Life." Los Angeles: United Synagogue of Conservative Judaism, Pacific South-West Region, 1990.

Fisch, Dov Aharoni. *Jews for Nothing*. New York: Feldheim, 1984.

Fishman, Sylvia Barack, and Goldstein, Alice. *When They Are Grown They Will Not Depart: Jewish Education and the Jewish Behavior of American Adults*. Waltham, MA: Brandeis University, 1994.

Fitzpatrick, Jean Grasso. *Something More: Nurturing Your Child's Spiritual Growth*. New York: Viking Penguin, 1991.

Fuchs, Stephen. "Outreach: Parameters and Prospects." Kiamesha, NY: Rabbinical Assembly Convention, 1992, audiotape.

——. "Reach Out—But Also Bring In." *Sh'ma* 21:12 (March 8, 1991): 10.

Gabbay, Alyssa. "Jews By Choice." *Baltimore Jewish Times*, June 1, 1990, pp. 52–53.

Gateways: An "Outreach" Program of the Jewish Theological Seminary. New York: Jewish Theological Seminary, 1995, promotional brochure.

Goldman, Ari. *The Search for God at Harvard*. New York: Ballantine Books, 1991.

Goodman-Malamuth, Leslie. Book review of *Mingled Roots: A Guide for Jewish Grandparents of Interfaith Grandchildren*, by Sunie Levin. *Dovetail* 1:4 (April/May 1993): 7.

Goodman-Malamuth, Leslie, and Margolis, Robin. *Between Two Worlds*. New York: Pocket Books, 1992.

Gordis, Daniel. *Am Kadosh: Celebrating Our Uniqueness*. New York: United Synagogue Youth, 1993.

Gordis, Robert, et al. *Emet Ve-Emunah: Statement of Principles of Conservative Judaism*. New York: Rabbinical Assembly, Jewish Theological Seminary, United Synagogue of Conservative Judaism, 1988.

Gordon, Albert I. *Intermarriage*. Boston: Beacon Press, 1964.

Gore, Albert, Jr. *Earth in the Balance: Ecology and the Human Spirit*. Boston: Houghton Mifflin, 1992.

Greenberg, Sidney, ed. *A Modern Treasury of Jewish Thoughts*. New York: Thomas Yoseloff, 1960.

Greenberg, Simon. *A Jewish Philosophy and Pattern of Life*. New York: Jewish Theological Seminary, 1981.

Greenberg, Susan. Letter to Editor. *Reform Judaism* 21:4 (Summer 1992): 56.

Grishaver, Joel. "December Dilemma." *Jewish Family* 1:1 (December 1992): 3.

——. *Forty Things You Can Do to Save the Jewish People*. Northvale, NJ: Jason Aronson, 1994.

Gross, David C. *The Jewish People's Almanac*. New York: Harper & Row, 1984.

Harlow, Jules. *The Rabbi's Manual*. New York: Rabbinical Assembly, 1968, pp. 13–16.

Hertzberg, Arthur. *Being Jewish in America*. New York: Schocken Books, 1978.

Heschel, Abraham J. *The Earth Is the Lord's*. New York: Harper Torchbooks, 1966.

——. *The Sabbath*. New York: Harper Trophy Torchbooks, 1966.

Hoffman, Mary. "Why Did I Convert to Judaism?" *The National Jewish Post and Opinion*, October 28, 1992, p. 11.

Huberman, Steven. "From Christianity to Judaism: Religion Changers in American Society." *Conservative Judaism* 32:1 (Fall 1982): 10–28.

Isaacs, Ronald. *Becoming Jewish*. New York: Rabbinical Assembly, 1994.

Jewish Family Service (MetroWest, NJ). "Outreach to the Intermarried." New York: Rabbinical Assembly and Jewish Family Service, 1989.

Johnson, Catherine. *Lucky in Love: The Secrets of Happy Couples and How Their Marriages Thrive*. New York: Viking, 1992.

Kaplan, Mordecai. *The Future of the American Jew*. New York: MacMillan, 1948.

Katzen, Lucy. "A Ten-Year Retrospective." *The Newly Jewish Family: A Newsletter*. MetroWest Jewish Family Service, September 1990.

Kaye, Deborah. "Grandma Wrestles with Santa." *The Jewish Monthly* 108:3 (December 1993): 36–40.

King, Andrea. *If I'm Jewish and You're Christian, What Are the Kids?* New York: Union of American Hebrew Congregations, 1993.

Kleiman, Nancy. "Religion as a Language." In Nina J. Mizrachi and Joel Oseran, eds., *Times and Seasons: A Jewish Perspective for Intermarried Couples—A Guide for Facilitators*. New York: Union of American Hebrew Congregations, 1987.

Kling, Simcha. *Embracing Judaism*. New York: Rabbinical Assembly, 1987.

Koch, Edward I. *Citizen Koch*. New York: St. Martins Press, 1992.

Kornhaber, Arthur, and Woodward, Kenneth L. *Grandparents and Grandchildren: The Vital Connection*. New Brunswick, NJ: Transaction, 1991.

Kroloff, Charles. "Love and Marriage." *Keeping Posted* 19:5 (February 1974): 3–7.

Kukoff, Lydia. *Choosing Judaism*. New York: Union of American Hebrew Congregations, 1992.

———. "Inviting Someone You Love to Become a Jew." New York: Union of American Hebrew Congregations, 1992, pamphlet.

Kukoff, Lydia, et al. *Working with Interfaith Couples: A Jewish Perspective—A Guide for Facilitators*. New York: Union of American Hebrew Congregations, 1992.

Kushner, Harold. *When All You've Ever Wanted Isn't Enough*. New York: Summit Books, 1986.

———. *Who Needs God?* New York: Summit Books, 1989.

Kushner, Lawrence. *God was in this PLACE and I, i did not know*. Woodmont, VT: Jewish Lights, 1993.

———. *Honey from the Rock*. San Francisco: Harper & Row, 1977.

Lamdan, Elimelech. "Judaism and Transcendental Meditation." In Simcha Cohen et al., eds., *Return to the Source*. New York: Feldheim, 1984, pp. 207–215.

Lamm, Maurice. *Becoming a Jew*. Middle Village, NY: Jonathan David, 1991.

Lebeau, William H. "The Interfaith Marriage Ceremony: A Time for Honesty—Not for Rabbis, Priests or Ministers," 1993, unpublished essay.

———. "To Learn, to Teach and to Observe: The Critical Role of Adult Education for Our Jewish Future." *Women's League Outlook* 63:4 (Summer 1992): 14–15.

———. "Ways to Express Ahavat Yisrael: Through Keruv." Newsletter of North Suburban Synagogue Beth El, Highland Park, IL, October 1985, p. 6.

Lee, Judith S. "Joining In: A Personal Account." *Reconstructionist* 51:7 (June 1986): 15–18.

Leifer, Penny, ed. *And Teach Them Diligently: Sisterhood Welcomes the Jew by Choice*. New York: Women's League for Conservative Judaism, 1994.

Lester, Julius. *Lovesong: Becoming a Jew*. New York: Henry Holt, 1988.

Levey, Larry. "Why I Embraced, Then Rejected Messianic Judaism." *The Jewish Monthly* 99:7 (April 1984): 18–21.

Levin, Sunie. _Mingled Roots: A Guide for Jewish Grandparents of Inter-faith Grandchildren_. Washington, DC: B'nai B'rith Women, 1993.

——. "When You Visit Your Grandchildren." _Kansas City Star_, April 28, 1993, p. 20.

Lindblad, Samantha. "A Convert to Judaism Tells Her Story." _The Jewish Post and Opinion_, October 16, 1981, pp. 3–4.

Maller, Allen. "Jews by Choice." _Reconstructionist_ 51:7 (June 1986): 22–24.

Mayer, Egon. "Why Not Judaism?" _Moment_ 16:5 (October 1991): 28–33.

Mayer, Egon, and Avgar, Amy. _Conversion Among the Intermarried_. New York: American Jewish Committee, 1987.

McCollister, John C. _The Christian Book of Why_. Middle Village, NY: Jonathan David, 1983.

Medved, Michael. _Hollywood vs. America: Popular Culture and the War on Traditional Values_. New York: HarperCollins, 1982.

Meir, Aryeh, ed. _The Intermarriage Crisis: Jewish Communal Perspec-tives and Responses_. New York: American Jewish Committee, 1991.

Miller, Arlene A. "An Exploration of Ethnicity in Marriages Between White Anglo-Saxon Protestants and Jewish Americans." Boston: Boston University, Ed.D thesis, 1993.

Miller, Avis. "Outreach to Intermarrieds: Parameters and Outlines." In Steven Bayme, ed., _Approaches to Intermarriage: Areas of Con-sensus_. New York: American Jewish Committee, pp. 3–4.

——. "Reaching Out: Dealing with Intermarried Families." _United Synagogue Review_ 42:1 (Fall 1989): 10.

——. "Support and Guidance for the Parents, Family, and Freinds of Intermarried and Interdating Couples." In Robert Rubin, ed., _Intermarriage: What Can We Do? What Should We Do?_ New York: United Synagogue of Conservative Judaism, 1992, pp. 23–24.

Moline, Jack. "Ten Things We Do Not Say Often Enough to Our Children." Kiamesha, NY: United Synagogue Convention, 1991, audiotape.

Nadich, Hadassah Ribalow. "The Art of Grandparenting." _Women's League Outlook_ 65:4 (Summer 1994): 22–24.

Ochs, Vanessa. _Words on Fire: One Woman's Journey into the Sacred_. New York: Harcourt Brace, 1992.

Osbourne, Ronald. "Marriage of Christians and Jews." *Plumbline* 13:3 (September 1985): 9–11.

Paskow, Shimon. "I Remember Bubbe: The Receipts of Righteousness." *Jewish News* (MetroWest, New Jersey), December 23, 1993, p. 3.

Pearl, Jonathan, and Pearl, Judith. "The Changing Channels of TV's Intermarriage Depictions." *Jewish Televimage Report* 1:1 (June 1991): 1.

Perel, Esther, and Cowan, Rachel. "A More Perfect Union: Intermarriage and the Jewish World." *Tikkun* 7:3 (May/June 1992): 59–64.

Petsonk, Judy, and Remsen, Jim. *The Intermarriage Handbook*. New York: William Morrow & Co., 1988.

Pogrebin, Letty Cottin. *Deborah, Golda, and Me*. New York: Crown, 1991.

Prager, Dennis. "Happiness Isn't Fun." *Ultimate Issues* 5:1 (January–March 1989): 13–16.

———. "Is There Such a Thing as 'Jews for Jesus'?" *Ultimate Issues* 5:4 (October–December 1989): 6–7.

———. "Judaism Seeks Converts." *Ultimate Issues* 7:1 (January–March 1991): 3–7.

———. "Raising a Jewish Child in a Christian Society." Los Angeles: 1993, audiotape.

———. "Why I Am a Jew: The Case for a Religious Life." *Ultimate Issues* 2:2–3 (Spring/Summer 1986): 1–35.

Prager, Dennis, and Telushkin, Joseph. *Nine Questions People Ask About Judaism*. New York: Simon & Schuster, 1981.

Rank, Perry. "Keruv, Covenant and Understanding Conservative Judaism." *Jewish News* (MetroWest, New Jersey), September 22, 1994, p. 13.

Reisman, Bernard. "Informal Jewish Education in North America." A report submitted to the Commission on Jewish Education in North America. New York, 1990.

Reuben, Steven Carr. *Raising Jewish Children in a Contemporary World*. Rochlin, CA: Prima Publishing, 1992.

Riskin, Shlomo. "With Law and Love." *Jewish Week* (New York), September 10, 1994, p. 23.

Romanoff, Lena. "How Does One Decide to Convert to Another Religion? *Dovetail* 2:3 (December 1993/January 1994): 3.

———. "Jewish Converts Network." Philadelphia: Jewish Converts Network, 1986, brochure.

———. *Your People, My People*. Philadelphia: Jewish Publication Society, 1990.

Roiphe, Anne. *Generation Without Memory*. Boston: Beacon Press, 1982.

Romano, Dugan. *Intercultural Marriages: Promises and Pitfalls*. Yarmouth, ME: Intercultural Press, 1988.

Rosen, James, and Zinner, Roslyn. Letter to the Editor on behalf of the Baltimore Board of Rabbis. *Baltimore Jewish Times*, December 3, 1993, p. 9.

Rosenberg, Elsa. "Why People Choose Judaism." *Reconstructionist* 51:7 (June 1986): 18–20.

Roth, Philip. *The Counterlife*. New York: Farrar, Straus, Giroux, 1986.

Rubin, Cheryl. "Grandparenting." *Your Child* 26:1 (Fall 1994): 4.

Rubin, Robert, ed. *Intermarriage: What Can We Do? What Should We Do?* New York: United Synagogue of Conservative Judaism, 1992.

Rudin, Jacob Philip. *A Harvest of Forty Years in the Pulpit*. New York: Bloch, 1971.

Rudin, James, and Rudin, Marcia. *Prison or Paradise: The New Religious Cults*. Philadelphia: Fortress Press, 1980.

Rusk, Tom, and Miller, Patrick D. *The Power of Ethical Persuasion*. New York: Viking Penguin, 1993.

Saint Pius School. "The Twelve Days of Christmas." Montville, NJ: Saint Pius School, 1992.

Saville, Gail. "Why I Chose to Become a Jew." *Reform Judaism* 12:1 (Fall 1983): 19–21.

Schneider, Susan Weidman. *Intermarriage*. New York: Free Press, 1989.

Schorsch, Ismar. Keynote speech to Conservative Movement Conference on Intermarriage and Conversion. New York, March 2–3, 1987.

Schreck, Alan. *Your Catholic Faith: A Question and Answer Catechism*. Ann Arbor, MI: Servant Publications, 1989.

Schulman, Zell. "A Modern Bubbe." *National Jewish Post and Opinion*, September 29, 1993, p. 9.

Schulweis, Harold. "The Hyphen Between the Cross and the Star." In Harold Schulweis, ed., *In God's Mirror: Reflections and Essays*. Hoboken, NJ: KTAV, 1990, pp. 168–177.

——, ed. _In God's Mirror: Reflections and Essays._ Hoboken, NJ: KTAV, 1990.

——. "My Zeyda, His Grandchildren, and the Synagogue." Wilstein Institute, _Comment and Analysis,_ p. 1.

——. "Peering into the Limbo of Judeo-Christian Beliefs." In Carol Diamant, ed., _Jewish Marital Status._ Northvale, NJ: Jason Aronson, 1989, pp. 238–245.

Seltzer, Sanford. "On Becoming a Jew." New York: Union of American Hebrew Congregations, 1986, pamphlet.

Shrage, Barry. "Bringing Federations Closer to Synagogues." In David Gordis, ed., _Federation and Synagogue: Toward A New Partnership._ Boston: Wilstein Institute, 1994.

Silberman, Charles E. _A Certain People: American Jews and Their Lives Today._ New York: Summit Books, 1985.

Silberman, Shoshanna. "Developing Jewish Rituals for Your Family." In Sharon Strassfeld and Kathy Green, eds., _The Jewish Family Book._ New York: Bantam Books, 1981, pp. 66–80.

Singer, Suzanne. "A 'Critical Mass' of Judaism May Prevent Intermarriage." _Moment_ 16:4 (October 1991): 4.

Sklare, Marshall. "American Jewry—The Ever-Dying People." _Midstream_ 22:6 (June–July 1976): 17–27.

Strassfeld, Sharon, and Green, Kathy, eds. _The Jewish Family Book._ New York: Bantam Books, 1981.

Tabachnik, Joseph, and Foster, Brenda. _Jews by Choice: A Study of Converts to Reform and Conservative Judaism._ Hoboken, NJ: KTAV, 1991.

Ticktin, Max. "The Blessings of Being a Grandfather." In Sharon Strassfeld and Kathy Green, eds., _The Jewish Family Book._ New York: Bantam Books, 1981.

Twerski, Abraham. "Animals and Angels: Spirituality in Recovery." Aliquippa, PA: Gateway Rehabilitation Center, 1990, videotape.

Waldoks, Moshe. _The Big American Book of Jewish Humor_ New York: Harper & Row, 1981.

Warren, Andrea, and Wiedenkeller, Jay. _Everybody's Doing It: How To Survive Your Teenager's Sex Life (And Help Them Survive It Too)._ New York: Viking Penguin, 1993.

Wasser, Joel. _We Are Family._ New York: United Synagogue Youth, 1993.

Wasserman, Michael. "The Convert and the Rabbi as 'Stress Absorbers.' " In Egon Mayer, ed., *The Imperatives of Jewish Outreach*. New York: The Jewish Outreach Institute, 1991.

Weintraub, Samuel. "Project Link: Principled, Sensitive, Conservative Outreach." *Conservative Judaism* 42:1 (Fall 1990): 38–45.

Weiss, Stephen. "Interview with Jew by Choice." New York: Jewish Theological Seminary Spring 1989, course paper.

Wiesel, Elie. "Pride in Being Jewish." In Dov Peretz Elkins, ed., *Loving My Jewishness*. Rochester, NY: Growth Associates, 1978, p. 19.

Winer, Mark. "Mom, We're Just Dating." In Carol Diamant, ed., *Jewish Marital Status*. Northvale, NJ: Jason Aronson, 1989, pp. 228–230.

Winer, Mark, and Meir, Aryeh. *Questions Jewish Parents Ask about Intermarriage: A Guide for Jewish Families*. New York: American Jewish Committee, 1993.

Wolfson, Ron. *The Art of Jewish Living: Hanukkah*. New York: Federation of Jewish Men's Clubs, 1990.

——. *Jewish Family Education*. Los Angeles: University of Judaism Series, 1990, pamphlet.

Wolpe, David J. *Explaining God to Children: A Jewish Perspective*. New York: Henry Holt, 1993.

Woocher, Jonathan. "Jewish Survival Tactics." *Hadassah Magazine* 74:10 (June–July 1993): 10–13.

Yankelovich, Daniel. *New Rules: Searching for Self-Fulfillment in a World Turned Upside Down*. New York: Random House, 1981.

Index

About the Author

Rabbi Alan Silverstein is the International President of the Rabbinical Assembly, the association of the 1,400 rabbis affiliated with Conservative Judaism's institutions. He received his Ph.D. in Jewish history at the Jewish Theological Seminary (JTS) and is the author of *Alternatives to Assimilation: The Response of Reform Judaism to American Culture, 1840–1930*, as well as dozens of articles, booklets, and essays. For the past ten years Rabbi Silverstein has taught Conservative Judaism's approach to intermarriage, conversion, and outreach to JTS rabbinical students. He has supervised pioneering programs in serving Jewish singles, in training and involving Jews by Choice, and in seeking to bring intermarried Jews closer to Judaism. He has lectured throughout North America on topics related to Jewish continuity. Rabbi of Congregation Agudath Israel in Caldwell, New Jersey, he resides in West Caldwell, with his wife, Rita, and their children, David and Rebecca.